In-Class Activities Guide
for
The Instructor's Survival Kit
to accompany
Marketing
Seventh Edition

Roger A. Kerin
Southern Methodist University

Eric N. Berkowitz
University of Massachusetts

Steven W. Hartley
University of Denver

William Rudelius
University of St. Thomas

Michael J. Vessey
Stewardship Marketing

Boston   Burr Ridge, IL   Dubuque, IA   Madison, WI   New York   San Francisco   St. Louis
Bangkok   Bogotá   Caracas   Kuala Lumpur   Lisbon   London   Madrid   Mexico City
Milan   Montreal   New Delhi   Santiago   Seoul   Singapore   Sydney   Taipei   Toronto

In-Class Activities Guide for The Instructor's Survival Kit to accompany
MARKETING
Roger A. Kerin, Eric N. Berkowitz, Steven W. Hartley and William Rudelius

Published by McGraw-Hill, an imprint of The McGraw-Hill Companies, Inc., 1221 Avenue of the Americas, New York, NY 10020. Copyright © 2003, 2000
by The McGraw-Hill Companies, Inc. All rights reserved.
The contents, or parts thereof, may be reproduced in print form solely for classroom use with
MARKETING
provided such reproductions bear copyright notice, but may not be reproduced in any other form or for any other purpose without the prior written consent of The McGraw-Hill Companies, Inc., including, but not limited to, in any network or other electronic storage or transmission, or broadcast for distance learning.

1 2 3 4 5 6 7 8 9 0 BKM/BKM 0 9 8 7 6 5 4 3 2

ISBN 0-07-246892-0

www.mhhe.com

ACKNOWLEDGMENTS

We have been heartened by the enthusiastic reaction by marketing instructors to our *In-Class Activities Guide* and *Instructor's Survival Kit* that accompanied *Marketing*, Fifth and Sixth Editions. These reactions have caused us to expand and update the set of In-Class Activities (ICAs) for our Seventh Edition, which includes 31 new or significantly revised ICAs.

Our *In-Class Activities Guide* benefits from our own classroom experiences, as well as those of our colleagues and graduate students who have contributed ICAs: David H. Gobeli, Amy Cox, Joann Peck, Mark Bergen, and Linda Rochford.

In developing these ICAs and our *Instructor's Survival Kit,* we received the continuing support of four members of our Irwin/McGraw-Hill team—former Executive Editor Gary Bauer, Development Editor Tracy Jensen, Production Supervisor Heather Burbridge, and Marketing Manager Kim Kanakes.

We especially want to thank the people who generously provided the items and other resources in our *Instructor's Survival Kit* that give special life in the classroom to a number of our ICAs. These include Karolyn Warfel and Kathy Fisher of Woodstream Corp. (Victor), John Chagnon of Chagnon's Outdoor World (Victor), Nicholas Skally of Benetton Sportsystem USA (Rollerblade), Kristin Casemore of Ten Speed Press, Traci Moscowitz of hotjobs.com, Sharon Gibson of the University of St. Thomas (Employment Questions), Michael Sandman of Fuld & Company, Inc., Chris Gorley of Starbucks Coffee Company, Leslie Letts of Sprint, Kerri Miller of MINIUSA, Daniel Sutton of Crispin, Porter, and Bogusky (MINI Cooper), Lisa Castaldo of Pepsico, Megan Betty and Cindy Hulett of Pillsbury (Big G Milk 'n Cereal Bar), Jim Laudenbach of Zebra Pens, Inc., Brian Jaquet of Handspring, Inc., Ken Hart, PhD. of 3M (VHB Tape), Greg Lee of Magnetic Poetry, Inc., Dr. Robert M. McMath of New Product Works, Ann Kreb of Golden Valley Microwave Foods (Act II Popcorn), Carol Watzke and Joanne Harms of CNS Inc., (Breathe Right), Stephen Bratspies and Shane Gillies of Frito-Lay (Go Snacks), Dave Ridley of Southwest Airlines, Karen McCall of Panasonic, Charles Smith of Kodak, Scott Wosniak and Bob Tess of Toro, George Koenig of easy2.com (Toro iMow), Kim Knutson of Fallon Worldwide, Bob Robinson and Joe McKesson of Apple, Robin Grayson of TBWA/Chiat/Day (Apple), Elizabeth Clendenin of Unilever (Caress), Nick Minnick of Valassis Communications, Inc. (Caress), Marsha Levine of A List Entertainment, Emily Richeda of Burson-Marsteller (Segway HT), Lisa Kuebelbeck and Linda Ousley of NewsAmerica Marketing (SmartSource), Teresa Bencivengo, Tom Stepanchak, and Carol Burrows of BMW USA, and Tom Johnson and David Eisen of General Mills (Wheaties). Additional thanks go to Karen Primak and Denise Brennan of IPAK, which produced the ISK. Finally, Daniel Hundley of Token Media, digitized many of the images in the ISK ICA PowerPoint CD.

We believe these activities will bring both excitement and enhanced understanding of key marketing concepts to your classroom.

Roger A. Kerin, Eric N. Berkowitz, Steven W. Hartley, William Rudelius, and Michael J. Vessey

CONTENTS

I. USING THE *IN-CLASS ACTIVITIES GUIDE* & *INSTRUCTOR'S SURVIVAL KIT*

Student Involvement Matters! 3
Why a Separate *In-Class Activities Guide*? 3
Elements of Each In-Class Activity 3
Kinds of In-Class Activities 4
The ICA PowerPoint CD 4
Items in the *Instructor's Survival Kit* 4
Where the In-Class Activities May Be Used 5

II. IN-CLASS ACTIVITIES (ICAs)

ICA	Description
1-1	What Makes a Better Mousetrap? (Part 1) 13
1-2	What is Marketing? 19
2-1	Marketing Yourself 24
2-2	What Makes a Better Mousetrap? (Part 2): The Role of Cross-Functional Teams in New Product Development 31
3-1	Questions That Cannot Be Asked Outright in a Pre-Employment Interview 42
3-2	Competitive Intelligence 45
4-1	Sustainable Development 48
4-2	What Is Ethical and What Is Not: A Survey of Your Opinions 52
5-1	Buying Process for Starbucks Coffee 56
6-1	Buying Center Role-Play 59
7-1	Are You an Ethnocentric Consumer? 64
7-2	Marketing Across Borders: Reintroducing the MINI® Brand to the U.S. 67
8-1	Pepsi vs. Coke Taste Test 74
8-2	Designing a Taste Test Questionnaire for a Howlin' Coyote® Chili ...79
8-3	Websurfing for Marketing Information 83
9-1	Product Categorization to Identify Market Segments and Competitors ...86
9-2	Product Positioning for Consumers and Retailers 89
9-3	Developing A Market–Product Grid for the Victor® Line of Mousetraps (Part 3) 96
10-1	Focus Group for Convergent Digital Devices 103
10-2	Communicating Important Points of Difference to Skeptical Design Engineers ..110
10-3	Using Method 6–3–5 to Find New Product Ideas for Magnetic Poetry® ...114
10-4	What *Were* They Thinking? Analyzing Some New Product Disasters 121

II. IN-CLASS ACTIVITIES (ICAs) CONTINUED

ICA	Description	
11-1	Managing the Product Life Cycle	128
11-2	Using Brainstorming and N/3 Techniques for Breathe Right® Nasal Strips	134
11-3	Creating Customer Value Through Packaging and Labeling	139
12-1	Airline Customer Service and Southwest Airlines	144
13-1	Pricing a Panasonic DVD Player	149
14-1	Extra Value Meal Bundle Pricing at McDonald's	153
15-1	Marketing Channels for Apple Computer	159
16-1	The "Foam Factory" Process Improvement Exercise	164
17-1	Retail Shopping Online: Comparing Prices for a Digital Camera	168
18-1	An IMC for the Toro® iMow™ Robotic Mower	172
18-2	An IMC for the Hermitage Museum	179
19-1	Recognizing Advertising Slogans	184
19-2	What Makes a Memorable TV Commercial?	187
19-3	Product Sampling Promotion	191
19-4	Product Placement in Movies and TV	197
19-5	Designing a Publicity Campaign for the Segway™ HT	201
20-1	Student Perceptions of Selling	206
20-2	Expense Account Role-Play	210
20-3	Personal Selling Process	215
21-1	Buying a BMW Z3 Roadster: "Marketplace" vs. "Marketspace" (Part 1)	221
21-2	Buying a BMW Z3 Roadster: "Build Your BMW" (Part 2)	226
22-1	Marketing Planning Worksheet	231
22-2	Brand Extensions: How Far Can General Mills Go?	235
22-3	Strategic Marketing Trends	240

I.

USING THE IN-CLASS ACTIVITIES GUIDE

AND

INSTRUCTOR'S SURVIVAL KIT

USING THE *IN-CLASS ACTIVITIES GUIDE* AND *INSTRUCTOR'S SURVIVAL KIT*

Student Involvement Matters!

Research shows that students who participate actively in their own learning—who are challenged to think, debate, and discuss—often retain and apply much more than students who are less involved. This edition of our *In-Class Activities Guide* contains In-Class Activities (ICAs) for instructors using our textbook. These activities encourage classroom discussion and involvement by adding an experiential component to the education process.

Why a Separate *In-Class Activities Guide*?

An *In-Class Activities Guide* to accompany *Marketing*, Seventh Edition is a result of the overwhelmingly positive reactions we have received from instructors using ICAs from previous editions. To facilitate their use, we have placed the ICAs in this separate *Guide* and provided detailed descriptions—often with some product samples and other "props," to enhance student involvement and learning. Also, most ICAs refer to websites, and for several accessing a website is integral to the ICA. Therefore, we encourage instructors to always recheck the websites and specific links referred to in each ICA before class since these are constantly changing.

Elements of Each In-Class Activity

Each ICA has nine (9) key elements to help instructors select and utilize these in-class activities:

- Learning Objectives. While the activities seek to increase student involvement and participation in the classroom, the most fundamental goal is enhanced learning. Making the key learning objectives explicit helps instructors select activities that are appropriate for their students.

- Definitions. From the glossary, these are provided for the key marketing terms mentioned in the activity.

- Nature of Activity. This is a snapshot summary of what the activity is and does.

- Estimated Class Time. Knowing the approximate time to complete an activity allows instructors to schedule the class period.

- Materials Needed. This describes what transparency masters in this *Guide* need to be made into transparencies, whether items in the *Instructor's Survival Kit* are available for the activity, what photocopies are needed for the class, and what ICA PowerPoint resources are tied to the activity.

- Preparation Before Class. This summarizes what instructors must do before teaching the activity in front of the class.

- <u>Instructions.</u> To simplify preparation for busy instructors, this element of each activity gives a step-by-step sequence to follow to achieve genuine instructional value. As instructors gain experience with an activity, they will often find ways to modify it to achieve their own special objectives in light of their students' backgrounds and interests.
- <u>Marketing Lessons.</u> This is the educational wrap-up—the "takeaway" for students.
- <u>Websites.</u> This lists the websites used in the ICA or suggests others for student use.

In some of the activities, supplementary information is provided to elaborate on the firm involved or identify where supplemental materials may be purchased.

Kinds of In-Class Activities

This *In-Class Activities Guide* contains a diverse array of ICAs that can meet a variety of classroom needs. While many involve team activities, several utilize responses of individual students. Examples of the activities include formal experiments, classroom surveys, student roll-plays, brainstorming, and visits to useful websites.

The ICA PowerPoint CD

Beginning with this edition, we have included two ICA PowerPoint CDs, each of which contains product shots, print ads, TV ads, etc. that either are integral to an ICA or provide additional context. These digital resources are contained in PowerPoint files on the CD, which is organized by chapter and ICA. Because a number of ICAs include digital resources, we have produced two CDs: Disc 1 contains ICA PowerPoints from Chapters 1 - 18; and Disc 2 contains ICA PowerPoints from Chapters 19 - 22.

To use the ICA PowerPoint CD, we recommend that PC users computers that have Windows 98 (Service Release Pack 1) or higher (Windows 2000 preferred) and Office '97 or higher (Office 2000 preferred). Because PowerPoint uses Windows Media Player to play the videos we included (which are in mpeg1 format), earlier versions of Windows or Office will not work or work well. If you need assistance to use the ICA PowerPoint CD, please contact the McGrawHill/Irwin toll-free technical support telephone number at **1-800-331-5094**. A support person should be able to answer your questions.

Items in the *Instructor's Survival Kit*

Besides the *In-Class Activities Guide*, and the ICA PowerPoint CDs, the *Instructor's Survival Kit* contains product samples, props, and other items that can be shown in class. These are described on the next page.

Items in the *Instructor's Survival Kit* Continued

Product Sample or Item	ICA
▪ Original Wooden Victor® 'Metal Bait Pedal' Mousetrap	1-1
▪ The 2002 Rollerblade® Collection brochure	1-2
▪ Victor® 'Easy Set®, Pre-Baited' Mousetrap with the "plastic cheese"	2-2
▪ Victor® 'Live-Catch' Mousetrap	2-2
▪ Victor® 'Quick-Kill' Mousetrap	2-2
▪ Starbucks Coffee Packet and Starbucks Card	5-1
▪ Sprint Prepaid Phone Card	6-1
▪ The 2002 MINI Cooper brochure	7-2
▪ Howlin' Coyote® Chili Challenge Taste Test Questionnaire	8-2
▪ Honey Nut Cheerios® Milk 'N Cereal Bar	9-1
▪ Zebra® Pen Corp. Jimnie® Gel Ink Rollerball Pen (black)	9-2
▪ Zebra® Pen Corp. Gel Sniff-itz® Pen (blueberry)	9-2
▪ Handspring Treo 180 Communicator brochure	10-1
▪ 3M® VHB™ Tape ad ("Screws in Skull" or "In Emergency Break Glass")	10-2
▪ Packet of 3M® VHB™ Tape Pull-tabs	10-2
▪ Original Magnetic Poetry Kit	10-3
▪ Golden Valley Microwave Foods ACT II® Extreme Butter Popcorn	11-1
▪ Golden Valley Microwave Foods ACT II® Kettle Corn Popcorn	11-1
▪ Breathe Right® Nasal Strips Package (2 strips each: tan, clear, kids)	11-2
▪ Frito Lay's Cheetos Asteroids Go Snack canister	11-3
▪ Southwest Airline's Inflatable Plane	12-1
▪ Toro iMow Robotic Mower brochure	18-1
▪ Caress/Valassis Newspac product sample	19-3
▪ Burston-Marsteller Press Releases for the Segway HT	19-5
▪ News America Marketing SmartSource Magazine	20-3
▪ The 2002 BMW Z3 Roadster brochure	21-1
▪ General Mills Wheaties® cereal box	22-2
▪ General Mills Wheaties Energy Crunch® cereal box	22-2

Where the In-Class Activites May Be Used

The tables on the next pages identify the primary chapter in *Marketing*, Seventh Edition, shown with a "**P**," for which an ICA was designed. An "**S**" shows a secondary chapter for which an ICA can be applied. The tables suggest the flexibility with which these ICAs may be adapted to an instructor's teaching style or learning objectives for a specific class.

CHAPTERS FOR WHICH IN-CLASS ACTIVITIES (ICAs) MAY BE USED

ICA	ACTIVITY DESCRIPTION	1	2	3	4	5	6	7	8	9	10	11	12	13	14	15	16	17	18	19	20	21	22
1-1	What Makes a Better Mousetrap? (Part 1)	P	S			S						S											S
1-2	What Is Marketing?	P	S						S	S		S						S					
2-1	Marketing Yourself		P																				S
2-2	What Makes a Better Mousetrap? (Part 2): The Role of Cross-Functional Teams in New Product Development		P			S						S	S			S							S
3-1	Questions That Can't Be Asked in a Pre-Employment Interview			P	S																S		
3-2	Competitive Intelligence		S	P	S				S	S	S							S					S
4-1	Sustainable Development	S	S		P			S	S						S	S	S						
4-2	What Is Ethical and What Is Not? A Survey of Opinions				P			S															
5-1	Buying Process for Starbucks Coffee					P			S				S						S	S		S		
6-1	Buying Center Role-Play						P										S					S		
7-1	Are You an Ethnocentric Consumer?					S		P															
7-2	Marketing Across Borders: Reintroducing the MINI Brand to the U.S.		S			S		P		S	S	S		S	S			S	S	S			S

P = Primary chapter for which activity is intended for use; S = Secondary (or alternative) chapters for which activity is intended for use.

CHAPTERS FOR WHICH IN-CLASS ACTIVITIES (ICAs) MAY BE USED (CONTINUED)

ICA	ACTIVITY DESCRIPTION	1	2	3	4	5	6	7	8	9	10	11	12	13	14	15	16	17	18	19	20	21	22
8-1	Pepsi vs. Coke Taste Test					S			P	S	S	S											
8-2	Designing a Taste Test Questionnaire for Howlin' Coyote Chili®								P	S	S	S											
8-3	Websurfing for Marketing Information					S			P	S	S	S	S										
9-1	Product Categorization to Identify Market Segments and Competitors					S	S		S	P	S	S						S					
9-2	Product Positioning for Consumers and Retailers					S	S		S	P	S	S						S					S
9-3	Developing A Market–Product Grid for the Victor® Line of Mousetraps (Part 3)					S				P	S	S											
10-1	Focus Group for Convergent Digital Devices					S				S	P	S		S	S				S	S			S
10-2	Communicating Important Points of Difference to Skeptical Design Engineers						S		S	S	P	S						S	S	S			S
10-3	Using Method 6–3–5 to Find New Product Ideas for Magnetic Poetry®		S					S			P	S							S	S			S
10-4	What *Were* They Thinking? Analyzing Some New Product Disasters					S			S	S	P	S											
11-1	Managing the Product Life Cycle		S								S	P								S			S
11-2	Using Brainstorming and N/3 Techniques for Breathe Right® Nasal Strips								S	S	S	P						S	S	S			
11-3	Creating Customer Value Through Packaging and Labeling			S	S	S					S	P		S	S		S	S					S

P = Primary chapter for which activity is intended for use; S = Secondary (or alternative) chapters for which activity is intended for use.

CHAPTERS FOR WHICH IN-CLASS ACTIVITIES (ICAs) MAY BE USED (CONTINUED)

ICA	ACTIVITY DESCRIPTION	\multicolumn{22}{c}{TEXTBOOK CHAPTER}																				
		1	2	3	4	5	6	7	8	9	10	11	12	13	14	15	16	17	18	19	20	21	22
12-1	Airline Customer Service and Southwest Airlines			S	S	S	S		S					S		S	S	S					
13-1	Pricing a Panasonic DVD Player			S		S				S	S	S	P	S				S					
14-1	Extra Value Meal Bundle Pricing at McDonald's								S	S	S	S	S	P	S			S					S
15-1	Marketing Channels for Apple Computer					S				S						P	S	S				S	
16-1	The "Foam Factory" Process Improvement Exercise						S				S					S	P						
17-1	Retail Shopping Online: Comparing Prices for a Digital Camera			S		S			S					S	S			P				S	
18-1	An IMC for the Toro® iMow™ Robotic Mower					S				S	S	S						S	P	S			S
18-2	An IMC for the Heritage Museum					S		S					S						P	S			S
19-1	Recognizing Advertising Slogans					S			S										S	P			
19-2	What Makes a Memorable TV Commercial?			S	S					S	S	S	S		S				S	P			S
19-3	Product Sampling Promotion					S			S	S	S	S		S						P			
19-4	Product Placement in Movies and TV									S	S	S								P			S
19-5	Designing a Publicity Campaign for the Segway™ HT					S	S			S	S	S							S	P			S

P = Primary chapter for which activity is intended for use; S = Secondary (or alternative) chapters for which activity is intended for use.

CHAPTERS FOR WHICH IN-CLASS ACTIVITIES (ICAs) MAY BE USED (CONTINUED)

ICA	ACTIVITY DESCRIPTION	1	2	3	4	5	6	7	8	9	10	11	12	13	14	15	16	17	18	19	20	21	22
20-1	Student Perceptions of Selling				S																P		
20-2	Expense Account Role-Play				S		S														P		
20-3	Personal Selling Process						S			S	S									S	P		
21-1	Buying a BMW Z3 Roadster: "Marketplace" vs. "Marketspace" (Part 1)			S		S	S							S	S			S				P	
21-2	Buying a BMW Z3 Roadster: "Build Your BMW" (Part 2)					S	S							S	S		S	S				P	
22-1	Marketing Planning Worksheet		S																				P
22-2	Brand Extensions: How Far Can General Mills Go?		S							S	S	S											P
22-3	Strategic Marketing Trends		S							S	S	S	S										P

P = Primary chapter for which activity is intended for use; S = Secondary (or alternative) chapters for which activity is intended for use.

II.

IN-CLASS ACTIVITIES (ICAs)

CHAPTER 1: DEVELOPING CUSTOMER RELATIONSHIPS AND VALUE THROUGH MARKETING

ICA1-1: IN-CLASS ACTIVITY

WHAT MAKES A BETTER MOUSETRAP? (PART 1)

Learning Objectives. To have students (1) discover the importance of "points of difference" in meeting a customer's wants and needs and (2) see how these may vary by market segment.

Definitions. The following marketing terms are referred to in this in-class activity (ICA):

- Customer Value: The unique combination of benefits received by targeted buyers that includes quality, price, convenience, on-time delivery, and both before-sale and after-sale service.

- Market Segments: The groups that result from the process of market segmentation; these groups ideally (1) have common needs and (2) will respond similarly to a marketing action.

- Points of Difference: Those characteristics of a product that make it superior to competitive substitutes.

Nature of the Activity. To have the instructor lead students through a humorous and involving mini-case in which students do in-class "marketing research" on why a better mousetrap failed more than two decades ago, which forms the basis of later ICAs for Chapter 2 (ICA2-2) and Chapter 9 (ICA9-3).

Estimated Class Time. 20 minutes.

Materials Needed.

- The original wooden Victor® Metal Bait Pedal mousetrap from the *Instructor's Survival Kit* box.[1]

- A transparency of TM1-1A (or use Slide 5 from ICA01-1.ppt of the ISK PowerPoint CD): Why Did the New Plastic Mousetrap Not Meet Sales Expectations?

- A transparency of TM1-1B (or use Slide 6 from ICA01-1.ppt of the ISK PowerPoint CD): Which of the Markets (A, B, C, or D) Was the Largest for Mousetraps 20 Years Ago?

- The ISK PowerPoint CD from the *Instructor's Survival Kit* box. See the instructions for use of this CD on page 4 of this manual if you use this CD in class.

---

[1] Mousetraps provided by Chagnon Outdoor World. See http://www.chagnonoutdoors.com.

Preparation Before Class. Follow the steps below:

1. Read the material below to give a background lecture.

2. Make transparencies of:

    a. TM1-1A (or use Slide 5 from ICA01-1.ppt of the ISK PowerPoint CD).

    b. TM1-1B (or use Slide 6 from ICA01-1.ppt of the ISK PowerPoint CD).

Instructions. Follow the steps below to conduct this ICA:

1. Give students this background mini-lecture (or show Slide 3):

    "If a man...makes a better mousetrap, the world will beat a path to his door."
    Ralph Waldo Emerson

    Let's excuse Mr. Emerson for his sexist statement, written over a century ago! But let's see if he was right!

    Over 20 years ago, Dick Woolworth, president of the Woodstream Corp., decided to take Emerson's adage to heart. Woodstream Corp.'s product was a 100 year-old wooden mousetrap that sold under the Victor® brand name in which peanut butter or cheese was placed on the metal bait pedal connected to the spring-loaded trap bar.

    Pass around the Victor® Metal Bait Pedal mousetrap (or show Slide 4).

    Woolworth decided that what the company needed to do was to build "a better mousetrap and wait for the world to beat a path to its door." He asked his engineers and scientists to study the eating, sleeping, and crawling habits of mice. They did and came up with a better mousetrap—one made of plastic.

    If we compare the new versus the old, the original Victor® Metal Bait Pedal trap sold in a package of 2 for 15 cents and was moderately efficient. The plastic trap sold individually for 25 cents and was very efficient. Thus, if 100 mice stepped on the old wooden trap, assume that 50 got caught (50% efficiency) while with the new plastic trap, assume that 90 got caught (90% efficiency). Woodstream Corp. introduced the new plastic trap in stores across the country. Now, for the sake of argument, suppose that the following problem emerged: Sales of the new better, plastic mousetrap did not meet sales expectations! Why do you suppose that happened?

2. Show transparency TM1-1A (or show Slide 5). Ask students to take 4 minutes to discuss their answers to the questions listed on the transparency with those sitting next to them. Call on the students to answer the following sequence of questions:

- Question 1: What triggers the decision to buy a mousetrap?

    Answer: Seeing nibbled boxes of cereal or mouse droppings on the floor triggers the "buy" decision.

- Question 2: Who in the family makes the decision to buy?

    Answer: The decision maker is the person most bothered by the mouse—often the "Mom" about 20 years ago, when the case takes place.

- Question 3: Who actually buys the mousetrap?

    Answer: The purchaser is the person asked to "take care of the problem"—often the "Dad" about 20 years ago, when the case takes place.

- Question 4: Where does the person buy the mousetrap?

    Answers: Mousetraps might be purchased in hardware stores (Ace), supermarkets (Safeway), mass-merchandisers (Wal-Mart, Target), home improvement stores (Home Depot), or the Internet (Chagnon's Outdoor World). This points out the need for different outlets for different buyers in the family, or different market segments.

- Question 5: Who in the family uses the mousetrap and how do they use it?

    Answers: This is the key question and should turn up two distinct market segments: (1) the "disposers" who dispose of the dead mouse and the trap by throwing both of them into the trash, and (2) the "reusers" who throw the dead mouse into the trash but reuse the trap.

- Question 6: What features do users want in a mousetrap?

    Answers: The "disposer" market segment wants a cheap and relatively efficient way to handle its mouse problem. So the important "points of difference" in its buying decision are low-cost and disposability. The "reuser" segment wants greater efficiency in resolving its persistent mouse problem and may be willing to pay more for a trap as a result.

    The key message: What potential buyers see as "better" is more important than what the scientists and engineers designing the product see as "better."

- Question 7: Why did sales of the "better" plastic mousetrap not meet sales expectations? [AGAIN, THIS IS FOR EDUCATIONAL PURPOSES.]

    Answers: Let the students suggest their answers and write them down on the blackboard. Then show the transparency TM1-1B (or show Slide 6). The answers are described below.

3. Twenty years ago, "efficiency" (the key "point of difference" or benefit) of the plastic trap was not an important feature to most buyers. The "disposer" segment was especially reluctant to throw the dead mouse and the 25-cent plastic trap into the trash can, but not at all hesitant to throw away the 7.5-cent wooden trap. If the wooden trap missed the mouse, these users just reset it. So the wooden trap provided greater <u>customer value</u> for most buyers. And because the largest market segments were "A" and "C" in the table above, the new "better" plastic traps gathered dust on retail shelves across the country. The plastic traps also had a very practical problem: disposing of a live mouse can be tricky (if the lid opened, the mouse may jump out) or time consuming (need to find a place far away from home to release the mouse).

[<u>NOTE</u>: Transparency TM1-1B is really a "market-product grid" that will be introduced in Chapter 9. However, this tool can help in this ICA since it allows students to answer the question: "What do we sell to whom?"]

<u>Marketing Lessons.</u> Customers define what a "better" product is and not the seller or its engineers! So, in a sense, Mr. Emerson was wrong! Key features or "points of difference" in the product provide customer value to users or market segments. These "points of difference" must be important to consumers and communicated to them in terms of (1) benefits to customers, (2) advantages relative to substitute products from competitors, and (3) features, which are given to the form's R&D engineers. Different market segments of buyers exist with different needs, but sometimes it is not possible to reach tiny market segments profitably. In Chapter 2, we'll fast-forward to Woodstream Corp.'s current line of mousetraps with ICA2-2.

<u>Websites.</u> To view Woodstream Corp.'s current product line of Victor® Brand Mousetraps, go to www.victorpest.com. To purchase additional mousetraps for this ICA, go to the Chagnon's Outdoor World website, which is www.chagnonoutdoors.com.

TM1-1A

WHY DID THE NEW PLASTIC MOUSETRAP NOT MEET SALES EXPECTATIONS?

OLD WOODEN TRAP	NEW PLASTIC TRAP
Wood	Plastic
2 for 15¢	25¢ each
50% efficiency	90% efficiency

Some Key Marketing Questions

1. What triggers the decision to buy a mousetrap?

2. Who in the family makes the decision to buy?

3. Who actually buys the mousetrap?

4. Where does the person buy the mousetrap?

5. Who in the family uses the mousetrap and how do they use it?

6. What features do users want in a mousetrap?

7. Why did the "better" plastic mousetrap not meet sales expectations?

© McGraw-Hill Companies, Inc., 2003

TM1-1B

WHICH OF THE MARKETS (A, B, C, OR D) WAS THE LARGEST FOR MOUSETRAPS 20 YEARS AGO?

Market Segment	Product: Kind of Mousetrap	
	Wooden Trap	Plastic Trap
"Disposers"	A	B
"Reusers"	C	D

© McGraw-Hill Companies, Inc., 2003

CHAPTER 1: DEVELOPING CUSTOMER RELATIONSHIPS AND VALUE THROUGH MARKETING

ICA1-2: IN-CLASS ACTIVITY

WHAT IS MARKETING?

Learning Objectives. To demonstrate to students the many activities that make up marketing.

Definitions. The following marketing terms are referred to in this in-class activity (ICA):

- Marketing: The process of planning and executing the conception, pricing, promotion, and distribution of ideas, goods, and services to create exchanges that satisfy individual and organizational objectives.

- Marketing Mix: The marketing manager's controllable factors, the marketing actions of product, price, promotion, and place that he or she can take to solve a marketing problem.

- Product Line: A group of products that are closely related because they satisfy a class of needs, are used together, are sold to the same customer group, are distributed through the same outlets, or fall within a given price range.

- Target Market: One or more specific groups of potential consumers toward which an organization directs its marketing program.

Nature of the Activity. To facilitate class discussion of students' perceptions of marketing. Use the Chapter 1 opening example about Rollerblade® and the discussion of the inline skating industry.

Estimated Class Time. 20 minutes.

Materials Needed.

- The 2002 Rollerblade Collection brochure from the *Instructor's Survival Kit*.

- Copies of the 2002 Rollerblade Collection: Segments, Benefits, Trends, and Marketing Program Handout for each student.

- The ISK PowerPoint CD from the *Instructor's Survival Kit* box. See the instructions for use of this CD on page 4 of this manual if you use this CD in class.

Preparation Before Class. Follow the steps below:

1. Read the Chapter 1 opening example, which contains a description of Rollerblade's marketing program and the current state of the inline skating industry.

2. Page through the 2002 Rollerblade Collection brochure that describes and shows the latest products from Rollerblade and the segments it has chosen to target.

3. Make copies of the 2002 Rollerblade Collection: Segments, Benefits, Trends, and Marketing Program Handout.

4. OPTIONAL: Make copies or color transparencies of selected pages of the 2002 Rollerblade Collection brochure to provide representative examples of the four P's from the inline skate and accessory marketers for two or three of the inline skating target markets listed (fitness, recreation, aggressive, female, kids, and speed) in the following handout that might be of most interest to your students.

Instructions. Follow the steps below to conduct this ICA:

1. Ask students what comes to their mind when they hear the word "marketing." If they have not yet read Chapter 1, they are likely to mention "advertising" or "selling." If they have read Chapter 1, they may also mention the four P's of the marketing mix.

2. Create a list of all the words/activities that students mention, which will provide a good starting point for discussing the many activities that make up marketing.

3. Ask students about their inline skating behavior and have them provide examples of marketing activities used by Rollerblade (or others) in the inline skating industry (K2, Roces, Salomon, Ultra Wheels, etc.) based on advertising awareness and personal experiences.

4. Pass around the 2002 Rollerblade Collection brochure (or show the following slides from ICA01-2.ppt of the ISK PowerPoint CD) that describe the market segments Rollerblade has targeted, the products it has developed to meet the needs of these segments, and ads it has designed to reach particular segments.

    a. Show Slide 3: A Rollerblade reminder print ad.

    b. <u>Fitness Segment</u>: Show Slides 4 – 6 (graphic, skate, pioneering print ad).

    c. <u>Recreation Segment</u>: Show Slides 7 – 8 (graphic, skate).

    d. <u>Aggressive (Street/Vertical) Segment</u>: Show Slides 9 – 10 (graphic, skate).

    e. <u>Women's Segment</u>: Show Slides 11 – 13 (graphic, skate, pioneering print ad).

    f. <u>Junior (Kids) Segment</u>: Show Slides 14 – 15 (graphic, skate).

    g. <u>Speed Segment</u>: Show Slides 16 – 17 (graphic, skate).

5. Discuss the benefits sought by, the trends occurring within, and marketing program used to target these segments.

6. Give students the 2002 Rollerblade Collection: Segments, Benefits, Trends, and Marketing Program Handout and briefly discuss the marketing mix Rollerblade has developed to reach its target market in 2002. [NOTE: For most segments, Rollerblade uses common promotions, such as advertising, trade shows, point-of-purchase displays in retail outlets, and sponsorships of regional, national, and international inline skating events. It also places its logo on items such as T-shirts, sandals, etc.]

Marketing Lessons. This exercise introduces students to the elements of the marketing mix. Most students will conclude that (a) marketing is much more than their initial perceptions, (b) they already know about marketing from their experiences as consumers (in this case, with inline skates, (c) most firms develop unique products for specific segments to meet their needs, and (d) firms such as Rollerblade select specific segments to target due to resource and marketing considerations.

Website. Rollerblade's website is www.rollerblade.com.

2002 Rollerblade Collection: Segments, Benefits, Trends, and Marketing Program Handout

BENEFITS, TRENDS, AND MARKETING PROGRAM	MARKET SEGMENT		
	FITNESS	RECREATION	AGGRESSIVE (STREET/VERT)
Benefits and Trends	<ul><li>Able to get a serious workout</li><li>Able to cross-train for hockey, ice skating, figure skating, etc.</li><li>Large and fast-growing segment</li><li>Focus on technology that allows for greater comfort and movement in ankles and legs</li><li>Ultra-light weight</li><li>Premium components</li><li>Customizable frames</li></ul>	<ul><li>Fun</li><li>Large and fast-growing segment</li><li>Value-oriented</li><li>Focus on the combination of greater comfort and support</li><li>ABT system for controlled braking</li></ul>	<ul><li>Comfort</li><li>High tech features</li><li>Performance</li><li>Image</li><li>Style similar to skateboard shoes</li><li>New skate parks opening</li><li>Now a sport: Gravity Games and X Games</li></ul>
Product	<ul><li>Rollerblade Models: Lightning 05, Core 09, & Core 07</li><li>Most firms have several skates in its product line</li><li>Other marketers include K2, Roces, Salomon, and UltraWheels</li></ul>	<ul><li>Rollerblade Models: EVO 08, EVO 07, EVO 04, & Fusion</li><li>Most firms have several skates in its product line</li><li>Other marketers include K2, Roces, Salomon, and UltraWheels</li></ul>	<ul><li>Rollerblade Models: Estilo TRS Pro, TRS Detail, TRS Access, & Swindler</li><li>Most firms have 1 to 3 skates in its product line</li><li>Other marketers include K2, Roces, Salomon, and UltraWheels</li></ul>
Price	<ul><li>Most prices: $200 - $700</li></ul>	<ul><li>Most prices: $50 - $200</li></ul>	<ul><li>Most prices: $180 - $350</li></ul>
Promotion	<ul><li>Workout plan on website</li></ul>	<ul><li>Tips on how to start</li></ul>	<ul><li>Inline skating events (skate ramps, street skating, etc.)</li><li>Sponsored athletes</li><li>Ads in local publications</li><li>E-mail outreach to inform customers of new products</li></ul>
Place	<ul><li>Specialty inline skate shops</li><li>Sporting goods stores</li><li>The Internet</li></ul>	<ul><li>Specialty inline skate shops</li><li>Sporting goods stores</li><li>Mass-merchandisers</li><li>The Internet</li></ul>	<ul><li>Specialty inline skate shops</li><li>Sporting goods stores</li><li>The Internet</li></ul>

2002 Rollerblade Collection: Segments, Benefits, Trends, and Marketing Program Handout

BENEFITS, TRENDS, AND MARKETING PROGRAM	MARKET SEGMENT		
	FEMALE	**KIDS**	**SPEED**
Benefits and Trends	• Fun • Fitness • Image • Growing segment	• Fun • Fitness/coordination • Sports conditioning • Self-confidence • Growing segment • No ice skating in summer • Durability • Value-conscious • Protective gear bought in conjunction with skates • Skates adjust as kid grows	• A small segment • Excitement • More product knowledge required • Probably started as a "fitness" inline or ice speed skater • Spends much more on equipment • Concern for snug boots • Focus on technology that allows both support and control in ankles
Product	• Rollerblade Models: Versions of men's but designed for women's specific fit • Focus on fitness • Marketers now targeting women with uniquely designed inline skates	• Rollerblade Models: Maxx 500 & BX 10 • Most firms do not offer • Other marketers include K2, Roces, and UltraWheels	• Rollerblade Models: Road Runner & Lightning 09 • "Speed" inline skates have 5 instead of 4 wheels • Other marketers include Bont Skates, K2, Salomon, Simmons Racing, and Verducci
Price	• Most prices same as men's inline skates	• Most prices: $30 - $130	• Most prices: $400 - $2,000, the highest average price
Promotion	• Show female inline skaters in ads • Female members in Performance Team	• Show kids inline skating and having fun • Developed Skate in School program to boost youth fitness and self-esteem • Developed Blade School™ to teach kids how to skate	• Sponsor national & international team competitions
Place	• Specialty inline skate shops • Sporting goods stores • Mass-merchandisers • The Internet	• Specialty inline skate shops • Sporting goods stores • Mass-merchandisers • The Internet	• Specialty inline skate shops since sales reps require more product knowledge • The Internet

CHAPTER 2: LINKING MARKETING AND CORPORATE STRATEGIES

ICA2-1: IN-CLASS ACTIVITY

MARKETING YOURSELF

Learning Objectives. To show students, especially non-marketing majors, that marketing is applicable to their future by using the strategic marketing process and marketing mix when looking for a job.

Definitions. The following marketing terms are referred to in this in-class activity (ICA):

- Marketing Mix: The marketing manager's controllable factors, the marketing actions of product, price, promotion, and place that he or she can take to solve a marketing problem.

- Positioning: The place an offering (or individual) occupies in a consumer's (employer's) mind with regard to important attributes relative to competitive offerings (other people).

- Situation Analysis: Taking stock of where the firm or product (or individual) has been recently, where it (he/she) is now, and where it (he/she) is headed in terms of the organization's (or person's) plans and the external factors and trends affecting it (him/her).

- Strategic Marketing Process: The approach whereby an organization (or individual) allocates its (his/her) marketing mix resources to reach its (his/her) target markets (employment opportunities).

- SWOT Analysis: An acronym describing an organization's (individual's) appraisal of its (his/her) internal strengths and weaknesses and external opportunities and threats.

Nature of the Activity. To have students apply the strategic marketing process to themselves as they seek employment.

Estimated Class Time. 20 minutes.

Materials Needed.

- Copies of the "Marketing Yourself" handout for each student.

- Copies of the "The Do-It-Myself Marketing Plan" worksheet for each student.

- The ISK PowerPoint CD from the *Instructor's Survival Kit* box. See the instructions for use of this CD on page 4 of this manual if you use this CD in class.

Preparation Before Class. Follow the steps below:

1. Read through Appendix C: Planning a Career in Marketing, which describes the process on how to "market yourself."

2. Make copies of the "Marketing Yourself" Handout and "The Do-It-Myself Marketing Plan" worksheet.

Instructions. Follow the steps below to conduct this ICA:

1. Show Slide 3: HotJobs.com TV ad (TRT: 0:30). This pioneering, humorous ad shows how being both qualified and prepared for the job interview can lead to a job that fits both the applicant and the employer.

2. Ask students about the type of jobs they hope to land after graduation and how they intend to find these jobs. Most students will describe a "shotgun approach" of aiming at any type of a job without really any focused or targeted effort at specific careers (product management, marketing research, advertising, sales, etc.) or positions (assistant product manager, marketing research analyst, etc.).

3. Contrast the difference between a shotgun approach and a targeted marketing effort. This is a good opportunity to explain how research can help students develop information to identify alternative "target markets." For example, students can learn about potential opportunities through networking, internships, informational interviewing, and many secondary sources.

4. Have students conduct a situation analysis, which involves taking stock of what they have done regarding their career search, where they are now, and where they are headed in terms of their existing plans and the external factors and trends affecting their employment prospects. A SWOT analysis should be used to appraise students' personal strengths and weaknesses as well as their opportunities for and threats (or barriers) to successful employment.

    a. To conduct an internal analysis, ask students what some of their strengths and weaknesses are in terms of the courses taken and grades received, work experience, extra-curricular activities involvement, honors received, etc.

    b. To conduct an external analysis, ask students which industries or types of jobs are growing or in demand that may be opportunities. Further, ask them what advantages or "points of difference" they have relative to other "competitors" (other students) seeking the same job opportunities, such as taking this marketing course, the reputation of this educational institution, etc. Finally, ask them what other external forces can impact their job search, for example a downturn in the economy, the need to be computer literate, etc. This type of focused approach helps to define potential market segments that can be targeted.

5. Ask students to identify elements of their marketing mix:

    - What type of "product" do you have to offer?

    - What sort of "pricing" is appropriate?

    - What "promotion" will be utilized?

    - What type of "place" or channel will be used? These include intermediaries such as on-campus career services, networking, employment agencies, and even the Internet, with firms such as HotJobs.com (or show Slide 4).

6. Pass out copies of the "Marketing Yourself" and "The Do-It-Yourself Marketing Plan" worksheets and ask students to spend 10 minutes filling them out.

7. Call on students and ask them to share portions of their personal marketing plan with the class. If students have few ideas about their marketing mix, ask about how information could be developed to help formulate an appropriate marketing mix.

8. Show Slides 5-7 from Richard Bolles' *2002 What Color is Your Parachute?*, which is the best-selling job-hunting book its 32nd edition, to provide students with a tangible resource for applying the strategic marketing process to themselves.

<u>Marketing Lesson.</u> The strategic marketing process can be applied to products, services, ideas, and even to marketing yourself!

<u>Websites.</u> To investigate some job possibilities, go to the HotJobs website, which is www.hotjobs.com. To view the Ten Speed Press website, go to www.tenspeed.com. For Richard Bolles' website, go to www.jobhuntersbible.com. There, you will find information on the latest edition of his best-selling book, *What Color is Your Parachute?* Bolles also has several other resources that may help students plan their careers and first job search.

MARKETING YOURSELF

Planning Phase

Situation Analysis

- Internal Assessment: What are your strengths and weaknesses? What can you do to enhance your strengths and minimize your weaknesses? What type of competitive advantage do YOU have? If you don't have one, can you develop one?

- External Analysis: What are the trends in the environmental factors that could impact your job search and career development? These consist of: socio-cultural, economic, technological, regulatory, and competitive factors.

- Competitive Analysis: What type of background, experiences, strengths, and weaknesses do your competitors have?

- Market Analysis: What market segments (job opportunities) have you identified as having the best potential? How do you fit into these markets? [NOTE: This means doing some research!]

Focus and Goal Setting

- What are your objectives? Make them specific and measurable! What is your target market? Examples might be large public accounting firms, business-to-business sales, and marketing research for a consulting firm in Chicago, etc.

Marketing Program

- Product: YOU. Know yourself well. Continually improve yourself. Understand how you can meet the needs of your target market—prospective employers!

- Pricing: What salary and compensation package do you want? What are you willing to settle for? What's the average salary received by competitors in your target market?

- Promotion: Very important. Think about the buying process. How will you create awareness for yourself? What can you do to "break through the clutter" and get the opportunity for an interview? Your personal selling skills will be important for telephone contacts and face-to-face interviews. Probe to find out about the needs of the organization before that "sales call" and during the interview. Have your questions prepared.

- Place: What channels have you developed to access your target market, such as associations, personal contacts, professors, etc? Do some careful research on these. Don't assume that intensive distribution is necessarily the way to go. Focus your efforts to those target markets that hold promise.

Implementation Phase

Develop a timetable and budget for research, wardrobe, résumés, and travel. Carry out your program. Contact your target market opportunities. Follow-up consistently. Remember that looking for a job requires a significant commitment of your time and effort.

Control Phase

Follow-up on all leads. Find out why you did or didn't make the cut. Ask at an interview what it was about your résumé that interested them. Even if you don't get the job, you have more insight. Similarly, when you call to follow-up on those cover letters and résumés that you sent out, ask when decisions will be made, when it would be appropriate to call back (and then do it). If you are rejected, call back and ask why. If you exhaust all of the possibilities in a given target market, go back to your situation analysis and identify new segments. Always send a "Thank You" note.

Resources:

- Your college placement office.

- Informational interviewing (a great opportunity to learn more about careers you are considering while you are still in school and can make some adjustments to your program).

- Internships. Good experience to build your résumé and potential contacts for positions. Even if you don't want to work there, they can possibly open doors for you elsewhere.

- From Appendix C, *Marketing*, 7th Edition, here are two important resources to consult:

    Richard N. Bolles, *The 2002 What Color is Your Parachute?: A Practical Manual for Job-Hunters and Career-Changers*, (Berkeley, CA: Ten Speed Press, 2001). A companion workbook is also available. See www.jobhuntersbible.com (Bolles' website) and www.tenspeedpress.com.

    Martin Yate, *Knock'em Dead 2002 Edition; Cover Letters That Knock 'Em Dead; and Resumes That Knock 'Em Dead*, (Holbrook, MA: Adams Media Corporation, 2002; 2001; 2001). See www. adamsmedia.com.

Websites. The following contain resources on job searches, résumé writing, interviewing, job postings, etc.

www.careercity.com   www.hotjobs.com

www.careerXroads.com   www.monster.com

www.careers-in-marketing.com   www.studentcentral.com

THE DO-IT-MYSELF MARKETING PLAN

STRATEGIC MARKETING PROCESS		MY OWN MARKETING PLAN		
P L A N N I N G P H A S E	Situational Analysis (SWOT)	Location of Factor	Kind of Factor	
			Favorable	Unfavorable
		Internal: Me • Personality • Formal Education • Job Experience • Motivation • Other:_____	My Strengths:	My Weaknesses:
		External: • Economic • Technical • Legal • Other:_____	Opportunities For Me:	Threats Affecting Me:
	Focus and Goal Setting	My Goals Upon Graduation	Personal Goals:	
		My Desired Position	Job Description:	
		My Target Industries, Organizations, and Locations	Industries:	
			Organizations:	
			Geographical Areas:	
		My Uniqueness (Points of Difference)	Personality:	
			Education & Experience:	
			Other:	
		My "Positioning"	How You Compare to Other Job Applicants:	

THE DO-IT-MYSELF MARKETING PLAN (CONTINUED)

	MARKETING PROGRAM	MY OWN MARKETING PLAN	
PLANNING PHASE	• Product Strategy (Actions to Improve My "Marketability")	Formal Education/Courses:	
		Job Experiences/Projects Completed:	
		Extra-Curricular/Volunteer Activities:	
		Obstacles To Overcome:	
	• Price Strategy	Compensation Sought:	
	• Promotion Strategy	Résumé, Personal Interviews, and Letters/Telephone Calls:	
	• Place Strategy	Networking for Contacts and References:	
IMPLEMENTATION PHASE	• Schedule/Budget	Actions to Take/Budget	Deadlines
	Marketing Actions (Courses to take, summer jobs to get, résumés to write, clothes to buy, travel arrangements to make, etc.)	1. 2. 3. 4. 5. 6.	1. 2. 3. 4. 5. 6.
CONTROL PHASE	• Evaluation	What Did and Didn't Work:	
	• Control	How to Modify Strategy:	

CHAPTER 2: LINKING MARKETING AND CORPORATE STRATEGIES

ICA2-2: IN-CLASS ACTIVITY

WHAT MAKES A BETTER MOUSETRAP? (PART 2): THE ROLE OF CROSS-FUNCTIONAL TEAMS IN NEW PRODUCT DEVELOPMENT

Learning Objectives. To have students (1) see the role cross-functional or multi-disciplinary teams play in new product development and (2) experience the importance of linking customer value and "points of difference" to features of a new product.

Definitions. The following marketing terms are referred to in this in-class activity (ICA):

- Cross-Functional Teams: A small number of people from different departments (marketing, accounting, finance, R & D, operations, manufacturing, etc.) in an organization who are mutually accountable to a common set of performance goals.

- Customer Value: The unique combination of benefits received by targeted buyers that includes quality, price, convenience, on-time delivery, and both before-sale and after-sale service.

- Points of Difference: Those characteristics of a product that make it superior to competitive substitutes.

Nature of the Activity. To have students role-play four different business functions that are represented on a cross-functional new product development team and to evaluate the product introduction of a new mousetrap design. This activity is the second part of the mini-case presented as an ICA for Chapter 1 (ICA1-1). The final part is an ICA for Chapter 9 (ICA9-3).

Estimated Class Time. 25 minutes.

Materials Needed.

- The Victor® Metal Bait Pedal, Live Catch, Easy Set®, Pre-Baited, and Quick Kill mousetraps from the *Instructor's Survival Kit* box.[1]

- A transparency of TM2-2A (or use Slide 8 of the ICA02-2 ISK PowerPoint CD): Roles and Responsibilities of Four Members of the "Better Mousetrap" Cross-Functional Teams.

- A transparency of TM2-2B (or use Slide 9 from ICA02-2.ppt of the ISK PowerPoint CD): The Two Tasks of the "Better Mousetrap" Cross-Functional Teams.

- A transparency of TM2-2C (or use Slide 10 from ICA02-2.ppt of the ISK PowerPoint CD): Cross-Functional New Product Develoment Teams: A Quick Look.

---

[1] Mousetraps provided by Chagnon Outdoor World. See http://www.chagnonoutdoors.com.

- The ISK PowerPoint CD from the *Instructor's Survival Kit* box. See the instructions for use of this CD on page 4 of this manual if you use this CD in class.

Preparation Before Class. Follow the steps below:

1. Review the material from ICA1-1: What Makes a Better Mousetrap? (Part 1).

2. Read the material below to give the background mini-lecture.

3. Make transparencies of:

    a. TM2-2A (or use Slide 8 from ICA02-2.ppt of the ISK PowerPoint CD).

    b. TM2-2B (or use Slide 9 from ICA02-2.ppt of the ISK PowerPoint CD).

    c. TM2-2C (or use Slide 10 from ICA02-2.ppt of the ISK PowerPoint CD).

Instructions. Follow the steps below to conduct this ICA:

1. Refresh students' memories of ICA1-1: What Makes a Better Mousetrap? (Part 1) for this mini-case. Focus on the features or benefits users want in a mousetrap. Pass around the Victor® Metal Bait Pedal mousetrap (or show Slide 3).

    The original wooden Victor® Metal Bait Pedal mousetrap is a spring-loaded trap with a metal bait pedal to place peanut butter or cheese. Consumers who buy this trap are part of the "disposer" market segment because they want a cheap and relatively efficient way to handle their mouse problem. So the important "points of difference" in this segment's buying decision are low-cost and disposability (convenience).

2. Give students this background mini-lecture:

    Dick Woolworth's negative experience 20 years ago has not stopped Woodstream Corp. (or other firms) from trying to invent a better mousetrap in an attempt to prove the validity of Emerson's adage. In recent years, new plastic mousetraps have appeared because research shows that some people do not want to see or touch a captured mouse while others prefer to humanely release a live, but captured mouse. **This newer plastic trap is different from the one discussed in ICA1-1**.

    The newer Victor® Live-Catch mousetrap allows a user to place some cheese or peanut butter at the back end of the trap, which then is placed on the floor with the open end touching the ground. When the mouse enters the trap, it tips it, which slams the door and traps the mouse. The user then picks up the plastic trap and to transport the live mouse outside. Finally, the user opens the door and lets the mouse out.

    Pass around the Victor® Live Catch mousetrap (or show Slide 4).

This newer plastic trap is even more efficient than the old plastic traps of twenty years ago. Now, almost 100 percent of mice are caught when they enter the plastic trap to eat the bait compared to 90 percent previously. Consumers who buy this trap are part of the "reuser" market segment because they want greater efficiency and a more cost-effective means to resolve a persistent mouse problem. So the important "point of difference" in this segment's buying decision is efficiency.

The new Victor® Live Catch plastic mousetrap is priced at $3.49 for a package of two at retail stores (home improvement, mass-merchandisers, hardware, etc.) while the original wooden Victor® Metal Bait Pedal mousetrap sells for about $1.00 for a package of two (or show Slide 5).

Now, we're going to discuss this recently introduced Victor® Live Catch mousetrap as a new product idea. To do that, we are going to ask you to play four different roles in a cross-functional new product development team.

3. Show transparency TM2-2A (or show Slide 6) and organize students into groups for role-play.

    Get into groups of four, and count off 1, 2, 3, and 4 within each group so that each person has a number. Now, in these groups, each student will play the role of a certain type of functional expert in the development of this plastic mousetrap. The overhead shows the roles students will play roles based on the number assigned:

    - Person #1 is the group leader, who is responsible for keeping the group on task, ensuring all questions are answered and all points of view are aired. This person will also report the results to the whole class at the end of the exercise.

    - Person #2 is the research and development or technical representative. This person should evaluate the Victor® Live-Catch mousetrap from a design perspective. How does the technology compare with the original wooden Victor® Metal Bait Pedal mousetrap? Is its performance better or worse? What new design ideas can be developed, consistent with past technological capabilities?

    - Person #3 is the marketing representative. This person should think about customer reactions to the Victor® Live-Catch mousetrap. Who are the customers? How do they use traps? What needs might this trap satisfy? What weaknesses or problems exist with both the plastic and wooden traps and what solutions or improvements can we find? What are the pricing and promotion strategies that can be used to sell the plastic trap? Where should these plastic traps be sold?

    - Person #4 is the manufacturing representative. This person is concerned about the durability and reliability of the product, and the ease with which it can be manufactured and assembled in the factory.

4. Show transparency TM2-2B (or show Slide 7) and have your teams focus on the two tasks shown.

   Task #1: Continue to pass the Victor® Live-Catch mousetrap around to the teams to evaluate it and re-show Slide 4: The Victor® Live Catch Mousetrap, if needed.

   Task #2: Have student teams search for benefits and corresponding features to design a better mousetrap! Remember which function or department you are representing, and be sure to get your concerns addressed in this discussion. The team leader will report to the class. Take about 15 minutes to cover this task.

5. Have each group report their conclusions. It is helpful to record these on the board or on a blank transparency. Points to raise or emphasize:

   Task #1: Evaluate the Victor® Live-Catch mousetrap.

   - Question 1: Who are the customers? How do they use traps? What needs might this trap satisfy?

     Answers: Target market segment is mousetrap "reusers". They are: environmentally-conscious, humane (don't want to kill the mice), and concerned about potential health or injury risks.

   - Question 2: How does the technology of the Victor® Live-Catch mousetrap compare with the Victor® Metal Bait Pedal mousetrap? Is its performance (efficiency) better or worse? Would you recommend introducing this new trap?

     Answers: There are "Pros" and "Cons" to the Victor® Live-Catch mousetrap:

     a. Pro's: Easy to set; no risk of injuring fingers from accidentally tripping the spring; more efficient at capture (weight shift of mouse inside trap closes door); simple, inexpensive design (1 moving part; 3 parts total); user protected from contamination from dead mouse; easy to remove (mouse slides out live).

     b. Con's: Live mouse to relocate (time consuming); higher unit price ($1.75 vs. $0.50); potential for mouse bite during removal.

   - Question 3: What are some reasons for or against offering the new plastic trap?

     Answers: There are both reasons to and not to introduce the new plastic trap:

     a. Reasons to introduce: Reach environmentally-conscious segment which does not want to touch or kill mouse; can reuse trap; easy disposal; relatively manufacturing and assembly due to few parts.

     b. Reasons not to introduce: Difficulties in switching manufacturing to this design, which uses different materials than wood.

Task #2: Search for benefits and corresponding features to design a better mousetrap!

- Question 1: What are some of the benefits and corresponding features in mousetraps that satisfy the needs of various markets?

    Answers: Benefits and features include:
    - Cheap
    - Not too messy
    - Kills mouse/doesn't kill mouse
    - Innovative design
    - Convenience
    - Reuse/dispose
    - Convenient
    - Value (price/performance)

- Question 2: What are some of the features to add to or improve upon existing mousetraps?

    Answers: Features to add to or improve upon existing mousetraps include:
    - Avoid need to replace peanut butter or cheese bait
    - Low kill rate (inefficient mousetrap)
    - What to do with the dead/live mouse
    - Trapping/catching more than one mouse before disposal
    - Using technologies that scare away mice from the dwelling

6. Woodstream Corp. has recently developed a new trap called the Victor® Easy Set®, Pre-Baited mousetrap, which improves on the basic wooden metal pedal trap.

    Pass around the Victor® Easy Set®, Pre-Baited mousetrap (or show Slide 8).

    As you can see, the Victor® Easy Set®, Pre-Baited mousetrap comes with a clever yellow plastic "Swiss cheese" pedal that requires no baiting because it is infused with a scent mice find irresistible! When the mouse sniffs and touches the cheese, it triggers the spring-loaded bar, killing the mouse. This trap is priced at $1.59 for a package of two, slightly higher than the original wooden Victor® Metal Bait Petal trap and can be found at home improvement, hardware, and mass- merchandiser stores.

    Task: Evaluate the Victor® Easy Set®, Pre-Baited mousetrap.

    - Question 1: Who are the customers? How do they use traps? What needs might this trap satisfy?

        Answers: Target market segment is mousetrap "disposers." They want to use a trap that is very easy to operate (don't even want to bait the trap with cheese or peanut butter). They also are price-conscious, concerned about efficiency (hopes the mouse is dead), and unconcerned about potential health or injury risks.

    - Question 2: What are the advantages and disadvantages of this trap?

        Answers: There are "Advantages" and "Disadvantages" to this trap:

- Advantages of the Victor® Easy Set®, Pre-Baited Mousetrap:
    - The permanent bait feature; they don't like the mess or risk of baiting a wooden, spring-loaded trap by hand for fear of accidental injury.
    - Modest price increase per unit over the original wooden trap for the added feature of impregnated cheese smell.
    - Longer lever arm—the cheese gives a longer lever arm, thereby making the trap more sensitive and more efficient at killing mice.
- Disadvantages of the Victor® Easy Set®, Pre-Baited Mousetrap:
    - Must buy the trap in a package of two.
    - Unsure as to whether the "plastic cheese" infused with a mouse attractant is more effective at luring mice than real bait.
    - Danger of contamination when disposing of mouse.

7. Recently, Woodstream invented the Victor® Quick-Kill mousetrap (with the "guillotine-like" killing bar), which is a completely new innovation. The black cover is lifted from the bait trough to place the bait. Next, the "killing bar" is lifted and locked into place. To get at the bait, the mouse must poke its head between the cover and the trough. As it lifts the cover with its head, the mouse then activates the killing bar, causing it to forcefully snap down on the mouse's head/neck and killing it instantly. This trap is priced at $4.29 for a package of two and can be found at home improvement, hardware, and mass-merchandiser stores.

    Pass around the Victor® Quick Kill mousetrap (or show Slide 9).

    [NOTE: When demonstrating this trap, be careful! The killing bar snaps down forcefully and could cause injury to fingers! After setting the killing bar, stick a pencil or pen in the hole created by the cover and trough to activate the mechanism. It will make a loud "SNAP!" To manually reset the trap, hold the bar while lifting up the bait cover. Lower the bar very slowly.]

    Task: Evaluate the Victor® Quick-Kill mousetrap.

    - Question 1: Who are the customers? How do they use traps? What needs might this trap satisfy?

        Answers: Target market segment is mousetrap "reusers". They want to use a trap that is very efficient (wants the mouse to be very dead)! Therefore, price is not as great a consideration and unconcerned about potential health or injury risks.

    - Question 2: What are the advantages and disadvantages of this trap?

        Answers: There are "Advantages" and "Disadvantages" to this trap:

- Advantages of the Victor® Quick-Kill Mousetrap:
    - The trap is extremely effective in killing mice.
    - Innovative design.
    - Durable design (tough plastic & metal; spring is of a higher gauge metal than wooden trap).
- Disadvantages of the Victor® Quick-Kill Mousetrap:
    - Unit cost is $2.15 per trap (package of two required).
    - Danger of contamination when disposing of mouse.
    - "Killing bar" creates the perception of the least humane method for solving the mouse problem.
    - Must be careful since the "killing bar" could injure fingers.

Marketing Lessons. A new product is better in the eye of consumers if it deals with their problem better. This is the essence of "customer value." The success of a new product depends on how well its design meets customer needs. Technological possibilities must be linked with market realities. Successful innovators have more insight into user applications and technological trends and are able to convert these insights into successful products.

Epilogue: Mini-lecture on Cross-Functional Teams. Show transparency TM2-2C (or show Slide 10). Every study that has examined new product development shows that collaboration among design, manufacturing, marketing, and other functional areas of an organization contributes to the success of a new product or service. Collaboration: (1) enhances the product design by linking the technology with the needs of the market; (2) improves the execution of the entire process from development to deployment; (3) makes assessment of the product's commercial viability easier, and (4) allows for the discovery of optimal design characteristics. This optimization occurs because each department has a unique perspective that is important to the overall process, and when it communicates with and challenges each other, the insights from each can be integrated to develop the best product possible.

One of the primary ways in which companies encourage this collaboration is the use of cross-functional new product development teams discussed throughout text. A cross-functional new product development team is a small group of people (8 to 10) representing a firm's various business functions or departments. The team is responsible for coordinating the design, engineering, and subsequent manufacture of components, subassemblies, or total systems that are part of the final product. The functions represented vary, but representatives from R&D, marketing, manufacturing, and finance are usually key players.

Firms do this in order to encourage parallel rather than sequential new product development. When all functions come on board at the beginning of a project, everyone can understand how decisions are arrived at and where ideas come from. It is then much easier to get commitment at a later stage. Being involved from the beginning also often leads to a greater sense of ownership of the project and a higher level of involvement. Development is also faster when done in parallel. All team members are working on their tasks at the same time, rather than waiting for something to be handed off to them, as in a serial process. Groups are generally felt to generate better solutions to complex problems than individuals. Group decisions are more creative because they integrate multiple viewpoints, and sharing ideas with others encourages comprehensive analysis of potential solutions to problems encountered.

<u>Websites.</u> To view Woodstream Corp.'s current product line of Victor® Brand Mousetraps, go to www.victorpest.com. To purchase additional mousetraps for this ICA, go to the Chagnon's Outdoor World website, which is www.chagnonoutdoors.com.

TM2-2A

ROLES AND RESPONSIBILITIES OF FOUR MEMBERS OF THE "BETTER MOUSETRAP" CROSS-FUNCTIONAL TEAMS

In your group of four, count off: 1, 2, 3, & 4

- ❑ Person #1: Team Leader Responsibilities:
  - Keep group on task; ensure that all views are aired
  - Report conclusions to class at end

- ❑ Person #2: Technical/R&D Responsibilities:
  - Focus on product design, technology, and performance
  - Make sure proposed ideas are consistent with past technological capabilities

- ❑ Person #3: Marketing Responsibilities:
  - Focus on the customer: Who are they? How do they use the trap? What needs are fulfilled?
  - Identify weaknesses and problems with present mousetraps and try to suggest solutions
  - Suggest pricing, promotion, and place strategies

- ❑ Person #4: Manufacturing Responsibilities:
  - Focus on durability, quality, and reliability
  - Consider ease of manufacture and assembly

© McGraw-Hill Companies, Inc., 2003

TM2-2B

THE TWO TASKS OF THE "BETTER MOUSETRAP" CROSS-FUNCTIONAL TEAMS

- Task #1: Evaluate the new Victor Pest mousetrap

    a. What is the target market segment and the needs this trap satisfies?

    b. What are the mousetrap's pros and cons? How does it compare with the wooden trap?

    c. Should we aggressively market this plastic mousetrap? Or withdraw it? Why?

- Task #2: Search for benefits and corresponding features to design a better mousetrap!

    a. What features (customer benefits) of the wooden and plastic traps you have seen that are good and should be retained or enhanced?

    b. What features (customer benefits) should be added or improved?

    c. Recommend a mousetrap with the features you identified in "a" and "b" above

© McGraw-Hill Companies, Inc., 2003

TM2-2C

CROSS-FUNCTIONAL NEW PRODUCT DEVELOPMENT TEAMS: A QUICK LOOK

- <u>Definition</u>: A small number of people from different departments in an organization who are mutually accountable to a common set of performance goals.

- <u>Functions represented</u>: Varies across firms and industries, but typically includes:

    - Product design/R&D
    - Materials management
    - Manufacturing
    - Accounting
    - Finance
    - Marketing
    - Operations

- Advantages of cross-functional teams for new product development:

    - Increases commitment
    - Eases implementation
    - Speeds up process
    - Integrates multiple perspectives for better solutions
    - Improves communications
    - Delegates tasks and fixes responsibilities

© McGraw-Hill Companies, Inc., 2003

CHAPTER 3: SCANNING THE MARKETING ENVIRONMENT

ICA3-1: IN-CLASS ACTIVITY

QUESTIONS THAT CANNOT BE ASKED IN A PRE-EMPLOYMENT INTERVIEW

Learning Objectives. To sensitize students to the kinds of questions they can or cannot ask in pre-employment interviews, thereby avoiding possible allegations of discrimination in hiring practices, a growing area in the legal/regulatory environment.

Definitions. The following marketing terms are referred to in this in-class activity (ICA):

- Laws: Society's values and standards that are enforceable in the courts.

- Regulations: Restrictions state and federal laws place on business with regard to the conduct of its activities.

Nature of the Activity. To have students indicate whether or not they believe an interviewer can ask them certain questions in a pre-employment interview.

Estimated Class Time. 30 minutes, which consists of:

- 10 minutes for distribution, completion, and return of the Pre-employment Interview Questionnaire (PIQ) during one class period.

- 20 minutes to discuss student responses during the subsequent class period.

Materials Needed. The Pre-Employment Interview Questionnaire.

Preparation Before Class. Read the material below and make copies of the Pre-Employment Interview Questionnaire (PIQ) for each student.

Instructions. Follow the steps below to conduct this ICA:

1. Ask students to check whether or not they believe it is appropriate to ask an interviewee each of the 16 questions listed on the PIQ.

2. Collect the PIQ and tabulate the responses for each question. Make a transparency of the PIQ to summarize the results during the following class period. Some time might be spent highlighting those questions that most students think can or cannot be asked.

3. Make a transparency of the PIQ to summarize the results.

4. Know that U.S. federal legislation, such as civil rights legislation and amendments (Title VII of the Civil Rights Act of 1964; Age Discrimination in Employment Act of

1967; Americans with Disabilities Act (ADA) of 1990; etc.), indicates that an interviewer <u>cannot ask any of the 16 questions posed on the PIQ in most situations.</u>

   a. Marital Status or Family Composition (Questions 1, 2, and 5).

   b. Creed or Religion (Question 10). You can ask if the applicant is available to work Saturday or Sunday.

   c. Organizations to which a person belongs (Question 7), where the name or character of the organization indicates race, creed, religion, national origin, sex, or ancestry of its member.

   d. Citizenship, National Origin, Ancestry, or Birthplace (Questions 12, 13 and 15), except to ask whether the applicant is legally entitled to work in the U.S.

   e. Relatives (Question 9).

   f. Physical Limitations (Question 8), except as they affect a person's ability to perform job-related functions. Violation of the ADA of 1990.

   g. Arrest Record and Convictions (Question 3), except felony convictions that reasonably relates to performing the job. The application must include a disclaimer that indicates a conviction does not automatically exclude an applicant.

   h. Financial Status (Questions 6 and 14).

   i. Photograph (Question 11).

   j. Educational Attainment (Question 4), unless there is a valid reason for having a certain educational background that is necessary to perform the job or position.

   k. Age (Question 16). Violation of the Age Discrimination in Employment Act of 1967. An employer can ask if the applicant is at least 18 years old (not a minor).

4. Tell students that the general rule for any question in an employment interview is: "Is this question job-related?" If it isn't, the question has a high probability of being discriminatory. Federal regulations now make it almost mandatory for employees to have well-defined job descriptions.

<u>Marketing Lessons.</u> Key lessons include:

1. While personal interviews are commonly used in hiring salespeople, interviewers cannot ask certain questions about interviewees. Knowledge of what cannot be asked is important for both the interviewer and interviewee.

2. Federal and state laws and regulations are constantly evolving. The U. S. Equal Employment Opportunity Commission has issued guidelines that explain laws and regulations pertaining to employment discrimination.

<u>Website.</u> For more information about appropriate interview guidelines, sexual harassment, and other discrimination issues, contact the EEOC website at www.eeoc.gov.

TM3-1

PRE-EMPLOYMENT INTERVIEW QUESTIONNAIRE

ASSIGNMENT: Please check whether you believe an interviewer can ask you each of the following questions in a pre-employment interview.

Interviewer:	Can Ask	Cannot Ask
1. Are you married?	_____	_____
2. Whom do you live with?	_____	_____
3. Have you ever been arrested or spent time in jail?	_____	_____
4. Are you a college graduate?	_____	_____
5. Do you plan to have children?	_____	_____
6. Do you own your home or do you rent?	_____	_____
7. Which clubs or social fraternities do you belong?	_____	_____
8. Are you handicapped in any way (e.g., poor hearing, poor eyesight)?	_____	_____
9. What are the names and addresses of your brothers and/or sisters?	_____	_____
10. Which religious holidays do you observe?	_____	_____
11. Do you have a photograph to place on your resume?	_____	_____
12. Are you a citizen of a country other than the U.S.?	_____	_____
13. What is the ethnic origin of your last name?	_____	_____
14. Are you currently receiving alimony from your former spouse?	_____	_____
15. In what city and state were you born?	_____	_____
16. How old are you/What is your birth date?	_____	_____

© McGraw-Hill Companies, Inc., 2003

CHAPTER 3: SCANNING THE MARKETING ENVIRONMENT

ICA3-2: IN-CLASS ACTIVITY

COMPETITIVE INTELLIGENCE

Learning Objectives. To enable students to collect vital information about competitors in a legal and ethical way and to demonstrate the opportunities and threats that information may present so that organizations can take pre-emptive or responsive marketing actions.

Definitions. The following marketing terms are referred to in this in-class activity (ICA):

- Code of Ethics: A formal statement of ethical principles and rules of conduct.

- Competitor Intelligence: According to Fuld & Company, Inc., "this phrase refers to legally and ethically collected information on a rival that has been analyzed to the point where you can make a decision."[1]

- Environmental Scanning: The process of continually acquiring information on events occurring outside the organization to and interpret potential trends.

Nature of the Activity. To have student teams access the Fuld & Company website that is devoted to competitive intelligence to learn how marketers benefit from this practice.

Estimated Class Time. 30 minutes, which consists of:

- 10 minutes to explain the nature of this ICA and distribute the Fuld & Company Handout to student teams.

- 20 minutes to present summaries by student teams during the subsequent class period.

- [NOTE: Students will spend 45 minutes outside class to complete their assignment.]

Materials Needed.

- Copies of the Fuld & Company Handout for each student.

- Student access to the Internet.

Preparation Before Class. Follow the steps below:

1. Read the material in Chapter 3 on the competitive forces that constitutes a critical element of an organization's environmental scan.

2. Familiarize yourself with the Fuld & Company competitive intelligence website.

3. Make copies of the Fuld & Company Handout for each student.

---

[1] See http://www.fuld.com/dictfiles/record7.html

Instructions. Follow the steps below to conduct this ICA:

1. Form students into four-person teams.

2. Pass out copies of the Fuld & Company Handout to each student.

3. Have the student teams go to the Fuld & Company website, which is www.fuld.com. Assign students the following tasks:

   a. Click on the "What Competitive Intelligence Is and Is Not" link at the top of the homepage to identify the 10 descriptions and misconceptions of intelligence.

      ASSIGNMENT: Have student teams write a 1/2-page brief that summarizes these 10 descriptions and misconceptions of intelligence.

   b. Click on the "Internet Intelligence Index" menu option, which "contains links to nearly 600 intelligence-related Internet sites."

      ASSIGNMENT: Have student teams select one item from "General Business Internet Resources" and one item from "Industry-Specific Internet Resources" and write a 1/2-page brief that summarizes the type of information found and the benefit it may have to marketers for each item selected.

   c. Click on the "CI Strategies & Tools" menu option.

      ASSIGNMENT: Have students write a 1/2-page brief that will be reported to their fellow classmates the next class period on each of the following:

      - Click on the "Intelligence Dictionary" link and write down the definitions of the following three (3) terms: Benchmarking, Economic Espionage Act, and Proprietary Information.
      - Click on the "Intelligence Pyramid" link. Then, click on the links for each of the three (3) steps and summarize some of the sources or activities cited.

   d. Have the student teams write a 1/2-page commentary on the benefits and concerns of competitive intelligence to an organization's marketing strategy development.

   e. Have the student teams hand in their summaries.

3. At the beginning of the next class period, select one student from 2 to 3 student teams to give a brief report on the competitive intelligence issues they summarized.

Marketing Lessons. While some people may object to competitive intelligence gathering as the ethical equivalent of spying (the latter being both unethical and illegal), organizations can and should use ethical means to gather, analyze, and act on information about their competition. Who is responsible for the environmental scanning of competitive forces? Usually mid-level managers and particularly those in the market research area.

Website. The Fuld & Company website is www.fuld.com.

ICA 3-2: COMPETITIVE INTELLIGENCE

FULD & COMPANY HANDOUT

❑ **Go to the Fuld & Company website (www.fuld.com) and perform the following tasks...**

1. Click on the "What Competitive Intelligence Is and Is Not" link at the top of the homepage to identify the 10 descriptions and misconceptions of intelligence.

    ASSIGNMENT: Write a 1/2-page brief that summarizes these 10 descriptions and misconceptions of intelligence.

2. Click on the "Internet Intelligence Index" menu option.

    ASSIGNMENT: Select one item from "General Business Internet Resources" and one item from "Industry-Specific Internet Resources" and write a 1/2-page brief that summarizes the type of information found and the benefit it may have to marketers for each item selected.

3. Click on the "CI Strategies & Tools" menu option.

    ASSIGNMENT: Write a 1/2-page brief for each of the following...

    - Click on the "Intelligence Dictionary" link and write down the definitions of the following three (3) terms: Benchmarking, Economic Espionage Act, and Proprietary Information.

    - Click on the "Intelligence Pyramid" link. Then, click on the links for each of the three (3) steps and summarize some of the sources or activities cited.

    - Write a 1/2-page commentary on the benefits and concerns of competitive intelligence to an organization's marketing strategy development.

❑ **Hand in your briefs and be prepared to present and discuss the issues of competitive intelligence during the next class period.**

CHAPTER 4: ETHICS AND SOCIAL RESPONSIBILITY IN MARKETING

ICA4-1: IN-CLASS ACTIVITY

SUSTAINABLE DEVELOPMENT

Learning Objectives. To have students learn how companies proactively balance shareholder value though environmental stewardship and corporate social responsibility in the markets they serve.

Definitions. The following marketing terms are referred to in this in-class activity (ICA):

- Social Responsibility: The idea that organizations are a part of a larger society and are accountable to that society for their actions.

- Sustainable Development: Conducting business in a way that protects the natural environment while making economic progress.

Nature of the Activity. To have students identify and analyze how Dow Chemical Company and Cargill, large, multi-national corporations, implement their commitment to sustainable development.

Estimated Class Time. 30 minutes, which consists of:

- 10 minutes to explain the nature of this ICA and distribute the World Business Council for Sustainable Development Handout to student teams.

- 20 minutes to present summaries by student teams during the subsequent class period.

- [NOTE: Students will spend 45 minutes outside class to complete their assignment.]

Materials Needed.

- Copies of the World Business Council for Sustainable Development Handout.

- Student access to the Internet and to Adobe's Acrobat Reader, which can be downloaded from Adobe's website at www.adobe.com.

Preparation Before Class. Follow the steps below:

1. Read the material in Chapter 4 on environmental quality, social responsibility, and sustainable development.

2. Familiarize yourself with the World Business Council for Sustainable Development website.

Instructions. Follow the steps below to conduct this ICA:

1. Give students this background mini-lecture:

According to the Dow Chemical Company, sustainable development "provides a framework for product development that goes beyond the economical and environmental impact of a product; it also considers the social impact."[1] It is a member of the World Business Council for Sustainable Development (WBCSD), which consists of a coalition of 150 multi-national firms from over 30 countries that are committed to the three tenets of sustainable development: economic growth, ecological balance, and social progress.

The WBCSD believes that there are significant opportunities for companies to use sustainable development practices to both manufacture and market profitable products and services in and to developing countries because such practices can reward firms with both growth opportunities and cost savings. The WBCSD has identified seven keys to implementing sustainable business practices:[2]

    a. <u>Innovate</u>. Technological and social innovation can do much to improve people's quality of life and tackle the depletion of resources and pollution.

    b. <u>Practice eco-efficiency</u>. This means creating more value with less impact. It can open up significant business opportunities and help economies grow.

    c. <u>Move from stakeholder dialogues to partnerships for progress</u>. This consists of alliances between business, government, and civil society to offer new solutions to common concerns.

    d. <u>Provide and inform consumer choice</u>. Individuals will change their consumption practices when they realize that they can gain financial benefits and better quality of life from sustainable behavior.

    e. <u>Improve market framework conditions</u>. Sustainability is hindered by monopolies, corruption, perverse subsidies, and prices that do not reflect real economic, social, and environmental costs. Legislation and regulations should promote competition, intellectual and physical property rights, reliable contractual terms, fair and transparent accounting standards, freedom and democracy, and full-cost pricing of goods and services.

    f. <u>Establish the worth of the Earth</u>. The market system needs to reflect the true environmental and social costs of goods and services. Proper valuation will help maintain the diversity of ecosystems, conserve natural resources, and prevent the build-up of toxic substances in the environment.

    g. <u>Make the market work for everyone</u>. Poverty and protectionism are the largest barriers to achieving sustainability through the market. Protectionism makes it harder for firms to seize profitable business opportunities and therefore increase consumer purchasing power.

2. Assign students into teams.

3. Give copies of the World Business Council for Sustainable Development Handout to each student.

---

[1] Recycle: Only One Component of Sustainable Development. See www.dow.com

[2] Sustainability Through the Market. See http://www.wbcsd.ch/projects/pr_marketsust.htm

4. Have the student teams go to the World Business Council for Sustainable Development (WBCSD) website, which is www.wbcsd.ch. Assign students the following tasks:

   a. Click on the "Case studies" link, which showcases some of the best global business practices for sustainable development.

   b. Click on the "All cases" menu option.

   ASSIGNMENT: Have student teams:

   - Select three case studies from any of the following categories, which relate to the seven keys to implementing sustainable business practices: Innovation & Technology; Eco-Efficiency, Managing and Understanding Change, Dialogue & Partnership, Providing and Informing Customer Choice, Corporate Social Responsibility, and Creating Sustainable Livelihoods.

   - Write a 1-page brief that summarizes the sustainable business practice implemented by the firm analyzed and the benefits to economic growth, ecological balance, and social progress plus a 1/2-page commentary on the benefits of sustainable development to an organization's marketing strategy.

   c. Hand in their summaries during the subsequent class period.

5. At the beginning of the next class period, select one student from 2 to 3 student teams to give a brief report on the sustainable business practices they wrote about.

Marketing Lessons. Many firms view sustainable development as an opportunity, not a threat. As these case studies show, organizations that invest in such practices can have a positive effect on economic growth, ecological balance, and social progress as well as their bottom line.

Website. The World Business Council for Sustainable Development website is www.wbcsd.ch.

ICA 4-1: SUSTAINABLE DEVELOPMENT

World Business Council For Sustainable Development Handout

☐ **Go to the World Business Council for Sustainable Development website (www.wbcsd.ch) and perform the following tasks...**

1. Click on the "Case studies" link, which showcases some of the best global business practices for sustainable development.

2. Click on the "All cases" menu option.

   ASSIGNMENT:

   - Select three case studies from any of the following categories, which relate to the seven keys to implementing sustainable business practices: Innovation & Technology; Eco-Efficiency, Managing and Understanding Change, Dialogue & Partnership, Providing and Informing Customer Choice, Corporate Social Responsibility, and Creating Sustainable Livelihoods.

   - Write a 1-page brief that summarizes the sustainable business practice implemented by the firm analyzed and the benefits to economic growth, ecological balance, and social progress plus a 1/2-page commentary on the benefits of sustainable development to an organization's marketing strategy.

☐ **Hand in your briefs and be prepared to present and discuss the issues of sustainable development during the next class period**

CHAPTER 4: ETHICS AND SOCIAL RESPONSIBILITY IN MARKETING

ICA4-2: IN-CLASS ACTIVITY

WHAT IS ETHICAL AND WHAT IS NOT: A SURVEY OF YOUR OPINIONS

Learning Objectives. To have students (1) move from an abstract understanding of ethical dimensions of marketing to actual situations they may experience as working professionals and (2) demonstrate the differences in opinions regarding what is and is not ethical.

Definitions. The following marketing terms are referred to in this in-class activity (ICA):

- Ethics: The moral principles and values that govern the actions and decisions of an individual or group.

- Moral Idealism: A personal moral philosophy that considers certain individual rights or duties as universal, regardless of the outcome.

- Utilitarianism: A personal moral philosophy that focuses on the "greatest good for the greatest number" by assessing the costs and benefits of the consequences of ethical behavior.

Nature of the Activity. To have students complete a survey in which they are asked to indicate their opinion about whether particular business and marketing practices are unethical. The comparison of student responses generates enthusiastic discussion and provides a vehicle for linking Chapter 4 to familiar business practices.

Estimated Class Time. 30 minutes.

Materials Needed.

- Copies of the "What is Ethical and What is Not Survey" for each student.

- A transparency of TM4-2: Comparison of Answers on Ethics Questionnaire Given by Sales Representatives and Students.

- A calculator to calculate the percentages from the survey.

Preparation Before Class. Follow the steps below:

1. Read the material below and in Chapter 4.

2. Make copies of the "What is Ethical and What is Not Survey."

3. Make a transparency of TM4-2.

Instructions. Follow the steps below to conduct this ICA:

1. Distribute the "What is Ethical and What is Not Survey" to each student.

2. Ask students to complete the survey by circling the number that corresponds to how they feel about whether each sales situation or practice listed represents an ethical dilemma.

3. Obtain a summary of the results using one of the following methods. For both methods fill in the results on the summary form TM4-2.

   a. Method 1: Collect the questionnaires from the students and have a student or a teaching assistant calculate the percentage of students answering "definitely yes" and "probably yes" to each of the questions.

   b. Method 2: Ask the students to self-report their responses in class.

4. Discuss the results with students. There will be a broad range of student opinions regarding what is unethical. In addition, the summary form allows comparison of the students' opinions with those from a survey of sales representatives.

Marketing Lessons. Key lessons include:

1. Students view situations and practices from different perspectives, leading to differences in opinions about whether they are unethical.

2. If Question B was unanswered: Many companies lack corporate policies about many of these situations and practices.

3. The more general the situation, the greater the percentage of salespeople (and usually students) who felt it posed an ethical question. For example, allowing personality differences to influence the terms of a sale is viewed as being unethical by more respondents than asking purchasers for information about competitors.

WHAT IS ETHICAL AND WHAT IS NOT SURVEY: HOW DO YOU FEEL ABOUT THE FOLLOWING SALES SITUATIONS OR PRACTICES?

Instructions: Assume you are a field sales representative for a large corporation. For each situation or practice listed below, circle the number corresponding to whether you feel it presents an ethical question.

Situation or Practice	Does the situation/practice present an ethical question?				
	Definitely Yes	Probably Yes	Maybe Yes Maybe No	Probably No	Definitely No
1. Allowing personalities—liking for one purchaser and disliking for another—to affect price, delivery, and other decisions regarding the terms of sale.	1	2	3	4	5
2. Having less competitive prices or other terms for buyers who use your firm as the sole source of supply than for firms for which you are one of two or more suppliers.	1	2	3	4	5
3. Making statements to an existing purchaser that exaggerates the seriousness of his problem in order to obtain a bigger order or other concessions.	1	2	3	4	5
4. Soliciting low priority or low volume business that the salesperson's firm will not deliver or service in an economic slowdown or periods of resource shortages.	1	2	3	4	5
5. Giving preferential treatment to purchasers who higher levels of the firm's own management prefer or recommend.	1	2	3	4	5
6. Giving physical gifts, such as free sales promotion prizes or "purchase-volume incentive bonuses" to a purchaser.	1	2	3	4	5
7. Using the firm's economic power to obtain premium prices or other concessions from buyers.	1	2	3	4	5
8. Giving preferential treatment to customers who are also good suppliers.	1	2	3	4	5
9. Seeking information from purchasers on competitors' quotations for the purpose of submitting another quotation.	1	2	3	4	5
10. Providing free trips meals, or other entertainment to a purchaser.	1	2	3	4	5
11. Attempting to reach and influence other departments (such as engineering) directly rather than go through the purchasing dept. when such avoidance increases the likelihood of a sale.	1	2	3	4	5
12. Gaining information about competitors by asking purchasers.	1	2	3	4	5

Source: Adapted from Alan J. Dubinsky, Eric N. Berkowitz, William Rudelius, "Ethical Problems of Field Sales Personnel," MSU Business Topics (Summer, 1980), p. 14.

TM4-2

COMPARISON OF ANSWERS ON ETHICS QUESTIONNAIRE GIVEN BY SALES REPRESENTATIVES AND STUDENTS

Respondents Replying "Definitely Yes" (1) or "Probably Yes" (2)

Situation or Practice	An Ethical Question?			
	Sales Reps		Students	
	Rank	Percentage	Rank	Percentage
1. Allowing personalities to affect decisions	1	52%		
2. Having less competitive prices for firms for which you are the sole source of supply.	2	50%		
3. Making statements to a purchaser that exaggerates the seriousness of his/her problem.	3	49%		
4. Soliciting low-priority business that won't be serviced in an economic slowdown or periods of resource shortages.	4	42%		
5. Giving preferential treatment to purchasers recommended by firm's own management.	5	41%		
6. Giving physical gifts to a purchaser.	6	39%		
7. Using the firm's economic power to obtain concessions from buyers.	7	37%		
8. Giving preferential treatment to customers who are also good suppliers.	8	36%		
9. Seeking information from purchasers on competitor's quotations to submit a new quotation.	9	34%		
10. Providing free trips, luncheons or dinners to a purchaser.	10	34%		
11. Attempting to reach and influence other departments directly rather than go through the purchasing department.	11	29%		
12. Gaining information about competitors by asking purchasers.	12	27%		

Source: Adapted from Alan J. Dubinsky, Eric N. Berkowitz, William Rudelius, "Ethical Problems of Field Sales Personnel," MSU Business Topics (Summer, 1980), p. 14.

© McGraw-Hill Companies, Inc., 2003

CHAPTER 5: CONSUMER BEHAVIOR

ICA5-1: IN-CLASS ACTIVITY

BUYING PROCESS FOR STARBUCKS COFFEE

Learning Objectives. To illustrate the consumer buying process when buying coffee.

Definitions. The following marketing terms are referred to in this in-class activity (ICA):

- Cognitive Dissonance: The feeling of postpurchase psychological tension or anxiety a consumer often experiences.

- Evaluative Criteria: Factors that represent both the objective attributes of a brand and the subjective ones a consumer uses to compare different products and brands.

- Evoked Set: The group of brands a consumer would consider acceptable from among all brands in the product class of which he or she is aware.

- Purchase Decision Process: The stages a buyer passes through in making choices about which products and services to buy.

Nature of the Activity. To relate the consumer buying process to purchasing a cup of Starbucks coffee.

Estimated Class Time. 20 minutes.

Materials Needed.

- The Starbucks Coffee packet from the *Instructor's Survival Kit* box.

- The Starbucks Card from the *Instructor's Survival Kit* box.

- A transparency of Figure 5-1 (or use Slide 5 from ICA05-1.ppt of the ISK PowerPoint CD): Purchase Decision Process.

- Blackboard or blank transparency to record student ideas.

- The ISK PowerPoint CD from the *Instructor's Survival Kit* box. See the instructions for use of this CD on page 4 of this manual if you use this CD in class.

Preparation Before Class. Follow the steps below:

1. Read the material in Case D-15 in Appendix D to give a background mini-lecture.

2. Make a transparency of Figure 5-1 (or use Slide 5 from ICA05-1.ppt of the ISK PowerPoint CD).

Instructions. Follow the steps below to conduct this ICA:

1. Give students this background mini-lecture (or show Slide 3):

   Starbucks Coffee Company is the leading retailer, roaster, and brand of specialty coffee in the world. For 2001, Starbucks had sales of $2.6 billion. As of early 2002, Starbucks had over 5,300 company-owned and franchised stores in North America, Europe, the Pacific Rim, and the Middle East. The firm plans to open over 1,200 more stores in the near future, both in existing and new markets, such as Mexico—its first stores in the Latin American market. Starbucks also operates two joint ventures: with Pepsi-Cola, it develops and distributes a Starbucks branded Frappuccino™ drink; and with Dreyer's Grand Ice Cream, Inc., it develops and distributes a Starbucks branded super premium ice cream.[1]

   Coffee is a commodity. People can buy a cup of coffee almost anywhere in the world or make it themselves. With most commodities, firms cannot charge a premium price. However, Starbucks can charge a higher price for its cup of coffee because it has created and delivered a brand promise to serve only the finest coffee. As a result, it has captured almost 7 percent of the U.S. coffee market.[2]

   Pass around the Starbucks coffee packet and the Starbucks Card (or show Slide 4).

   Starbucks recently introduced the Starbucks Card. This "smart card", which comes in denominations of $5 to $500, is designed to improve customer service by shortening checkout lines. These cards also enable Starbucks to obtain advanced sales, allowing the firm to earn interest on the unused balances. Moreover, customers will be able to order their coffees by cell phone or via the Internet, thus eliminating any wait time.[3] Finally, some businesses are using it to reward employees.

2. Tell the students that you would like to get their ideas on the process they use for buying a cup of coffee. Ask each student (or teams of students) to rank the top three factors that influence their decision to buy a cup of coffee. You may ask students to write these down and turn them in or just solicit their ideas orally. Write these down on the blackboard or a blank transparency for the entire class to see.

3. Show transparency Figure 5-1 (or show Slide 5). Call on students to describe their coffee purchase decision process based on the following questions:

- <u>Question 1</u>: What triggers the decision to buy a cup of coffee? Is it a need? A want?

   <u>Answers</u>: Thirsty, saw an ad, part of a routine, etc.

---

[1] Information obtained from Starbucks website.

[2] Shirley Leung, "Starbucks Plans Mexican Stores by End of Year," *The Wall Street Journal*, February 26, 2002.

[3] Stanley Holmes, Starbucks' Card Smarts, *BusinessWeek*, March 18, 2002, p. 14.

- Question 2: How do you seek information about the purchase of a cup of coffee, knowing that coffee is a commodity?

    Answers: Use past experiences recalled from memory (internal search). Also may ask family & friends, consult a product-rating organization (Consumer Reports, local newspaper review, etc.), and/or ads or store signage (external search).

- Question 3: What evaluative criteria do you use when deciding to purchase a particular coffee brand?

    Answers: Taste, price, location, convenience (wait time), atmospherics (comfortable), service, etc.

- Question 4: What is your evoked set of coffee brands?

    Answers: Make at home: Folgers, etc. Buy at retailer: Starbucks, Caribou Coffee, etc.

- Question 5: When and where do you buy a cup of coffee?

    Answers: Multiple responses and use situations possible.

- Question 6: With respect to the purchase of your last cup of coffee, did you experience any cognitive dissonance? If dissatisfied, what was deficient? Did you tell anyone? Will you go back? What marketing activities could be undertaken to reduce this?

    Answers: Marketers have several options regarding the kinds of activities they can do, such as redesigning the product, reworking the advertising message or retraining salespeople if the product is being oversold, improving customer service, offering refunds, etc.

- Question 7: Do any of you own a Starbucks Card now? What are the benefits to you? What are the benefits to Starbucks?

    Answers: The principal benefit to consumers is convenience, since the card is designed to speed up the check out process. For Starbucks, the card encourages repeat purchases and brand loyalty (less likely to go to Caribou's) and Starbucks receives consumers' money in advance in the amount of the card.

Marketing Lesson. Marketers must understand each step in the consumer purchase decision process as it applies to their products or services. By doing so, they can develop better marketing programs with which to target their customers more effectively.

Website. To view Starbucks' current product line of coffees and other products and services, go to www.starbucks.com.

CHAPTER 6: ORGANIZATIONAL MARKETS AND BUYER BEHAVIOR

ICA6-1: IN-CLASS ACTIVITY

BUYING CENTER ROLE-PLAY

Learning Objectives. To have students (1) understand the cross-functional nature of the organizational buying process and (2) identify the key roles within the buying center.

Definitions. The following marketing terms are referred to in this in-class activity (ICA):

- Buying Center: The group of people in an organization who participate in the buying process and share common goals, risks, and knowledge important to a purchase decision.

- New Buy: The first-time purchase of a product or service, involving greater potential risk.

- Organizational Buying Behavior: The decision-making process that organizations use to establish the need for products and services and identify, evaluate, and choose among alternative brands and suppliers.

Nature of the Activity. To have several students conduct a role-play by assuming different characters to discuss an organizational purchase of Sprint's FonPromotions program.

Estimated Class Time. 20 minutes.

Materials Needed.

- The Sprint Pre-Paid Phone Card from the *Instructor's Survival Kit* box.

- 7 copies of the script that appears at the end of this ICA.

- 7 name cards, one for each of the student participants in the role-play.

- The ISK PowerPoint CD from the *Instructor's Survival Kit* box. See the instructions for use of this CD on page 4 of this manual if you use this CD in class.

Preparation Before Class. Follow the steps below:

1. Read the material below for background.

2. Prepare name cards for each of the characters.

3. Make 7 copies of the role-play, one for each of the participants, and highlight the particular parts for each character's script.

4. Set up a table and chairs in front of the classroom for the "meeting."

Instructions. Follow the steps below to conduct this ICA:

1. Recruit students to play the seven characters in the role-play. Seat the characters at a table in front of the class and give each the corresponding "script."

2. While the role-playing students are reviewing the scripts, the instructor should give the following background and then introduce the characters:

"You are about to see a glimpse inside FarNorth, Inc., a successful manufacturer of golf accessories (bags, apparel, gloves, etc.) for men and women that are sold to golf pro shops, golf superstores, and sporting goods stores in the U.S. FarNorth's management has asked Lisa Ludwig, the sales representative for Sprint FonPromotions, to present a proposal for a marketing program to stimulate sales and motivate the firm's sales people. However, Sprint FonPromotions, which costs $100,000, is more than what was budgeted for advertising and sales promotion for the current fiscal year (show Slide 3).

Before we listen in to the conversation between Lisa and the co-workers that constitute FarNorth's buying center for marketing programs, let me introduce you to our cast:"

Character	Job Title	Role in FarNorth's Buying Center
Lisa Ludwig	Sales Representative, Sprint	SUPPLIER: Sprint FonPromotions
Carol Woods	President and CEO, FarNorth	INFLUENCER
Lynn Tan	VP - Marketing, FarNorth	DECIDER/INFLUENCER
Sam Hawthorne	Purchasing Manager, FarNorth	GATEKEEPER/BUYER/INFLUENCER
Neil Vanathan	Sales Manager, FarNorth	USER/INFLUENCER
Thor Sandholm	Advertising Manager, FarNorth	USER/INFLUENCER
Basil Winters	Finance Manager, FarNorth	INFLUENCER

3. Introduce the cast and his/her job title and role in the FarNorth buying center.

4. Have the students read the buying center role-play script in front of the class. (Show Slides 4-5 during the presentation).

5. When finished with the role-play, say: "So we now leave FarNorth's marketing promotions buying center. Let's discuss what we've observed by answering some questions."

6. Ask students the questions below to facilitate the buying center discussion:

- Question 1: What buying center roles did each of the participants play? Which characters were Influencers? Gatekeepers? Deciders? Buyers? Users?

  Answers: See above.

- Question 2: Who do you feel is the key buying influence for this decision? Why?

  Answers: Lynn Tan (VP – Marketing) and Thor Sandholm (Advertising Manager) are probably the key buying center constituents for this decision. They raise the most questions that require answers before a decision can be made. Neil Vanathan (Sales Manager) is also a key player since he is directly responsible for implementing the program. The CEO, Carol Woods, appears to seek Lynn's approval for going ahead with the program.

- Question 3: What are the marketing challenges that face Lisa Ludwig or any business-to-business sales person with a buying center such as this?

  Answer: One of the biggest challenges for a business-to-business sales person is to determine the people who constitute the organization's buying center and what roles they play. Different roles are concerned about different issues. It is a challenge to attempt to address all of these different needs at the same time. Sales people need to prepare, research, and learn about a potential customer's buying center participants in order to effectively meet their needs and generate the sales they desire.

Marketing Lesson. Organizational buying decisions can be more complex than those for consumers because of the number of individuals involved and their differing needs and perspectives within the buying center. This complexity is particularly evident in a "new buy" situation, such as the one illustrated.

Website. To learn more about Sprint's FonPromotions program, go to its website, which is www.sprint.com/fonpromotions.

SCRIPT: BUYING CENTER ROLE-PLAY

Lisa: In summary, the Sprint FonPromotions program, with its Sprint Prepaid Business Card and Prepaid Phone Card, would accomplish the following marketing objectives for FarNorth:

- First, to build brand awareness among customers and prospects, the Sprint Prepaid Business Card looks like your regular business card but offers 20-minutes of free domestic long-distance calls (show Slide 4). On the front of the card is your sales person's contact information. On the back are the telephone and ID numbers that allows your customers and prospects to make their free calls. The Sprint Prepaid Business Card encourages these customers and prospects to think you and the free long distance minutes they received every time they view your unique business card.

- Second, to generate excitement and motivate sales people and other FarNorth employees, the Sprint Prepaid Phone Card can be used to create an interactive sweepstakes. Each would receive a free, 30-minute Sprint Prepaid Phone Card (show Slide 5). On the card would be a toll-free number that employees would use to enter the contest. Participants then enter a six-digit number of their choice, and if it matched the winning numbers, they instantly win a prize ranging from a weekend get-a-way to a free Sprint Prepaid Phone Card.

Sam: Thank you for your presentation, Lisa. I'm sure that there are a few questions.

Lynn: Yes, Sam. Lisa, have those sales improvement figures been verified by an independent agency? I can't believe that we would see those increases in our situation.

Lisa: Yes, they have Lynn. That information is in Appendix II of the sales proposal, which you each have in front of you. However, according to a recent study from one of our clients that you may contact, sales increased by 10 percent over the six-month promotional period.

Neil: What about procedures? Our sales people haven't had any experience with this type of promotional program and we're very busy at the moment. What level of support or training does Sprint provide?

Lynn: We can't afford time for training. This is the prime selling season for our golf accessories.

Thor: We have already made our media buys for the season. We're going to have to increase our budget to…

Basil: Wait a minute! You want more money for advertising? Can't you just reallocate from one budget category to another?

Thor: Not really. We have signed contracts with our advertising agency so our budget is basically spent for this selling season. Increasing our budget for this Spring FonPromotions program could sufficiently increase sales to cover any increase we need if Lisa's projections are on target.

Basil: But that's a lot of money. Can't you defer some advertising until the next fiscal year?

Lynn: That could be difficult given our marketing plan, Basil.

Thor: Marketing has very ambitious goals for this year, Basil. Not spending the already allocated funds on advertising could have very serious implications on this year's sales.

Neil: Well, if we did implement Lisa's program, it could increase sales from new and existing customers since they and our employees would be even more motivated.

Sam: Excuse me, but are there more questions for Lisa concerning the specifics of the Sprint FonPromotions program?

Lisa: I'd like to answer Neil's question about procedures. I would work closely with Lynn, Neil, and Thor to customize the design of the program. We have 2 customer service reps (one for marketing that would train your sales people and one for data processing that would interface with your data processing people) that would help you implement the program. We would manage the reporting of all sales activity. You would receive daily sales updates by region, channel member, etc. via our link to FarNorth's intranet.

Basil: Do you have any "canned" or turnkey programs? Any programs that have already been developed for other clients that we could reuse with only minor modifications?

Thor: [Thor gives Basil a dirty look.]

Lisa: I think that you would be interested in the financial projections that I've prepared. At your current sales rates, the Sprint FonPromotions program would pay for itself in less than 9 months.

Carol: I find these projections in Appendix II very compelling, Lisa. What do you think about the program, Lynn? Given our current sales figures, we could project the impact of the purchase. Sam, could you develop a cost-benefit analysis of the program based on Lisa's projections?

[End of the Role-Play]

CHAPTER 7: REACHING GLOBAL MARKETS

ICA7-1: IN-CLASS ACTIVITY

ARE YOU AN ETHNOCENTRIC CONSUMER?

Learning Objectives. To have students (1) discover their personal orientation toward foreign-made products and (2) consider the implication of consumer ethnocentrism for global marketing.

Definition. The following marketing term is referred to in this ICA:

- Ethnocentrism: According to the Encyclopedic Dictionary of Sociology, it is "the tendency to view the norms and values of one's own culture as absolute and to use them as a standard against which to judge and measure all other cultures."

Nature of the Activity. To expose students to the dimensions of consumer ethnocentrism and generate discussion about consumer attitudes toward foreign-made products.

Estimated Class Time. 40 minutes, which consists of:

- 20 minutes to distribute, complete, score, and return the Consumer Sentiment Questionnaire (CSQ) during one class period.
- 20-minutes to discuss the results of the CSQ in the subsequent class period.

Materials Needed.

- Copies of the Consumer Sentiment Questionnaire.
- A calculator to calculate the percentages and means from the survey.
- [OPTIONAL: A computer with a statistical program (SPSS, STAT PAC, or Excel) to calculate the percentages and means for the survey.]

Preparation Before Class. Follow the steps below:

1. Read the material below to provide background for the ICA and subsequent discussion.

2. Make copies of the Consumer Sentiment Questionnaire for each student.

Instructions. Follow the steps below to conduct this ICA:

1. Distribute the Consumer Sentiment Questionnaire to the class period prior to the lecture related to Chapter 7.

2. Have students respond to all 17 items. Once done, ask students to pass their completed forms to the instructor. [OPTIONAL: Hand out the surveys at the beginning of the class period. After students have completed the survey, collect them. Then, during the time between classes, input the data into a statistical program and calculate the percentages, means, crosstabulations, and t-tests for the survey. Make overheads and discuss the results.]

3. Tally the scores and create a frequency distribution and calculate the means. The numerical range of scores is from 17 to 102.

4. When presenting the final results, instructors might note that there is positive relationship between scores on the Consumer Sentiment Questionnaire and the following variables: patriotism, political-economic conservatism, dogmatism, domestic car ownership, intention to buy a domestic car, and country-of-origin importance. There is a negative relationship between scores on the CSQ and education, income, and consumer attitudes toward foreign-made products.

5. For additional reading on consumer ethnocentrism, see Subhash Sharma, Terence A. Shimp, and Jeongshin Shin, "Consumer Ethnocentrism: A Test of Antecedents and Moderators," Journal of the Academy of Marketing Science (Winter, 1995), pp. 26-37.

Marketing Lessons. Key lessons include:

1. Consumer ethnocentrism can be measured.

2. Attitudes toward domestic and foreign-made products are often related to attitudes toward a country's world trade policies.

3. Attitudes toward domestic and foreign-made products are often linked to actual purchase behavior.

CONSUMER SENTIMENT QUESTIONNAIRE

Please indicate the extent to which you agree with the following 17 statements:

	Statement	Strongly Agree	Agree	Neither Agree nor Disagree	Disagree	Strongly Disagree
1.	American people should always buy American-made products instead of imports.	☐	☐	☐	☐	☐
2.	Only those products that are unavailable in the U.S. should be imported.	☐	☐	☐	☐	☐
3.	Buying U. S. -made products keeps us working.	☐	☐	☐	☐	☐
4.	American products, first, last, and foremost.	☐	☐	☐	☐	☐
5.	Purchasing foreign-made products is un-American.	☐	☐	☐	☐	☐
6.	It is not right to purchase foreign products, because it puts Americans out of jobs.	☐	☐	☐	☐	☐
7.	A real American should always buy American-made products.	☐	☐	☐	☐	☐
8.	We should purchase products manufactured in America instead of letting other countries get rich off us.	☐	☐	☐	☐	☐
9.	It is always best to purchase American products.	☐	☐	☐	☐	☐
10.	There should be very little trading or purchasing of goods from other countries unless out of necessity.	☐	☐	☐	☐	☐
11.	Americans should not buy foreign products, because this hurts American businesses and causes unemployment.	☐	☐	☐	☐	☐
12.	Curbs should be put on all imports.	☐	☐	☐	☐	☐
13.	It may cost me in the long run but I prefer to support American products.	☐	☐	☐	☐	☐
14.	Foreigners should not be allowed to put their products on our markets.	☐	☐	☐	☐	☐
15.	Foreign products should be taxed heavily to reduce their entry into the U.S.	☐	☐	☐	☐	☐
16.	We should buy from foreign countries only those products that we can't obtain in our own country.	☐	☐	☐	☐	☐
17.	American consumers who purchase products made in other countries are responsible for putting their fellow Americans out of work.	☐	☐	☐	☐	☐

CHAPTER 7: REACHING GLOBAL MARKETS

ICA7-2: IN-CLASS ACTIVITY

MARKETING ACROSS BORDERS:
REINTRODUCING THE MINI® BRAND TO THE U.S.

Learning Objectives. To have students (1) determine whether the MINI brand, which is owned by the BMW Group and sells two models: the MINI Cooper® and MINI Cooper® S® in the U. S., is an international firm (extends its domestic marketing strategy), a multinational firm (uses a multi-domestic marketing strategy), or a transnational firm (employs a global marketing strategy), (2) identify the problems global marketers face when selling a product—in this case a well-known British car—to American consumers, and (3) discuss any marketing mix modifications that MINI might need to make to appeal to American consumers.

Definitions. The following marketing terms are referred to in this in-class activity (ICA):

- Global Marketing Strategy: The practice of standardizing marketing activities when there are cultural similarities and adapting them when cultures differ.

- Multidomestic Marketing Strategy: A multinational firm's offering as many different product variations, brand names, and advertising programs as countries in which it does business.

Nature of the Activity. To have students assess selected elements of the MINI brand's marketing mix contained in (1) a copy of the new MINI Cooper and MINI Cooper S brochure, (2) a PowerPoint presentation, and (3) background information provided by the instructor to discuss the typical problems that global marketers face when targeting American consumers.

Estimated Class Time. 30 minutes.

Materials Needed.

- The MINI product brochure from the *Instructor's Survival Kit* box.

- A transparency of TM7-2 (or use Slide 15 from ICA07-2.ppt of the ISK PowerPoint CD): Marketing Actions to Improve the MINI Brand's Chances of Successfully Entering the U.S. Market.

- The ISK PowerPoint CD from the *Instructor's Survival Kit* box. See the instructions for use of this CD on page 4 of this manual if you use this CD in class.

Preparation Before Class. Follow the steps below:

1. Read through the MINI product brochure that describes and shows the MINI Cooper and MINI Cooper S automobiles.

2. Make a transparency of TM7-2 (or use Slide 15).

Instructions. Follow the steps below to conduct this ICA:

1. Give students this background mini-lecture on global marketing strategy alternatives:

   While many U. S. companies engage in global marketing and trade with consumers in foreign countries, the reverse is also true. The U. S. can be a fertile place to expand sales and profits for foreign companies. All companies engaged in global commerce may be characterized as either: (1) an <u>international firm</u>, which engages in trade and marketing in different countries as an extension of the marketing strategy it uses in its home country; (2) a <u>multinational firm</u>, which uses a **multidomestic marketing strategy** that creates as many different product variations, brand names, and advertising programs as countries in which they do business; and (3) a <u>transnational firm</u>, which uses a **global marketing strategy** that standardizes its marketing practices across all countries to the extent possible, modifying it only when there are cultural differences.

   When a firm looks for new markets for its products in foreign countries, it often encounters unexpected problems—often because of a lack of understanding of the language, culture, and habits of consumers in the new country. Let's assume you are marketing consultants to MINI's International Marketing Team (a division of the BMW Group) that wants to export its MINI Cooper and MINI Cooper S automobiles to U.S. consumers.

2. Provide students with the following historical background of the MINI brand (or show Slide 3, which is narrated by John Cooper, the creator of the Mini Cooper; TRT = 2:52):

   In the late 1950's, there was a fuel crisis caused by tensions in the Middle East. Therefore, to compete with the growing number of small fuel-efficient cars, Sir Leonard Lord challenged Alec Issigonis to design and engineer a fuel efficient car capable of carrying four adults within the economic reach of just about anyone. The first Classic Mini was first sold in 1959 for approximately $800 (USD) and became Britain's most popular car, selling over 5.3 million units during its 40+ years. In 1999, an international panel of judges ranked the Classic Mini the #2 global car of the 20th century. Ford's Model T was ranked #1.[1]

   Mini Cooper got its name in 1961 when racecar driver John Cooper modified the Classic Mini and developed a high performance model. In 1964, 1965, and 1967, the Mini Cooper won the prestigious Monte Carlo race over other European sports cars.

   From 1960 - 1967, about 10,000 Classic Mini Coopers were sold in the U.S. In 1968, the U.S. government issued more restrictive safety and emissions regulations, and the Mini was withdrawn from the market. In September 2000, the all new MINI premiered at the Mondial De L'Automobile Show in Paris. Days later, the last Classic Mini rolled off the line in Longbridge, UK. Mini became MINI. The new MINI made its European debut in September 2001 and was reintroduced to the U.S. in March 2002 (or show Slide 4; TRT = 1:49).

---

[1] Information from the MINIUSA.com website.

The new MINI Cooper and MINI Cooper S are manufactured in Oxford, England. The BMW Group, the owner of the MINI brand, expects to sell a total of 20,000 units in the U.S. during the 2002 calendar year.

3. Pass around the MINI Cooper and MINI Cooper S brochure (or show Slides 5-12) that shows the MINI Cooper and MINI Cooper S.

4. Discuss the following "product" attributes of the MINI Cooper and MINI Cooper:

   a. Is 142.84" long (bumper-to-bumper) by 66.5" wide (wheel-to-wheel), or one-third larger than the Classic Mini. Has go-kart like handling with the wheels at the four corners.

   b. Has either a 1.6 liter, transverse 4-cylinder, 115 horsepower engine (MINI Cooper) or a 163 horsepower supercharged engine (MINI Cooper S).

   c. "Sips" gas: fuel economy is 28 mpg city and 37 mpg highway (MINI Cooper with manual transmission).

   d. Has six standard airbags with Smart Technology that is able to sense which airbags need to inflate, when they need to inflate, and how much they need to inflate.

   e. Can "Build-to-Order" via the MINIUSA.com website with 40+ paint combinations, MINI Motoring-Gear, Genuine MINI Motoring Accessories, and other options are available online.

   f. Incorporates the latest generation 4-channel, Anti-Lock Braking System (ABS).

   g. Has front wheel drive.

   h. Uses multi-link rear suspension, a technology that is borrowed from rear-wheel drive sports cars.

5. Discuss the following "price" attributes of the MINI Cooper and MINI Cooper S:

   a. MSRP is $16,850 (MINI Cooper) or $19,850 (MINI Cooper S), including destination charges.

   b. Options and accessories are extra.

   c. Financing is available from MINI Financial Services.

6. Discuss the following "promotion" attributes of the MINI Brand:

   a. Demographics are insignificant since people from 16 to 60 find themselves attracted to the MINI. Instead, it's about the mindset.

   b. Placed an abridged version of the "Book of Motoring" as an insert in selected magazines (or show Slide 13). This publication relies on a combination of "cheeky" humor, the motoring philosophy, and product substance highlights to communicate the marketing message.

c. Instead of allocating money for TV ads, MINI will use other traditional media in non-traditional ways: billboards with the message "The SUV Backlash Officially Starts Now" or "Let's Sip Not Guzzle"; magazine ads, such as buying the margin around a news story in *Rolling Stone* and *Motor Trend* for its 'Cornering ads' that say, "Nothing Corners Like a MINI" (show Slide 14); guerilla sightings (mounting MINIs atop SUVs and drive around major metropolitan cities); and video ads on the MINIUSA.com website.

d. "Starred" in the 2002 Austin Powers III movie.

7. Discuss the following "place" (or distribution) attributes of the MINI Cooper and MINI Cooper S:

a. Sold through a network of approximately 70 MINI dealers located primarily in major metropolitan areas in the U.S.

b. MINI dealership showrooms are distinctly separate from BMW dealership showrooms. One dealer located its MINI dealership in a regional shopping center (Minneapolis, MN: Southdale Mall).

8. Randomly assign students into teams.

9. Show transparency TM7-2 (or show Slide 14) and ask the students to spend 5 minutes (1) identifying the issues or problems in global marketing and (2) recommending an action or solution for each of four marketing mix elements:

a. Product modifications.

b. Price modifications.

c. Promotion modifications.

d. Place (distribution or dealer network) modifications.

10. Write down students' ideas on transparency TM7-2 (or show Slide 14 and discuss orally). Here are some points that may emerge in the discussion:

Marketing Mix Element	Issue/Problem	Action/Solution
Product Improvements	<ul><li>In England, car is small</li><li>In England, steering wheel on the right (wrong!) side</li><li>U.S. fuel economy standards</li><li>U.S. safety standards</li><li>Comfort</li><li>Ability to customize</li></ul>	<ul><li>Make car larger</li><li>Design MINI with steering wheel on left side</li><li>Design a fuel-efficient engine</li><li>Conform to U.S. safety standards</li><li>Focus on technology that allows for greater comfort and movement in upper body and legs</li><li>Offer "Build-to-Order" via website that offers features & accessories that American prefer (CD players)</li></ul>
Pricing Improvements	<ul><li>Currency exchange risks since cars are produced in England (£) and exported to the U.S. ($)</li><li>Price of options higher to keep base price under $20,000</li></ul>	<ul><li>Price guarantees for a fixed period of time</li><li>Show comparison prices of similar options for selected competitor cars</li></ul>
Promotion Improvements	<ul><li>No TV ads; Americans like TV</li><li>Austin Powers III movie may not be seen by target market</li><li>Non traditional use of traditional media may not appeal to target customers</li><li>British humor, if used, may not be fully appreciated by Americans</li></ul>	<ul><li>Must use very creative alternative media to inform potential target customers, such as magazine ads, billboards, public relations, etc.</li><li>Use multiple product placement situations that are consistent with brand image</li><li>Use humor that is culturally accepted</li></ul>
Place (Distribution) Improvements	<ul><li>Dealers in only 70 major U.S. cities</li><li>MINI dealer showrooms separate from BMW dealer showrooms</li></ul>	<ul><li>Ability to order a car via the Internet</li><li>MINI is a unique brand personality that needs to be separate from BMW</li></ul>

11. Ask students to classify MINI, the firm that sells the MINI Cooper and MINI Cooper S automobiles in the U.S., either as an international firm, a multinational firm, or a transnational firm.

The MINI Brand should be classified as a <u>transnational firm</u> because it uses a **global marketing strategy**. The BMW Group and the MINI International marketing Team have standardized the marketing practices for its MINI Cooper automobiles in the U.S. to the extent possible, modifying them only when there are cultural or legal differences to those employed in England (its home country) and the other European countries it targets.

For example, the MINI Cooper and MINI Cooper S have the same overall body style and technologies regardless of where the cars are sold. However, one significant product modification is the position of the driver and location of the steering wheel (in England, it's on the right and in America, it's on the left). Also, the humor is culturally determined; therefore, what may be humorous in England may not be in America due to the cultural context within which it is presented.

Marketing Lessons. It is very difficult to take a product from one country to another without making changes in the product, pricing, advertising, and distribution. Because of the potential pitfalls inherent in executing any kind of marketing program across borders, marketing, brand, and product managers should conduct marketing research when seeking to enter new global markets.

Websites. If you want to obtain a price quote for a new MINI Cooper or MINI Cooper S or build one online, visit MINIUSA.com. To view the new 2002 car introductions from the major automobile marketers, go to the MSN Carpoint website that it developed for the North American International Auto Show, which is www.naias.com.

TM7-2

MARKETING ACTIONS TO IMPROVE THE MINI® BRAND'S CHANCES OF SUCCESSFULLY ENTERING THE U.S. MARKET

MARKETING STRATEGY AREA	ISSUE/PROBLEM	ACTION/SOLUTION
Product Improvements		
Pricing Improvements		
Promotion Improvements		
Place (Dealer) Improvements		

CHAPTER 8: TURNING MARKETING INFORMATION INTO ACTION

ICA8-1: IN-CLASS ACTIVITY

PEPSI VS. COKE TASTE TEST

Learning Objectives. To have students (1) run an experiment, collect data, and interpret the results; (2) replicate the "Pepsi Challenge" with Pepsi Cola and Coca-Cola, and (3) develop and analyze simple cross-tabulations based on the experimental data they collected.

Definitions. The following marketing terms are referred to in this in-class activity (ICA):

- Cross-tabulation: A method of presenting and relating data having two or more variables to analyze and discover relationships in the data.

- Data: The facts and figures pertinent to the problem, comprised of primary and secondary data.

- Experiment: Obtaining data by manipulating factors under tightly controlled conditions to test cause and effect.

Nature of the Activity. To have students conduct an in-class taste test by comparing Pepsi and Coke.

Estimated Class Time. 30 minutes.

Materials Needed.

- Copies of the Pepsi – Coke Taste Test Questionnaire.

- A sufficient number of 2-liter bottles of Pepsi Cola and Coca-Cola so that each student in the class can participate in the experiment.

- A sufficient number of 2-ounce Dixie® paper cups for each student in the class.

- 1 box of regular crackers (e.g. Nabisco's Original Premium® Saltines).

- A marker to write letters on the side or bottom of each cup.

- 1 large container of water.

- [OPTIONAL: 2 or 4 blindfolds (depending on the size of your class) so that students cannot see the color of the soft drink. Since each brand is a slightly different shade of green, heavy users of these products could discern which cup contained which brand.]

- [OPTIONAL: A computer with a statistical program (SPSS, STAT PAC, or Excel) to calculate the percentages and cross-tabulations for the survey.]

- The ISK PowerPoint CD from the *Instructor's Survival Kit* box. See the instructions for use of this CD on page 4 of this manual if you use this CD in class.

Preparation Before Class. Follow the steps below:

1. Purchase a sufficient number of 2-liter bottles of Pepsi Cola and Coca-Cola. To calculate the number of each soft drink needed, count the number of students, multiply by 2 ounces, and then divide by 88, the number of ounces in a 2-liter bottle.

2. Purchase a package of 2-ounce Dixie paper cups and 1-2 boxes of saltine crackers.

3. Write a "B" on 1/3 of the paper cups, an "N" on another 1/3 of the paper cups, and a "W" on the last 1/3 of the paper cups with a marker.

4. Refrigerate the bottles of Pepsi and Coke until just before class.

5. Make copies of the Pepsi – Coke Taste Test Questionnaire.

6. Arrange for a pitcher of cool water to be brought to class on the day of the taste test.

7. [OPTIONAL: Buy or make 1 to 3 blindfolds to create a true "blind" taste test.]

8. Before class starts, set up two taste test stations at the front of the classroom that consists of a shield (to prohibit taste-testers from identifying the soft drink brands being evaluated), labeled cups, water, saltines, surveys, and (optional) blindfolds.

9. At the start of class, select two teams of 1- 2 students at random to manage each taste test stations. Recruit students who are responsible to perform this task. Have them randomly assign the letters "B" or "N" to either Pepsi or Coke.

10. [OPTIONAL: In your statistical program, create the study design, variables, and statistical procedures before you collect the data based on the Pepsi – Coke Taste Test Questionnaire.]

Instructions. Follow the steps below to conduct this ICA:

1. Give this background mini-lecture (and show Slide 3; TRT: 0:30):

   During the late 1970s and early 1980s, Pepsi Cola conducted a nationwide comparative taste test known as the "Pepsi Challenge." Pepsi set up stations on college campuses and at other public events to have consumers compare the taste of Pepsi to Coca-Cola (the original brand, now known as "Coca-Cola Classic"). This "blind" taste test was conducted in the following manner:

   a. Two small cups were labeled "B" and "N". To prohibit taste-testers from identifying which cola was poured into which cup, one was filled with Pepsi and the other one with Coke behind a cardboard backdrop or shield.

   b. Next, a taste-tester was asked to take a sip from cup "B". Then, the taste-tester was required to eat one saltine cracker and take a sip of water to remove any aftertaste in his/her mouth. Lastly, the taste-tester took a sip from cup "N". Since both colas were brown in color, no blindfold was necessary.

c. When finished, the taste-tester was asked to state (verbally and on a brief survey) which tasted better: cola "B" or cola "N". After recording the result, the taste-tester was informed of the identity of the cola in each cup and asked for her/his reaction. The presumption was that since Coca-Cola had a greater market share than Pepsi, more taste-testers would prefer Coke to Pepsi. According to Pepsi, the results of the taste test were just the opposite: more people preferred the taste of Pepsi because it was sweeter than Coke.

In 1985, Coca-Cola decided to conduct its own Coke Taste Test when it compared a reformulated, sweeter "New" Coke with the original Coca-Cola formula. Based on results obtained from blind taste tests run on almost 200,000 people:

- Consumers preferred New Coke to the original Coke 55 percent to 45 percent.
- Consumers preferred New Coke to Pepsi Cola 52 percent to 48 percent.
- However, after New Coke was introduced, new studies showed only 30 percent of consumers liked New Coke.

Thus, consumers preferred the taste of "new" Coke over "old" Coke, and more importantly, over Pepsi. As astute marketers, Coca-Cola made the decision to pull "old" Coke from the market and replace it with "new" Coke to reinvigorate the brand and gain market share.

However, the results of this strategy were disastrous for Coca-Cola! During the taste test, Coca-Cola had failed to assess the impact on the results if its customers/testers were told that "old" Coke would be pulled off the market if consumers in general preferred the "new" Coke to both "old" Coke and Pepsi. Brand-loyal consumers, who highly valued both the history and somewhat bitter taste of the old Coca Cola brand, rebelled when Coca-Cola pulled "old" Coke. They boycotted Coca-Cola products and generated a massive write-in campaign demanding that "old" Coke be reinstated. After a brief period, Coca-Cola reintroduced the old formulation as "Coca-Cola Classic" and ultimately removed New Coke from the market.[1]

Today, we are going to replicate the Pepsi Challenge and Coke Taste Test experiments (or show Slide 4).

2. Behind a shield, have Team 1 put Pepsi in cup "B and Coke in cup "N". Team 2 will put Coke in cup "B" and Pepsi in cup "N". All teams will fill the "W" cups with water.

3. To begin the taste test, have students come down by rows. Have students from odd numbered rows go to station 1 and those from even rows go to station 2. Then, place a blindfold on the student. Next, take one "B", "N", and "W" cup from behind the shield and place them in front of the student.

---

[1] Robert F. Hartley, "Marketing Mistakes and Successes," 8th edition (New York: John Wiley & Sons, 2001), pp. 11-14.

4. With the blindfold on, have each taste-tester take a small sip from cup "B". Then, have him/her take a bite of a saltine cracker and a sip of water. Next, have her/him repeat the process for cup "N". When finished, place the used cups behind the shield before you tell the tester to remove his/her blindfold. Hand the student a copy of the Pepsi – Coke Taste Test Questionnaire with the station number printed on it.

5. When finished the taste test, have each student fill out and hand in the Pepsi – Coke Taste Test Questionnaire. When all students have completed the test and turned in their surveys, take a poll by station number as to which brand (cup "B" or cup "N") tasted the better and record the results on the blackboard or a blank overhead transparency. Finally, inform them which brand was in which cup for each station or wait until the end of (or next) class period when the survey results have been tabulated.

6. Have someone tabulate the results during the middle of class and discuss the results at the close of class. Some ideas for cross-tabulations are mentioned below.

Some Controls Built into the Experiment. You may want to point out two controls built into the taste test experiment and others that were omitted:

- Randomly assigning letters to the brands. This is done to eliminate students guessing which letter would be given a particular brand. However, this does not overcome the potential problem of a student preference for one letter in the alphabet over another.

- Eating a saltine cracker and drinking water between tastes. This is done to avoid a possible lingering "aftertaste" that might be caused from tasting the previous brand.

Tabulating the Results. The simplest analysis is based on tabulating the taste test results on a blank copy of the form and calculating the percentages for each question with a calculator. In addition, especially if the sample were larger, the answers to Questions 1 – 2 could be cross-tabulated with stated preferences, behaviors, and gender in Questions 3 – 5.

Strategy Decisions. Tabulations of Questions 1 and 2 tell how the two brands compare with each other in paired-comparison tests. An in-class discussion led by the instructor might initially assume that the class test results were consistent with the shares reported in the surveys. Ask students how they might explain the discrepancy between their stated preferences and the results from the in-class taste test experiment.

Marketing Lessons. Intentions expressed in an experiment do not always translate well into actual practice.

- The experimental condition itself can affect results (the Hawthorne effect; people know they're being evaluated).

- Measuring only one element of the marketing mix (the "product") does not provide the whole marketing mix context within which consumers may evaluate products and make purchase decisions of how consumers will react to the entire offering).

Websites. Pepsi's website is www.pepsiworld.com. Coca-Cola's website is www.coca-cola.com.

PEPSI– COKE TASTE TEST QUESTIONNAIRE

STATION NUMBER: _____

1. In comparing the tastes of brand "B" and brand "N":

    I prefer "B" ..... ☐   I am indifferent between "B" and "N" ..... ☐   I prefer "N" ..... ☐

2. Based on your station number, which soft drink brand is "B" and which is "N"?

    "B" is: _____   "N" is: _____

3. Are you a "Heavy", "Medium", "Light" or "Non" user or consumer of soft drinks?

    Heavy User ..... ☐   Medium User... ☐   Light User .... ☐   Non User .... ☐

4. Which is your preferred brand: "Pepsi," "Coca-Cola," or "None"?

    Pepsi .... ☐   Coca-Cola .... ☐   None .... ☐

5. What is your gender: Male .... ☐   Female ...... ☐

© McGraw-Hill Companies, Inc. 2003

CHAPTER 8: TURNING MARKETING INFORMATION INTO ACTION

ICA8-2: IN-CLASS ACTIVITY

DESIGNING A TASTE TEST QUESTIONNAIRE FOR HOWLIN' COYOTE® CHILI

Learning Objectives. To have students (1) design three questions for a taste test questionnaire of a possible new Howlin' Coyote® chili and (2) compare their questions with those actually used in the taste test.

Definitions. The following marketing terms are referred to in this in-class activity (ICA):

- Questionnaire Data: Facts and figures obtained by asking people about their attitudes, awareness, intentions, and behaviors.

- Scale: A fixed alternative question with three or more choices that measures the variation or intensity in a respondent's attitude, opinion, and/or behavior.

Nature of the Activity. To have students design questions for a survey, each using a scale to measure the attitudes and behaviors and appreciate the difficulty in developing questions that assess consumer attitudes, opinions, and/or behaviors.

Estimated Class Time. 20 minutes.

Materials Needed.

- A transparency of TM8-2 (or use Slide 4 from ICA08-2.ppt of the ISK PowerPoint CD): Try Your Hand at Designing a Chili Taste Test Questionnaire.

- The Howlin' Coyote® Chili Challenge Taste Test Questionnaire from the *Instructor's Survival Kit* box.

- A transparency of the Howlin' Coyote® Chili Challenge Taste Test Questionnaire (or use Slide 5 from ICA08-2.ppt of the ISK PowerPoint CD).

- Copies of the Howlin' Coyote® Chili Challenge Taste Test Questionnaire.

- The ISK PowerPoint CD from the *Instructor's Survival Kit* box. See the instructions for use of this CD on page 4 of this manual if you use this CD in class.

Preparation Before Class. Follow the steps below:

1. Read Appendix A, which is located at the end of Chapter 2 in the text.

2. Review the Howlin' Coyote® Chili Challenge Taste Test Questionnaire.

3. Make a transparency of TM8-2 (or use Slide 4).

4. Make a transparency of the Howlin' Coyote® Chili Challenge Taste Test Questionnaire (or use Slide 5).

5. Make copies of the Howlin' Coyote® Chili Challenge Taste Test Questionnaire.

Instructions. Follow the steps below to conduct this ICA:

1. Give this background mini-lecture (and show Slide 3):

   Paradise Kitchens® (see Appendix A) often does taste tests to evaluate a new chili that might be added to its Howlin' Coyote® line. As a part of the taste test, participants are asked to complete a short questionnaire that summarizes their feelings. This questionnaire must be simple and worded very carefully so that participants are able to provide the information requested.

2. Show transparency TM8-2 (or show Slide 4). Ask students to take 5 minutes and design each of the three scales or questions requested on TM8-2.

3. Have several students suggest their proposed scales for each of the three TM8-2 questions, and perhaps have them write them on the blackboard.

4. Show the transparency made from Howlin' Coyote® Chili Challenge Taste Test Questionnaire (or show Slide 5) and pass copies of it around to the class. Make these points about the three questions posed on TM8-2:

   - Question #1. As shown in Questions 1 and 2 in the Howlin' Coyote® Chili Challenge Taste Test Questionnaire, the six scale points are:

     - Dislike extremely – Neutral   – Like very much
     - Dislike somewhat   – Like somewhat   – Like extremely

     Point out (1) the "neutral point" is <u>not</u> in the center of the scale, thereby giving more scale points and discrimination to the positive reactions; instead, a "5-point" scale should have been used if a neutral point is desired and (2) the "faces" on the scale are intended to make the question less threatening to respondents and serve as surrogates for verbal descriptors.

   - Question #2. This should have been easy for students. The chili spiciness scale is:

     – Mild   – Medium   – Hot

   - Question #3. See Question 8 in the Howlin' Coyote® Chili Challenge Taste Test Questionnaire. Point out to the class that (1) the time period covered is the past <u>6 months</u> (not a year, which would be more difficult for participants to remember) and (2) the scale points are "none", "1 to 5 times", and "6 or more times". Clearly, the heavy users (6 or more times) are of greatest interest to Paradise Kitchens®.

5. Ask students to comment on or critique other parts of the actual Howlin' Coyote® Chili Challenge Taste Test Questionnaire. Also, ask them to develop marketing actions that each question could lead to.

- Opening Statement. Offering "valuable coupons" and a "raffle entry to win prizes" may entice some respondents to not only complete the survey (+) but also potentially provide more favorable responses to the questions asked than they normally would in hopes of receiving the coupons or winning the prize, thus skewing the survey results (–).

- Questions #1 & #2. Adding the faces to the verbal adjectives for the scales in these questions is a good idea because some respondents process information visually and view these cues as helpful.

- Question #3. "choose" should be capitalized.

- Question #5. A comma should be placed after "chili."

- Question #7. Seems out of sequence. Better survey design needed.

- Question #9. Age ranges are not mutually exclusive (what if a respondent is 35 years old, which response option would be checked: 22 – 35 or 35 – 55?) or exhaustive (what if a respondent is 18 years old? or is 56 – 60 years old?)

- Overall Questionnaire Design. Too many questions bunched at the bottom of the page. Either use two pages (front and back) or eliminate a question or two and use just one page.

Marketing Lessons. It is critically important that marketing research questionnaires (1) be simple, (2) be precisely worded, (3) be visually appealing, and (4) most importantly, lead to tangible marketing actions.

Website. Paradise Kitchens does not have a website.

TM8-2

TRY YOUR HAND AT DESIGNING A CHILI TASTE-TEST QUESTIONNAIRE

1. You have a respondent taste a new Howlin' Coyote® chili being considered for manufacture. Suggest names for the <u>six</u> scale points seeking the respondent's reaction, where one of the scale points is "neutral."

   _____   _____   _____   _____   _____   _____

2. Suggest three names on a "spiciness scale" to evaluate the new chili.

   _____   _____   _____

3. You are especially interested in reactions to consumers who frequently eat chili. Compose a question to measure a respondent's frequency of consuming chili.

CHAPTER 8: TURNING MARKETING INFORMATION INTO ACTION

ICA8-3: IN-CLASS ACTIVITY

WEBSURFING FOR MARKETING INFORMATION

Learning Objectives. To have students experience the wide variety of marketing information that is available on the Internet and World Wide Web.

Definitions. The following marketing terms are referred to in this in-class activity (ICA):

- Internet: An integrated global network of computers that gives users access to information and documents.

- World Wide Web: A part of the Internet that supports a retrieval system that formats information and documents into Web pages.

Nature of the Activity. To have students visit three websites that have been discussed in the text or are likely to be of interest to marketing students and then select one website they find interesting and summarize the kinds of information that this website offers.

Estimated Class Time.

- If Internet access is available in the classroom, 20 minutes of "surfing" and discussion should be adequate.

- If Internet access is not available, two class sessions—one for assigning websites to visit and one for discussion—will be necessary.

Materials Needed.

- A transparency of TM8-3: Websites of Interest to Marketing Students.

- Internet access in the classroom.

- Computer and projection equipment the classroom that will allow the websites to be shown on an overhead screen.

Preparation Before Class. Follow the steps below:

1. Read the Web Link on p. 215 in Chapter 8.

2. Access each of the websites identified in TM8-3.

3. Make a transparency of TM8-3.

4. Make copies of TM8-3.

Instructions. Follow the steps below to conduct this ICA:

1. Ask students about their experience "surfing" the Internet. Solicit examples of what Internet websites interest them.

2. Hand out copies of TM8-3.

3. Show transparency TM8-3.

4. If the classroom has Internet access, select 2 – 3 websites to visit, such as the American Marketing Association's marketingpower.com and the U.S. government's portal, firstgov.gov. If the classroom does not have Internet access, assign 1 – 2 websites to students or teams of students, and ask them to visit these websites before the next class.

5. Discuss the marketing implications of the websites.

Marketing Lessons. The websites listed on TM8-3 demonstrate the wide variety of marketing information and activities available on the Internet. The American Marketing Association and American Advertising Federation websites are resources for marketing students and professionals. Firstgov.gov and the Wall Street Journal Interactive Edition websites demonstrate the growing access to marketing information. Finally, the McGraw-Hill Higher Education website provides information about this and other marketing books!

Websites. See those listed in TM8-3.

TM8-3

WEBSITES OF INTEREST TO MARKETING STUDENTS

[NOTE: "http://" is assumed before "www"]

1. The American Marketing Association — www.marketingpower.com

2. The American Advertising Federation — www.aaf.org

3. Ad Forum.com (15,000 print & TV ads) — www.adforum.com

4. eBay (on-line auction) — www.ebay.com

5. McGraw-Hill Higher Education — www.mhhe.com/kerin

6. HotJobs.com (careers) — www.hotjobs.com

7. iVillage.com (portal for women) — www.ivillage.com

8. Pollstar (concert locator) — www.pollstar.com

9. The Drudge Report (political news) — www.drudgereport.com

10. Amazon.com (purchase books, CDs) — www.amazon.com

11. Business Week (business news) — www.businessweek.com

12. Wall Street Journal Interactive Edition — www.wsj.com

13. Yahoo! (portal) — www.yahoo.com

14. Google (search engine) — www.google.com

15. Firstgov.gov (U.S. government portal) — www.firstgov.gov

© McGraw-Hill Companies, Inc. 2003

CHAPTER 9: IDENTIFYING MARKET SEGMENTS AND TARGETS

ICA9-1: IN-CLASS ACTIVITY

PRODUCT CATEGORIZATION TO IDENTIFY MARKET SEGMENTS AND COMPETITORS

Learning Objectives. To have students: (1) discover the process of categorization and how different people categorize the same objects in different ways; (2) explore some of the reasons for these differences; and (3) understand the importance of categorization in identifying both market segments and competitors.

Definitions. The following marketing terms are referred to in this in-class activity (ICA):

- Product Class: The entire product category or industry.

- Product Form: Variations of a product within a product class.

- Product Item: A specific product as noted by a unique brand, size, or price.

- Product Line: A group of products that are closely related because they satisfy a class of needs, are used together, are sold to the same customer group, are distributed through the same outlets, or fall within a given price range.

Nature of the Activity. To have the instructor lead students through a fun and informative activity in which two students independently group some snack and candy items into different categories. Students in the class are able to observe the differences in the ways different people group items and discuss some of the reasons for these differences.

Estimated Class Time. 20 minutes.

Materials Needed.

- The Honey Nut Cheerios® Milk 'n Cereal bar from the *Instructor's Survival Kit* box.

- A variety of several candies and other food items, such as

    - M&M's (Plain, Almond, Peanut, Peanut Butter, & Crispy)
    - Snickers
    - A package of Frito Lay sunflower seeds
    - A package of Planter's mixed nuts
    - A Quaker Oats Chewy granola bar
    - A package of Fruit Rollups
    - An apple, banana, or orange

- The ISK PowerPoint CD from the *Instructor's Survival Kit* box. See the instructions for use of this CD on page 4 of this manual if you use this CD in class.

Preparation Before Class. Follow the steps below:

1. Read the material below.

2. Purchase the above-mentioned items.

Instructions. Follow the steps below to conduct this ICA (or show Slide 3):

1. Lay the assortment of "snack items" out on a table in the front of the classroom.

2. Ask for two student volunteers. The students must go out of the room. One student is shown in and given the following instructions:

   "Your task is to take these objects and group them together in any way that you wish. The only requirement is that there must be at least two objects in each group."

3. Ask the student why he or she grouped items in the manner described. For example, there may be one group with items that contain chocolate or one with items that contain nuts…or perhaps the student has a "healthy snack group." Either the instructor or another student should write down the way the items are categorized by the student and the rationale given for grouping these items.

4. Have that student sit down, bring in the other student, and repeat the grouping process. The student's explanation of the grouping should also, once again, be recorded. The groupings by the two students will more than likely be very different.

5. Use these discussion points:

   a. The way items are categorized by one person is usually very different than the way another person may group the items. Ask students what some of the factors are that may account for the differences. Common answers include:

   - Prior experience with the items (those with nuts vs. those that have caramel).

   - Knowledge (those items which are more nutritional).

   - Appearance or packaging (some students may group all brown colored packages together).

   - Personal preferences or attitudes towards different items (groups based on items the person likes or dislikes).

   - Advertising or position the product has in the consumer's mind. With no personal experience with an item, a student may think that granola bars are healthy based on advertisements for the items.

   - Brand name (even if a student has never seen or tasted the Honey Nut Cheerios Milk 'n Cereal bar, the student may assign a positive value to the product based on the Cheerios® brand name).

b. Ask students the following questions:

- Question 1: What are the product items?

    Answer: The Honey Nut Cheerios Milk 'n Cereal bar, M&M's (Plain, Almond, Peanut, Peanut Butter, & Crispy), Snickers, Frito Lay sunflower seeds, Planter's mixed nuts, a Quaker Oats granola bar, Fruit Rollups, and an apple, banana or orange.

- Question 2: What are the product forms?

    Some Answers: "Candy," "fruit," and "granola/nuts/seeds."

- Question 3: What are the product lines?

    Answer: M&M's (Plain, Almond, Peanut, Peanut Butter, & Crispy).

- Question 4: What is/are the product class(es)?

    Answer: "Snacks."

c. Ask students why product categorization is important in marketing. The answer is that items grouped together by an individual may be considered substitutes for each other by that individual, which helps define the class of products, the market segments, and the competitors to these segments.

   For example, if a student groups a granola bar, Fruit Rollups, and a piece of fruit together as "healthy" snacks, this student probably would accept a granola bar in place of a piece of fruit. However, another student may group the granola bar with "candy" items and consider them all junk food. When this student craves a "healthy" snack (the "market segment"), a granola bar will not substitute for a piece of fruit since it is outside the "product grouping" for acceptable substitutes.

d. Finally, ask students the products with which the Honey Nut Cheerios Milk 'n Cereal bar must compete most directly. Also, have the class discuss the special promotional strategies suggested by this competitive set. By the time you discuss this in class, you may see an ad for the Honey Nut Cheerios Milk 'n Cereal bar!

Marketing Lessons. Marketers need to understand how consumers categorize objects because it helps define both the market segments, acceptable substitutes in the product grouping, and the competitors to these segments. Marketers, through advertising, packaging, and branding, can influence the way consumers categorize products. This influence is especially critical for new products that consumers may be unfamiliar with.

Websites. The Honey Nut Cheerios Milk 'n Cereal bar and Fruit Rollups do not have websites; see the General Mills website, which is www.generalmills.com. Websites for products referred to in this ICA are: M&M's (www.m-ms.com); Snickers (www.snickers.com); Frito Lay (www.fritolay.com); Planters (www.planters.com); and Quaker Oats (www.quakerchewy.com).

CHAPTER 9: IDENTIFYING MARKET SEGMENTS AND TARGETS

ICA9-2: IN-CLASS ACTIVITY

PRODUCT POSITIONING FOR CONSUMERS AND RETAILERS

Learning Objectives. To have students: (1) observe the product, branding, and packaging strategies of Zebra® Pen Corp., a writing instrument company; (2) identify the benefits to both consumers and retailers; and (3) suggest positioning statements for the company.

Definitions. The following marketing terms are referred to in this in-class activity (ICA):

- Branding: Activity in which an organization uses a name, phrase, design, or symbols, or combination of these, to identify its products and distinguish them from those of competitors.

- Packaging: Any container in which a product is offered for sale and on which label information is communicated.

- Product Positioning: The place an offering occupies in consumers' minds on important attributes relative to competitive offerings.

Nature of the Activity. To have students look at a "blister cards" of a 1-pack black pen sample and a 2-pack specialty pen sample from Zebra Pen Corp., a writing instrument firm. Students will suggest consumer benefits and retailer benefits, and compose a product positioning statement.

Estimated Class Time. 25 minutes.

Materials Needed.

- The Jimnie® Gel Roller black pen (1-pack blister card) and the Gel Sniff-itz™ blueberry pen (2-pack blister card) from the *Instructor's Survival Kit* box.

- Copies of the **back** of Jimnie Gel Roller and the Gel Sniff-itz blister cards.

- A transparency of TM9-2A: Jimnie Gel & Gel Sniff-Itz Product & Branding Strategies.

- A transparency of TM9-2B: Jimnie Gel & Gel Sniff-Itz Packaging Strategies.

- Copies of TM9-2A and TM9-2B.

- A transparency of TM9-2C: How Zebra Pen's Product and Brand Strategies Benefit Consumers and Retailers.

- A transparency of TM9-2D: How Zebra Pen's Packaging Strategies Benefit Consumers and Retailers.

- Copies of TM9-2C and TM9-2D.

- The ISK PowerPoint CD from the *Instructor's Survival Kit* box. See the instructions for use of this CD on page 4 of this manual if you use this CD in class.

Preparation Before Class. Follow the steps below:

1. Read the material below.

2. Study the blister cards for the two Zebra pens to discuss the benefits to both consumers and retailers and compose a product positioning statement.

3. Make copies of the **back** of the Jimnie Gel Roller and the Gel Sniff-itz blister cards.

4. Make transparencies and copies of TM9-2A, TM9-2B, TM9-2C, and TM9-2D.

Instructions. Follow the steps below to conduct this ICA:

1. Divide students into two sets of 4-person teams. Designate half the teams the "product and brand team" and the other half the "packaging team."

2. Show and briefly discuss transparency TM9-2A and handout copies to members of the "product and brand" team. Then, show and briefly discuss transparency TM9-2B and handout copies to members of the "packaging" team.

3. Pass around the Jimnie Gel Roller black pen in the 1-pack blister card and the Gel Sniff-itz blueberry pen in the 2-pack blister card (or show Slide 3).

4. Give students this background mini-lecture:

    "The Jimnie Gel Roller is available in black, blue, red, green, pink, and violet colors and in 1-, 2-, 4-, and 12-packs at office supply superstores (Office Max, Staples) and mail order firms (Quill). The 1-pack is only carried in small office supply and stationery stores (or show Slide 4).

    The Gel Sniff-itz is available in four "Fruity" scents (blueberry, orange, green apple, and peach) and four "Passion" scents (vanilla, mint, lavender, and soap). It is sold in 2- and 4-packs at office supply superstores" (or show Slide 5)."

5. Pass out copies of the **back** of the Jimnie Gel Roller and the Gel Sniff-itz blister cards.

6. Allow 10 minutes for both the "product and brand" and the "packaging" teams to:

    a. Complete the "benefit/importance" boxes on their TM9-2A and TM9-2B forms for both consumers and retailers that may carry Zebra Pen Corp.'s 1-pack Jimnie Gel Roller and Gel Sniff-itz 2-pack pens.

    b. Compose a "positioning statement" of not more than 15 words for consumers and retailers that may carry the product.

7. Have both the "product and brand" and "packaging" teams each contribute their ideas to the class for 5 minutes. Write these ideas on the transparencies made from TM9-2A and TM9-2B. Use the two respective "answers and discussion points" tables on the following pages (TM9-2C and TM9-2D) to direct the discussion.

8. Ask both the "product and brand" and "packaging" teams for a 15-word positioning statement directed at consumers and retailers. Stress to the class that reasonably priced writing instruments are often seen by both consumers and retailers as commodities. Zebra Pen Corp. has used its creativity and marketing expertise to add value to both consumers and retailers.

    Two short positioning statements might be:

    - For consumers: "Writing instruments that are comfortable, socially-responsible, express my creativity, and innovative."
    - For retailers: "A writing instruments line with a recognized brand name and logo, creative packaging, and high potential volume."

    These positioning statements help Zebra Pen Corp. distinguish its products in the minds of consumers and retailers from competitive products, as discussed at the end of Chapter 9.

Marketing Lessons. Firms selling convenience products that are traditionally seen as "commodities" can break through the clutter by using creative product, branding, and packaging strategies to achieve a strong position in the minds of consumers and retailers.

To Obtain Other or More of Zebra Pen Corp. Writing Instruments. Instructors wishing to show other Zebra Pen Corp. writing instruments to their class can buy them at an office supply superstore or contact Zebra Pen Corp. at 1-800-247-7170.

Website. Connect to Zebra Pen Corp. at www.zebrapen.com.

TM9-2A

JIMNIE GEL & GEL SNIFF-ITZ PRODUCT & BRANDING STRATEGIES

(a) Identify benefit and importance to consumers and retailers and (b) compose a positioning strategy?

Product and Branding Strategy	Benefit/Importance to Consumers	Benefit/Importance to Retailers
1. Kinds of writing instruments: ball point pens, retractable pens, roller pens, mechanical pencils, highlighters & markers, and combination instruments		
2. For Gel Roller Pens: Color Xchanger, Gel Sniff-itz, Jell3 Roller, Jimnie Gel Antique, Jimnie Gel Metallic, Jimnie Gel Retractable, Jimnie Gel Roller, J-Roller, Sarasa Bold, Super Marble Gel Ink		
3. Zebra logo and Jimnie brand		
4. Features: listed on the front and back of the package		
5. Design: gel ink, rubber grip, colors, see-through barrel	⇩	⇩
Positioning statement suggested by above strategies:		

© McGraw-Hill Companies, Inc. 2003

TM9-2B

JIMNIE GEL & GEL SNIFF-ITZ PACKAGING STRATEGIES

(a) Identify benefit and importance to consumers and retailers and
(b) compose a positioning strategy?

Packaging Strategy	Benefit/Importance to Consumers	Benefit/Importance to Retailers
1. "Blister card" can hold varying numbers of writing instruments		
2. Thicker, stronger blister cards and shells		
3. Can package products in blister cards or in bulk (boxes)		
4. Unique Zebra graphics on package for each product, while retaining a cohesive look to its product line	⇩	⇩
Positioning statement suggested by above strategies:		

© McGraw-Hill Companies, Inc. 2003

TM9-2C

ANSWERS & DISCUSSION POINTS

HOW ZEBRA PEN'S PRODUCT AND BRAND STRATEGIES BENEFIT CONSUMERS AND RETAILERS

Product and Branding Strategy	Benefit/Importance to Consumers	Benefit/Importance to Retailers
1. Kinds of writing instruments: ball point pens, retractable pens, rollerball pens, mechanical pencils, highlighters & markers, and combination instruments	• Makes it possible for customer to find writing instrument that serves her/his unique needs	• Provides a complete product mix • Can use fewer suppliers rather than several
2. For Gel Roller Pens: Color Xchanger, Gel Sniff-itz, Jell3 Roller, Jimnie Gel Antique, Jimnie Gel Metallic, Jimnie Gel Retractable, Jimnie Gel Roller, J-Roller, Sarasa Bold, Super Marble Gel Ink	• Makes it possible for customer to find roller pen that serves her/his unique needs	• Provides a complete product line • Offers fine and medium roller sizes
3. Zebra logo and Jimnie brand	• Aids consumer recognition and recall of company and brand	• Helps convince retail buyer of product's marketability
4. Features: listed on the front and back of the package	• Communicates value perception • Stimulates point of purchase buying decision	• Helps convince retail buyer of product's marketability
5. Design: gel ink, rubber grip, colors, see-through barrel	• Encourages consumer loyalty, repeat purchases, frequent purchases	• Helps retailer see opportunity for follow-on sales

© McGraw-Hill Companies, Inc. 2003

TM9-2D

ANSWERS & DISCUSSION POINTS

HOW ZEBRA PEN'S PACKAGING STRATEGIES BENEFIT CONSUMERS AND RETAILERS

Packaging Strategy	Benefit/Importance to Consumers	Benefit/Importance to Retailers
1. "Blister card" can hold varying numbers of writing instruments	• Provides economic purchase quantity for consumers	• Uses common blister card sizes to make display easier, more convenient
2. Thicker, stronger blister cards and shells	• Looks more substantial to consumers; enhances consumers' perceptions of quality; protects instruments	• Avoids writing instruments breaking out of blister cards during shipment • Makes blister cards look neat and clean on display rack
3. Can package products in blister cards or in bulk (boxes)	• Customers can obtain quantity discounts, if desired (particularly small business and corporate customers)	• Permits sellers to obtain writing instruments in quantities and packaging they desire
4. Unique Zebra and other graphics on package for each product, while retaining a cohesive look to its product line	• Provides aesthetically pleasing, attention-getting package • Enhances consumers' perceptions of quality	• Helps establish greater credibility with retail buyers

© McGraw-Hill Companies, Inc. 2003

CHAPTER 9: IDENTIFYING MARKETS SEGMENTS AND TARGETS

ICA9-3: IN-CLASS ACTIVITY

DEVELOPING A MARKET–PRODUCT GRID FOR THE VICTOR® LINE OF MOUSETRAPS (PART 3)

Learning Objectives. To have students analyze the Victor® lines of mousetraps manufactured by Woodstream Corp. and to position the traps in a market–product grid.

Definitions. The following marketing terms are referred to in this ICA:

- Market–Product Grid: A framework to relate the segment of a market to products offered or potential marketing actions by the firm.

- Market Segments: The groups that result from the process of market segmentation; these groups ideally (1) have common needs and (2) will respond similarly to a marketing action.

- Points of Difference: Those characteristics of a product that make it superior to competitive substitutes.

Nature of the Activity. To have students learn the importance of using a market-product grid to identify and select target market segments and then develop marketing actions to reach these segments. This activity complements ICAs in Chapter 1 (ICA1-1) and Chapter 2 (ICA2-2).

Estimated Class Time. 20 minutes.

Materials Needed. Use the following items from the *Instructor's Survival Kit* and make copies and overheads of the following to hand out or use:

- The Victor® Metal Bait Pedal, Live Catch, Easy Set®, Pre-Baited, and Quick Kill mousetraps from the *Instructor's Survival Kit* box.[1]

- Copies of the "Product Descriptions for Selected Victor® Mousetraps" handout.

- Copies of TM9-3A: Market–Product Grid for Mousetraps (Blank).

- A transparency of TM9-3A (or use Slide 10 from ICA09-3.ppt of the ISK PowerPoint CD): (Blank) Market–Product Grid for Mousetraps.

- A transparency of TM9-3B (or use Slide 11 from ICA09-3.ppt of the ISK PowerPoint CD): Market–Product Grid for Victor® Brand Mousetraps.

---

[1] Mousetraps provided by Chagnon Outdoor World. See http://www.chagnonoutdoors.com.

- The ISK PowerPoint CD from the *Instructor's Survival Kit* box. See the instructions for use of this CD on page 4 of this manual if you use this CD in class.

Preparation Before Class. Follow the steps below:

1. Review background material from ICA1-1: What Makes a Better Mousetrap? (Part 1) and ICA2-2: What Makes a Better Mousetrap? (Part 2).

2. Review the website (www.victorpest.com) to direct the class discussion.

3. Make copies of the "Product Descriptions for Selected Victor® Mousetraps" handout.

4. Make copies of TM9-3A: Market–Product Grid for Mousetraps (Blank).

5. Make transparencies of:

    a. TM9-3A (or use Slide 10).

    b. TM9-3B (or use Slide 11).

Instructions. Follow the steps below to conduct this ICA:

1. Refresh students' memories of the background for this ICA from ICA1-1: What Makes a Better Mousetrap? (Part 1) and ICA2-2: What Makes a Better Mousetrap? (Part 2). Review the market segments and benefits users want in a mousetrap.

    The "disposer" market segment wants a cheap and relatively efficient way to handle its mouse problem. So the important "points of difference" in its buying decision are low-cost and disposability (a surrogate for convenience). The "reuser" segment wants greater efficiency and a more cost-effective means to resolve a persistent mouse problem. However, users are willing to pay more for a trap so they don't have to worry about contamination or injury, as is the case when releasing a mouse from a wooden, spring-loaded trap.

2. Give the following mini-lecture:

    Woodstream Corp. and other firms have been trying to invent the better mousetrap for over 100 years to prove Ralph Waldo Emerson's adage that "If a man...makes a better mousetrap, the world will beat a path to his door." Over the years, these firms have introduced new mousetraps to satisfy the needs of people who do not want to see or touch a captured mouse and prefer to humanely release a live, but captured mouse.

    Pass around the Victor® Metal Bait Pedal, Live Catch, Easy Set®, Pre-Baited, and Quick Kill mousetraps from the *Instructor's Survival Kit* (or show Slide 3).

    We will now see how Woodstream Corp. has chosen to solve the mice problems of prospective customers. Here are the four Victor® mousetraps we have see before.

These traps are positioned as "Poison Free" to offer consumers alternatives to chemically-based traps.

3. Form students into teams.

4. Give students copies of the "Product Descriptions for Selected Victor® Mousetraps" handout (or show the following slides):

   a. Slide 4: The Victor® Quick Set Mousetrap.

   b. Slide 5: The Victor® No See™ Mousetrap.

   c. Slide 6: The Victor® Sonic Pest Chaser.

   d. Slide 7: The Victor® Sonic Pest Chaser Ad.

   e. Slide 8: The Victor® Rodent Glue Tray.

   f. Slide 9: The Victor® Rat (Mouse) Zapper Trap.

5. Give students copies of TM9-3A: Market–Product Grid for Mousetraps (Blank).

6. Show transparency TM9-3A (or show Slide 10). Have students classify each of these Victor® mousetraps according to the kind of mousetrap it is (Wooden, Plastic, or Other) and the most likely target market segment it is trying to reach (Disposer or Reuser). This is a "market–product grid" that was introduced in Chapter 9. Explain this "Victor® mousetrap" market–product grid to students.

7. Solicit and write down the market–product classification students come up with for each Victor® mousetrap on the TM9-3A overhead.

8. Show transparency TM9-3B (or show Slide 11) to compare students' responses.

9. Ask students these questions:

   Question #1: What other bases might be used to segment the mousetrap market?

   Answers: Other ways to segment the mousetrap market include these bases:

   - "Humane-Conscious", those don't want to kill the mouse, just remove it versus those who don't care or want it dead.

   - "Magnitude of the Mouse Problem", those who have one or a few mice to deal with versus those who have many mice or a persistent mouse problem.

   - "Safety-Conscious", those who have children or pets that may be injured (total safety) versus those who are careful with potentially more hazardous mousetraps.

   - "Price-Conscious", those who want the least expensive mousetrap versus those who are willing to spend more for a mousetrap that may be more efficient.

Question #2: What other ways (besides "Wooden" vs. "Plastic" vs. "Other") might Woodstream Corp. use to form the products into groupings or clusters?

Answers: Other ways to group product types may include:

- "Technology," such as "Spring-loaded," "Glue," "Sonic," and "Electric."
- "Magnitude of the Mouse Problem," such as traps that catch/kill only one mouse at a time versus those that can catch/kill two or more mice.
- "Price Sensitivity," such as traps that cost < $5.00 vs. those that cost ≥ $5.00.

10. Encourage students to come up with other bases of segmentation and product groupings. Students may take two of these variables and position the various Victor® mousetraps on a perceptual map like that shown for chocolate milk at the end of Chapter 9 in the textbook. Point out that the "best" segmentation base and product grouping may vary with the marketing options available.

Marketing Lessons. Key lessons include:

1. A "better" product is in the eye of the customer, not the seller. Therefore, marketers, such as Woodstream Corp., will strive to develop and offer products that satisfy the needs of their targeted market segments better than the offerings of their competitors. In the process, marketers may offer a variety of products using different technologies. (So, in a sense, Mr. Emerson is right!)

2. Key features or "points of difference" in the product provide customer value to users.

3. Different market segments of buyers exist due to the different needs that may be satisfied by different product offerings. These segments and products may be displayed in a market–product grid. There is often no one "correct" market-product grid since the most useful one may vary with the marketing conditions involved.

Websites. To view Woodstream Corp.'s current product line of Victor® Brand Mousetraps, go to www.victorpest.com. To purchase additional mousetraps for this ICA, go to the Chagnon's Outdoor World website, which is www.chagnonoutdoors.com.

PRODUCT DESCRIPTIONS FOR SELECTED VICTOR® MOUSETRAPS HANDOUT

<u>Victor® Metal Bait Pedal Mousetrap</u>: The original wooden mousetrap with the spring-type metal bait pedal to handle gumdrops, peanut butter, cheese, or other natural mouse attractants. Price: $1.00 per 2-pack.

<u>Victor® Easy Set®, Pre-Baited Mousetrap</u>: This wooden snap trap with its clever "Swiss cheese" pedal requires no baiting because the trigger is infused with a scent mice find irresistible! Price: $1.59 per 2-pack.

<u>Victor® Live Catch Mousetrap</u>: Some people do not want to see or touch a captured mouse while others prefer the option of harmlessly releasing the captured mouse. Price: $3.49 per 2-pack.

<u>Victor® Quick Kill Mousetrap</u>: This trap is designed with a "power bar" that is designed for a quick, humane kill. It also has a safety latch built in. Price: $4.29 per 2-pack.

<u>Victor® Quick Set Mousetrap</u>: The Quick Set snap trap is very easy to set, bait, and dispose. Simply squeeze the trap to release the mouse. Price: $4.29 per 2-pack.

<u>Victor® No See™ Mousetrap</u>: This mousetrap has a unique covered design so you don't have to see or touch the mouse. Mice can enter from either direction when the trap is placed along the wall. The trap mechanism tells you when a mouse is caught. Price: $3.29 per 2-pack.

<u>Victor® Rodent Glue Trap</u>: This trap is pre-baited, ready to use, and are available in a wide variety of styles including flat boards, trays, and "no see" alternatives. Price: $3.25 per 4-pack.

<u>Victor® Sonic Pest Chaser</u>: This device emits a high-frequency sound that drives rodents crazy but cannot be heard by humans or pets! Covers up to 400 square feet. Plugs directly into an outlet. Price: $10.99 per unit.

<u>Victor® Rat (Mouse) Zapper Trap</u>: This electronic device delivers a lethal dose of electricity to mice. It detects mice and instantly releases stored electrical energy to kill the mouse. The set of 4 AA batteries will kill 10-20 rodents. The Rat Zapper is a safe alternative compared to standard traps, glue boards, and poison. The Rat Zapper is difficult for a child or a pet to trigger it. If a child or pet was able to trigger the Rat Zapper, the voltage will cause their muscles to contract, forcing them to pull their arm or paw away from it. Since the amount of energy produced by the Rat Zapper is intentionally limited by use of batteries and circuit design, we have virtually eliminated the possibility of an injury occurring from the Rat Zapper. Price: $74.99 per unit.

TM9-3A

MARKET–PRODUCT GRID FOR MOUSETRAPS

MARKET SEGMENT	PRODUCT GROUPING: KIND OF MOUSETRAP			
	Wooden Traps	Plastic Traps	Other Traps	
"Disposers"				
"Reusers"				

© McGraw-Hill Companies, Inc., 2003

TM9-3B

MARKET–PRODUCT GRID FOR VICTOR® BRAND MOUSETRAPS

	PRODUCT GROUPING: KIND OF MOUSETRAP									
	Wooden Traps			Plastic Traps				Other Traps		
MARKET SEGMENT	Basic Spring-Loaded Trap	Enhanced Spring-Loaded Trap	Covered Spring-Loaded Trap	Basic Spring-Loaded Trap	Enhanced Spring-Loaded Trap	Covered Live Catch Trap	Basic or Covered Glue Trap	Sonic Trap	Electric Trap	Poison Bait Pellets and Chemicals Trap
"Disposers"	Victor® Metal Bait Pedal Mousetrap	Victor® Easy Set® "Swiss Cheese" Mousetrap	Victor® No See™ "Covered" Mousetrap	Victor® Quick Set Mousetrap			Victor® No See "Covered" Glue Mousetrap			
							Victor® Mouse Glue Tray			
							Victor® Mouse Glue Board			
"Reusers"					Victor® Quick Kill Mousetrap	Victor® Live-Catch Mousetrap		Victor® Sonic "Pest Chaser"	Victor® Rat (Mouse) "Zapper" Trap	

© McGraw-Hill Companies, Inc., 2003

CHAPTER 10: DEVELOPING NEW PRODUCTS AND SERVICES

ICA10-1: IN-CLASS ACTIVITY

FOCUS GROUP FOR CONVERGENT DIGITAL DEVICES

Learning Objectives. To have students demonstrate the use of focus groups as a marketing research method to test new product ideas and concepts.

Definitions. The following marketing terms are referred to in this in-class activity (ICA):

- 3G: Third generation mobile telecommunications services that may include voice, high-speed data transfer, such as messaging, wireless Internet access and web browsing, paging, etc., still (pictures) and motion video (games, movies, etc.), music, e-commerce (ordering and payment of products and services), personal organizer applications, such as contact lists, date book, memos, etc., and business productivity software, such as word processing, spreadsheet, etc.

- Focus Group: An informal session of 6 to 10 past, present, or prospective customers in which a discussion leader, or moderator, asks their opinions about the firm's and its competitors' products.

Nature of the Activity. To have the instructor moderate a focus group with 5 or 6 students to explore reactions to a new convergent handheld device.

Estimated Class Time. 30 minutes.

Materials Needed.

- The Handspring® Treo™ 180 Communicator brochure from the *Instructor's Survival Kit* box.

- A transparency of TM10-1A: Features or Applications Desired in a New Convergent Digital Device.

- A transparency of TM10-1B (or use Slide 6 from ICA10-1.ppt of the ISK PowerPoint CD): Summary of Features for the Handspring Treo 180 Communicator.

- A transparency of TM10-1C: Likes and Dislikes of the Handspring Treo 180 Communicator.

- Blank name cards and markers for making nametags for focus group participants.

- A table and enough chairs for the moderator, recorder, and focus group members.

- The ISK PowerPoint CD from the *Instructor's Survival Kit* box. See the instructions for use of this CD on page 4 of this manual if you use this CD in class.

Preparation Before Class. Follow the steps below:

1. Read the section in Chapter 9 on focus groups (p.217). Conduct this in-class activity before you lecture on Chapter 10.

2. Read the material below.

3. Make transparencies of TM10-1A, TM10-1B (or use Slide 6 from ICA10-1.ppt of the ISK PowerPoint CD), and TM10-1C.

4. Make copies of the Handspring Treo 180 Communicator brochure to give to the focus group participants.

Instructions. Follow the steps below to conduct this ICA:

1. Give the following mini background lecture:

    "Marketers today use a variety of primary research methods (experiments, interviews, surveys, etc.; see Chapter 9) to help them design new or refine existing products and services. One such method is the focus group. Today, we will conduct a brief focus group to evaluate a new product.

    Recall that focus groups: (1) start with general background questions and then focus more specifically on the main topic of interest; (2) cost less than personal depth interviews or mail surveys; (3) can stimulate new ideas through group interaction; (4) usually involve 8 to 10 participants; (5) may last 1-2 hours; and (6) participants receive payment for their time."

2. Recruit 5 or 6 students for the focus group on convergent digital devices. Seat them in the front of the room and have them write their names on the cards. Recruit another student to record the focus group participants' responses to the questions asked by the moderator on the blackboard or a blank transparency.

3. When all have been seated, welcome the focus group by thanking them for agreeing to participate in this activity. Tell the participants that they will be asked to give their opinions on a new digital device. You will act as the moderator, the person who facilitates the focus group discussion.

4. Tell the focus group participants that the only rules are: (1) no opinion or idea is to be thought of as foolish; and (2) everyone in the group must have a chance to share his/her opinions.

5. As the moderator, have the focus group participants answer the following questions:

- Question 1: Do any of you use any type of method to keep track of your assignments, appointments, activities, and other personal information? Explain.

  Answers: Methods may include: memory, notebook, calendar, personal digital assistant (PDA) computer, DayTimer, etc.

- Question 2: What do you like about your method of keeping track of personal info? Dislike?

  Answers: Likes may include: ease-of-use, convenience, cost, habit, etc. Dislikes may include: entering data is cumbersome or takes too long, the device is expensive, etc.

- Question 3: What kinds of personal information do you think people want to keep track of?

  Answers: Kinds may include addresses, phone numbers, to-do lists, appointments, expenses, e-mail addresses, passwords, "dates", notes, etc.

- Question 4: Do any of you use a cellular or mobile phone? Why or why not?

  Answers: If yes: the need and freedom to communicate with anyone anywhere, safety, need for work, talk with a lot of friends, etc. If no: no need or can wait, device too expensive, fear of losing it, don't want to be bothered, want all-in-one device, etc.

- Question 5: What kinds of features do you think people want in a mobile phone?

  Answers: Features may include large memory for phone numbers or voice messages, speed dial, call waiting, three-way calling, receive messages or e-mail, have the unit and services reasonably priced, small enough to fit into pocket or purse, etc.

- Question 6: If you were to design an integrated or 3G (third generation) personal information and communications device, what kinds of information, functions, or applications would you want or need, regardless of how feasible it may be? Remember, no idea is "off the wall" and ignore what the cost might be.

  Answers: Have the student recorder write down the group's ideas on TM10-1A.

6. Show Slide 3: Jeff Hawkins and the Handspring Treo Communicator (TRT: 1:41).

7. Show the focus group a description of the Handspring Treo 180 Communicator.

   a. Show them the Handspring Treo 180 Communicator brochure (or show Slide 4).

   b. Have each member spend up to 1 minute reading the brochure.

   c. Show Slide 5 that depicts the Handspring Treo 180 Communicator.

   d. Show TM10-1B (or show Slide 6), which summarizes the features of the Handspring Treo 180 Communicator.

8. Show the transparency made from TM10-1C.

   a. Ask focus group members what they like and dislike about the Handspring Treo 180 Communicator.

   b. Have the student recorder write down these likes and dislikes on TM10-1C.

   c. Ask the focus group participants whether they would buy the Handspring Treo 180 Communicator at the specified price ($399 with service activation or $599 for just the unit itself) and the reason(s) for their response.

9. Thank the focus group participants for evaluating the new convergent digital device and excuse them from the focus group.

10. Acting as the instructor, have the entire class answer the following questions:

    - Question 1: How was the interaction among the focus group participants? Did you think everyone had a chance to share his/her opinions?

      Answers: If interaction is good, many diverse opinions can lead to ideas to develop new or improve existing products. If interaction is poor, it diminishes the value of this marketing research technique and perhaps conducting personal depth interviews or administering a survey would have had better results.

    - Question 2: What do you think about the convergence of digital devices? Would you buy one of these 3G devices today? Why or why not?

      Answers: Many possible responses exist.

11. The Handspring Treo Communicator product development team used a variety of methods to design the Treo 180 (or show Slide 7; TRT: 1:49).

12. Show Slides 8-9: In May 2002, the Handspring Treo product development team launched the Handspring Treo 90 (organizer only; color screen; $299) and Treo 270 Communicator (phone, organizer, e-mail, web; color screen; $499 w/ activation or $699 without).

Marketing Lessons. Methods such as focus groups are useful in generating new product ideas or evaluating of new product concepts in very early stages of development before a great deal of time, effort, and resources are expended. They are also used to evaluate existing products to assess quality, whether all the features are necessary or if others ones are needed, etc. However, focus groups are based on small, nonprobability samples that can limit the ability to generalize the results to an entire target market.

Website. Go to www.handspring.com to learn more about the line of Handspring Treo devices.

TM10-1A

FEATURES OR APPLICATIONS DESIRED IN A NEW CONVERGENT DIGITAL DEVICE

-
-
-
-
-
-
-
-
-
-

-
-
-
-
-
-
-
-
-
-

© McGraw-Hill Companies, Inc. 2003

TM10-1B

SUMMARY OF FEATURES FOR THE
THE HANDSPRING TREO™ 180 COMMUNICATOR

Mobile Phone	
Integrated Dialing from PhoneBook	Yes
Speed; 3-Way Dialing	Yes
Speakerphone; Hands Free Headset	Yes
Vibrating Call Alert System/Sound Mute	Yes
Personal Organizer	
Memory	16 Mb
Applications	Date Book Plus; Advanced Calculator; PhoneBook; To Do List; Memo Pad
HotSync	USB to PC/Mac
Wireless	
E-Mail	Yes, with Treo Mail ($49.99 - $99.99 per year)
Short Message Service	Yes
Internet Access	Yes, with Blazer browser
Product Specifications	
Battery	Rechargable Lithium; 2.5 hours of talk time
Screen Display	Monochrome
Keyboard	Yes
Protective Flip Cover	Yes
Size/Weight	Credit card-sized; 5.2 oz.
Operating System	Palm OS
Price	$399 w/ Service Activation ($19.99 - $99.99/mo.) $599 for just the unit itself

© McGraw-Hill Companies, Inc. 2003

TM10-1C

LIKES AND DISLIKES FOR THE HANDSPRING TREO™ 180 COMMUNICATOR

EVALUATION	Handspring Treo™ 180 Communicator
LIKES	
DISLIKES	

© McGraw-Hill Companies, Inc. 2003

CHAPTER 10: DEVELOPING NEW PRODUCTS AND SERVICES

ICA10-2: IN-CLASS ACTIVITY

COMMUNICATING IMPORTANT POINTS OF DIFFERENCE TO SKEPTICAL DESIGN ENGINEERS

Learning Objectives. To have students study a 3M marketing program for its innovative 3M® VHB™ (Very High Bonding) Tape to discover (1) how skeptical students and design engineers might respond to 3M's VHB Tape, (2) what key points of difference 3M stresses in its recent brochure and advertisement, and (3) how 3M can effectively communicate these points of difference.

Definitions. The following marketing terms are referred to in this in-class activity (ICA):

- Evoked Set: The group of brands that a consumer would consider acceptable from among all the brands in the product class of which he or she is aware.

- Points of Difference: Those characteristics of a product that make it superior to competitive substitutes.

Nature of the Activity. To have the instructor lead students through a practical new product exercise that involves demonstrating a key point of difference for 3M's VHB Tape (an incredibly effective ability to hold two smooth surfaces together) in a very creative way by providing a sample of the 3M's VHB Tape, which consists of two thin "pull-apart" materials, and challenging students to pull them apart.

Estimated Class Time. 20 minutes.

Materials Needed.

- The package of 3M's VHB Tapes from the *Instructor's Survival Kit* box.

- Either one of two 3M VHB Tape brochures from the *Instructor's Survival Kit* box:

    a. "Screws in the Skull."

    b. "In Emergency Break Glass."

    c. [NOTE: Due to limited supplies, only one of these two brochures is in the *Instructor's Survival Kit* box. However, both brochures are contained in the ICA10-2.ppt folder of the ISK PowerPoint CD.]

- Copies of the front and back of the unfolded 3M's VHB Tape brochure for each student (or show Slides 3-8).

- Copies of the "Screw on the Psychiatrist's Couch" ad, identified as VHBCouchad.pdf file located in the pdf folder in the ICA10-2 folder (or show Slide 9).
  [NOTE: Adobe Acrobat Reader is required to print the ad.]
- The ISK PowerPoint CD from the *Instructor's Survival Kit* box. See the instructions for use of this CD on page 4 of this manual if you use this CD in class.

Preparation Before Class. Follow the steps below:

1. Read the material below to give a background lecture.

2. Make copies of:

   a. the front and back of the unfolded 3M VHB Tape brochure.

   b. the "Screw on the Psychiatrist's Couch" ad.

Instructions. Follow the steps below to conduct this ICA:

1. Give students this background mini-lecture:

   "For 20 years, 3M has asked skeptical engineers to 'Imagine your world without rivets, screws, and welding!' when it developed very high bonding, double-sided foam VHB Tape. 3M's VHB Tape is intended to replace these mechanical fasteners for a variety of applications, such as applying steel strips to aluminum airplane wings to joining truck cab frames to the body (or show Slides 3-8).

   Sound like an exaggeration? This is exactly the problem 3M faces when marketing its VHB Tape to design engineers, who for years have been specifying more traditional fasteners in their new designs. Typically, design engineers see foam tapes as useful only in non-critical, lightweight attachment applications, such as for mounting posters or soap dispensers. 3M has tried to counter this perception by developing creative advertising, such as the "Screws in the Skull" and "In Emergency Break Glass" brochures or the "Screw on the Psychiatrist's Couch" ad (or show Slide 9).

2. Conduct a quick "Yes" or "No" market research survey by asking the class whether they believe 3M's claims about its VHB Tape. [NOTE: If there are engineers in the class, the instructor might tabulate their answers separately!]

   a. Write the results of the survey on the board.

   b. Ask students to explain their answers.

3. Ask the engineering students (if there are any) and the class the following questions:

    - Question 1: What special concerns might design engineers have in specifying 3M's VHB Tape in their new designs?

        Answers: Students may suggest strength, durability, test results under various use conditions, etc.

    - Question 2: What kinds of applications might design engineers consider using 3M's VHB Tape?

        Answers: Students may suggest small appliances or other applications where stress forces aren't that great and/or safety is not an issue if the VHB Tape fails.

    - Question 3: What kinds of applications might design engineers be very hesitant to use 3M's VHB Tape?

        Answers: Students may suggest applications with a lot of stress and where failure of the adhesive might be life threatening.

4. Pass out copies of 3M's VHB Tape brochure from the *Instructor's Survival Kit*. This brochure has been placed in several technical magazines targeted at design engineers. Ask students what "points of difference" the ad identifies for the 3M's VHB Tape. The key points of difference are:

    a. Provides strong, reliable, durable adhesive bonding.

    b. Reduces corrosion.

    c. Absorbs impact.

    d. Lessens metal fatigue.

    e. Eliminates weight.

    f. Dampens sound.

    g. Reduces parts inventory.

    h. Simplifies manufacturing processes/eliminates labor-intensive processes.

    i. Increases design freedom.

5. Ask students what is the single most critical point of difference for most design engineers. The answer: "a" in the list above, which is "strong, reliable durable adhesive bonding." This is the <u>necessary condition</u>—the essential requirement—for many design engineers to allow 3M's VHB Tape into their "evoked set" of fastening alternatives and to be genuinely considered for use in an engineering design. Unless 3M's VHB Tape has this attribute, all other attributes are secondary. The reason is that safety, appearance, durability, etc. all depend on this point of difference.

6. Pass out copies of the "Screw on the Psychiatrist's Couch" ad for 3M's VHB Tape.

7. Give two students a tear-apart sample from the *Instructor's Survival Kit*. Ask them to try to pull or tear the two strips apart. Then ask the class two final questions:

   - Question 1: Why did 3M include actual "tear-apart" strips in its brochure (see inside panel 2)?

     Answers: To (l) gain attention for 3M's VHB Tape and (2) directly address the skepticism that many design engineers have about the adhesive power of 3M's VHB Tape.

     [NOTE: Some students may be able to pull the strips apart and conclude the VHB Tape doesn't work. The tear-apart strips are an attention-getter, not a formal test! In real applications, the VHB Tape is subjected to tension and compression forces that it handles very well and **NOT** the shear forces to which the students may be subjecting the VHB Tape.]

   - Question 2: What does 3M have in its "Screw on the Psychiatrist's Couch" ad to trigger immediate action by design engineers?

     Answers: Having grabbed an engineer's attention, the brochure provides the opportunity for two immediate actions: To (l) call 3M using the 800 number at the bottom of the ad and (2) visit its website.

Marketing Lessons. It often takes creative marketing and advertising programs to overcome the tradition-bound inertia among both ultimate consumers and business-to-business customers for these potential buyers to genuinely consider innovative new products that can satisfy their wants and needs.

Website. To obtain the latest information on 3M's VHB Tape, go to 3M's website at www.3M.com/vhb.

CHAPTER 10: DEVELOPING NEW PRODUCTS AND SERVICES

ICA10-3: IN-CLASS ACTIVITY

USING METHOD 6–3–5 TO FIND NEW PRODUCT IDEAS FOR MAGNETIC POETRY®

Learning Objectives. To have students (1) participate in Method 6–3–5,[1] an idea generation technique and as a result (2) develop new product ideas for Magnetic Poetry®.

Definitions. The following marketing terms are referred to in this in-class activity (ICA):

- Brand Extension: The practice of using a current brand name to enter a completely different product class. Example: Having Fisher-Price, a toy-maker, launch a line of children's shampoos and conditioners.

- Idea Generation: Developing a pool of concepts as candidates for new products.

- Line Extension: The practice of using a current brand name to enter a new market segment in its product class. Example: Adding Frosted Cheerios to build on the brand equity of the Cheerios name and try to reach the segment that likes sweetened cereal.

Nature of the Activity. To have students participate in small groups to generate ideas for line and brand extensions for Magnetic Poetry.

Estimated Class Time. 20 minutes.

Materials Needed.

- The original Magnetic Poetry kit from the *Instructor's Survival Kit* box.

- A transparency of TM10-3A (or use Slide 4 from ICA10-3.ppt of the ISK PowerPoint CD): Ground Rules for Method 6-3-5.

- Copies of TM10-3B: Using Method 6-3-5 to Find New Product Ideas for Magnetic Poetry.

- A transparency of TM10-3C (or use Slides 5 -6 from ICA10-3.ppt of the ISK PowerPoint CD): Some Existing Line and Brand Extensions for Magnetic Poetry.

- The ISK PowerPoint CD from the *Instructor's Survival Kit* box. See the instructions for use of this CD on page 4 of this manual if you use this CD in class.

Preparation Before Class. Follow the steps below:

1. Read the material below to give a background lecture.

---

[1] Bryan Mattimore, "Eureka: How to Invent a New Product," *The Futurist* (March-April 1995), pp. 34-38.

2. Make transparencies of:

   a. TM10-3A (or use Slide 4 from ICA10-3.ppt of the ISK PowerPoint CD).

   b. TM10-3C (or use Slides 5 - 6 from ICA10-3.ppt of the ISK PowerPoint CD).

3. Make copies of TM10-3B to hand out in class.

Instructions. Follow the steps below to conduct this ICA:

1. Pass around the Original Magnetic Poetry Kit (or show Slide 3).

2. Give students this background mini-lecture based on Magnetic Poetry press releases:

   "The story behind the creation of Magnetic Poetry has taken on the quality of urban legend, but this one is true, and the man who sneezed it into being is Dave Kapell.

   Yes, Dave (at the time a cash-poor songwriter and ex-cab driver) was cutting up things, like old letters and newspaper articles in ransom-note style, as a lyric writing experiment. When Dave sneezed, it sent all of his carefully arranged words and letters flying. They spawned the idea of gluing a piece of magnet to the back of each tiny slip and sticking the newly "magnetized" words to a cookie sheet. From there, the first Magnetic Poetry Kit was born.

   Since that auspicious day in 1993, Magnetic Poetry has grown into a seven million dollar-per-year business with 25 employees and more than 100 different products. Magnetic Poetry has been sighted on the fridge in Hugh Grant's apartment in "Notting Hill," in "Conspiracy Theory," Seinfeld," and "Caroline in the City." And as reported in *Newsweek*, all but 4 words from Madonna's hit single "Candy Perfume Girl" are contained in Magnetic Poetry's Sequel Kit. Coincidence? A linguistic expert and a professional mathematician figured out the odds. A conservative estimate put the odds at 1 in 4.2 trillion that she didn't use the kit."

3. Introduce the Method 6-3-5 exercise as follows:

   "We've all heard of brainstorming as a technique for generating ideas. Organizations use these techniques to develop or improve products or advertising campaigns (see ICA11-2). Like brainstorming, Method 6-3-5 encourages creative thinking.

4. Tell the students they will be asked to come up with new line and brand extensions of the Original Magnetic Poetry Kit that the company might bring to market. [NOTE: The goal is to come up with good new product ideas. Students can debate later whether a product idea is really a line or brand extension.]

5. Assign students to teams (ideally 6 on each team) and have them sit together (in a circle works best). Pass out the handouts made from TM10-3B.

6. Show transparency TM10-3A (or show Slide 4) and explain the rules of Method 6–3–5. Each student on the team of <u>6</u> is given <u>3</u> minutes to come up with <u>5</u> ideas for new products for Magnetic Poetry. After 3 minutes, students are to pass their ideas on to the team member on their left. That team member is to elaborate and expand on the original 5 ideas. This is repeated a second time. This could continue all the way around the circle of 6 but after 2 iterations, the students have a good idea of how Method 6–3–5 works.

7. Ask each team to share 3 of their better ideas with the class and discuss what they thought of Method 6–3–5 for generating ideas. Did the opportunity to elaborate on other team members' ideas help to refine those ideas or generate more new ideas?

8. Show transparency TM10-3C (or show Slides 5 - 6), which highlights some of the line and brand extensions now offered by Magnetic Poetry. Detailed descriptions of these are:

   a. <u>Line Extensions or (show Slide 5)</u>.

   - Foreign language kits.

   - Specialized kits. For cooks, artists, dog lovers, etc.

   - Face kits. To transform photos of faces.

   - Destination kits. For cities such as New York or London.

   - StoryMaker™. A colorful collection of over 150 words and phrases to let young children learn to compose sentences.

   - College kits. For colleges and universities; Harvard and Yale have their own kits.

   b. <u>Brand Extensions (or show Slide 6)</u>.

   - Poetry Stones™. A kit for making tinted, word-bearing concrete cobblestones to border gardens or walkways.

   - Magnetic Poetry: The Game. A fast-paced board game where teams earn points creating poetry.

   - Poetry Beads. A kit for making necklaces with personalized messages.

<u>Marketing Lessons</u>. Method 6–3–5 demonstrates one of many techniques used to develop new products and services or to improve on existing products and services. Method 6–3–5 is a form of group idea generation, as opposed to other techniques, such as brainstorming.

<u>Website</u>. To view Magnetic Poetry's product line, go to www.magneticpoetry.com.

TM10-3A

GROUND RULES FOR METHOD 6–3–5

1. Use teams of <u>6</u> people each and sit in a circle.

2. In <u>3</u> minutes, have each team member come up with <u>5</u> ideas (written down on TM10-3B).

3. After 3 minutes, have each team member pass their ideas on to the team member to the left who spends 3 minutes elaborating and improving on the 5 ideas on the paper in front of them.

4. After 3 minutes, repeat Step 3 (above) again.*

* This could be repeated all around the circle, but to save time only 2 improvement iterations are done here.

TM10-3B

USING METHOD 6-3-5 TO FIND NEW PRODUCT IDEAS FOR MAGNETIC POETRY®

IDEA	ORIGINAL IDEA	FIRST REWORK	SECOND REWORK
#1			
#2			
#3			
#4			
#5			

© McGraw-Hill Companies, Inc. 2003

TM10-3C

SOME EXISTING LINE AND BRAND EXTENSIONS FOR MAGNETIC POETRY®

Line Extensions.

- Foreign Language kits

- Specialized kits

- Destination kits

- StoryMaker™

- College/University kits

Brand Extensions.

- Poetry Stones™

- Magnetic Poetry: The Game

- Poetry Beads

© McGraw-Hill Companies, Inc. 2003

CHAPTER 10: DEVELOPING NEW PRODUCTS AND SERVICES

ICA10-4: IN-CLASS ACTIVITY

WHAT *WERE* THEY THINKING? ANALYZING SOME NEW PRODUCT DISASTERS

Learning Objectives. To have students study six new product failures and in each case assess (1) who the target market was, (2) some likely reasons it failed, and (3) what simple marketing research might have been done to identify and avert these problems early.

Definitions. Although many of the marketing terms below are not formally listed as "key terms" in the textbook, they are central to the successful completion of this in-class activity (ICA). These are the seven marketing reasons for new product failures shown on pp. 274 – 278 of *Marketing*, 7th edition. Note that all have significant areas of subjectivity.

- Insignificant "Point of Difference": Characteristics of a product that make it superior to substitutes.

- Incomplete Market and Product Definition Before Product Development Starts: A new product needs to precisely define the target market, its needs, wants, and preferences, and what it will be and do.

- Too Little Market Attractiveness: The market is too small and/or has too many competitors to warrant the expense to reach it.

- Poor Execution of the Marketing Mix: The critical elements, such as the name, package, price, promotion, and/or distribution are deficient, leading to lackluster sales.

- Poor Product Quality or Sensitivity to Customer Needs on Critical Factors: The product is defective or fails to meet customer expectations on 1 or 2 key features.

- Bad Timing: The product is introduced too soon, too late, or at a time when consumer tastes had shifted dramatically.

- No Economical Access to Buyers: The costs of advertising, creating a distribution network, or other necessary costs of reaching prospective customers are prohibitive.

Nature of the Activity. To have students work in teams to identify key reasons for the failure of six—sometimes outrageous—consumer products. These examples, and the accompanying photos, are adapted from Robert M. McMath's book "What *Were* They Thinking?" and his website (www.newproductworks.com).[1]

Estimated Class Time. 20 minutes.

---

[1] Robert M. McMath and Thom Forbes, "What *Were* They Thinking?" (New York: Times Business, 1998). See also New Product Works at www.newproductworks.com.

Materials Needed.

- A transparency of TM10-4A (or use Slides 3 - 8 from ICA10-4.ppt of the ISK PowerPoint CD): Six Consumer Products With Problems.

- Copies of TM10-4A: Six Consumer Products With Problems.

- A blank transparency of TM10-4B: Worksheet to Analyze Why Six Consumer Products Failed.

- Copies of TM10-4B: Worksheet to Analyze Why Six Consumer Products Failed.

- A transparency of TM10-4C: Worksheet to Analyze Why Six Consumer Products Failed.

- The ISK PowerPoint CD from the *Instructor's Survival Kit* box. See the instructions for use of this CD on page 4 of this manual if you use this CD in class.

Preparation Before Class. Follow the steps below:

1. Review Chapter 10, especially pp. 274 – 278 on why new products succeed and fail.

2. Read the material below to give a background lecture.

3. Make transparencies of TM10-4A (or use Slides 3 – 8 from ICA10-3.ppt of the ISK PowerPoint CD), TM10-4B, and TM10-4C.

4. Make copies of TM10-4A and TM10-4B to handout in class.

Instructions. Follow the steps below to conduct this ICA:

1. Review the seven critical marketing factors that often separate new product successes and failures that are discussed on pp. 274 – 278 of the text.

2. Show transparency TM10-4A (or show Slides 3 - 8) and hand out copies of it to students. Provide a brief overview of each of the six products, describing what the product was and what it was intended to do.

3. Form students into four-person teams.

4. Pass out the handouts made from TM10-4B. Ask half of the teams to analyze products A, B, and C and ask the other half to analyze products D, E, and F.

5. Give the teams 7 minutes to complete the following in the TM10-4B worksheet:

    a. Under the "Target Market" column, have students identify to whom they think each product was targeted.

b. Under columns 1 – 7 for each product, have the respective teams (A – C or D – F) check the one or more reason (s) why the product failed.

c. Suggest some possible marketing research activities that the firm could have done to avoid the failure.

d. [NOTE: If a team finishes the analysis of its three products early, let it work on the remaining products.]

6. For each product listed on TM10-4B, have a team share its analysis for a given product (row) and obtain comments from other students about the analysis (agree/disagree; why?).

7. Study TM10-4C. This might be made into a transparency and shared in the class or used simply as background for the class discussion. TM10-4C reflects comments made by Robert M. McMath (see earlier footnote) and the subjective assessments of the co-authors of *Marketing*, 7th edition. The following points should be made:

   a. Body Smarts. A photo of the product appears on p. 12 of the textbook, along with a brief discussion on pp. 12 – 13. The textbook material was written in December 2001. However, in early 2002, Adams pulled the product off retailer shelves despite a $70 million market-introduction campaign that involves advertising, in-store promotions, and national sampling. The big problem (as the text suggested) was: The taste was not good enough to satisfy nutrition-conscious consumers!

   b. Surge. Starting with a $50 million promotional launch in 1995, Surge faced difficulties in beating out Pepsi Cola's strongly entrenched Mountain Dew in the citrus drink category, both in terms of gaining consumer preference and space on retailers' shelves.

   c. Wheaties Dunk-A-Balls Cereal. C'mon! A cereal that encourages kids to "shoot baskets" with it around the kitchen? Introduced in 1994, Mom (and Dad!) didn't want "Sis" or "Junior" playing with their cereal before eating it.

   d. Garlic Cake. Introduced in 1989, the product was supposed to be served as an hors d'oeuvre with sweet breads, spreads, and meats. But the company never adequately explained this to prospective customers, who spent their time wondering what garlic cake was and when to eat it.

   e. Special K Plus cereal (with more calcium). Launched in the fall of 1999 with a $15 million campaign, the product's extra calcium may have been an important point of difference for a significant number of consumers. But the resealable milk carton-like package was a big part of the problem. While it contained the same number of servings as a regular cereal box, consumers thought it contained less. And the smaller shelf facings were not very attention-getting on grocery shelves.

    f. <u>Dr. Care Toothpaste.</u> Think about this for three seconds: Turning a six-year old loose in the bathroom with a toothpaste-filled aerosol can? The vanilla-mint flavor may have been OK, but parents saw the aerosol can as a "show-stopper."

<u>Marketing Lessons.</u> Introducing successful new products is difficult, but (1) having a clear product concept and definite point of difference, (2) knowing traditional marketing reasons for failure, and (3) conducting simple marketing research can reduce the new product risks.

<u>Epilogue: Monday Morning Quarterbacking.</u> As Robert M. McMath asks, "What ***Were*** They Thinking?" Or, how could these (and other) product disasters have happened, especially since many of the problems are so obvious afterwards? Listed below are a few partial explanations:

1. <u>Pressure to increase revenues.</u> Product managers face extreme pressures to generate increased revenues, often turning to new products for the quick answer.

2. <u>Short deadlines.</u> Pressures to increase revenues often force product managers to "go to market" with products they know have not received adequate marketing research.

3. <u>"Groupthink".</u> New product teams—like all teams—are under pressure to develop cohesiveness. So when a team member asks embarrassing questions about a new product concept, he or she can get ostracized from the group and not be seen as a "team player." So knowledgeable team members "bite their tongues" and don't ask the tough questions so that they can remain a respected member of "the team," or what has sometimes been labeled as "groupthink."

<u>Website.</u> To view more examples of new product failures (and successes), go to Robert M. McMath's New Product Works website, which is www.newproductworks.com.

TM10-4A

SIX CONSUMER PRODUCTS WITH PROBLEMS

A. **Body Smarts**: Produced by Adams (a division of Pfizer). Nutritional crunch bars and fruit chews.

B. **Surge**: Produced by Coca-Cola. High caffeine, citrus-flavored soft drink.

C. **Wheaties Dunk-A-Balls**: Produced by General Mills. Basketball-shaped sweetened corn and wheat puffs breakfast cereal.

D. **Garlic Cake**: Produced by Gunderson & Rosario. A hors d' oeuvre for cocktail parties.

E. **Special K Plus**: Produced by Kellogg's. An extension of Special K cereal with more calcium, packaged in a recloseable milk carton-like container.

F. **Dr. Care**: Produced by Dairimetrics, Ltd. A vanilla mint-flavored toothpaste in an aerosol container.

© McGraw-Hill Companies, Inc. 2003

TM10-4B

WORKSHEET TO ANALYZE WHY SIX CONSUMER PRODUCTS FAILED

PRODUCT	TARGET MARKET	REASON(S) FOR FAILURE							POSSIBLE MARKETING RESEARCH
		1 Bad Pt. of Diff.	2 Bad Prod/ Mkt Def.	3 Too Small Mkt	4 Bad Mkt Mix Exec	5 Poor Prod Qual	6 Bad Time	7 Poor Access to Buyers	
A. Body Smarts	Nutrition-conscious adults								
B. Surge	18 – 34 year old males								
C. Wheaties Dunk-A-Balls	Kids								
D. Garlic Cake	Adults								
E. Special K Plus	Health-conscious adults								
F. Dr. Care Toothpaste	Families								

© McGraw-Hill Companies, Inc. 2003

TM10-4C

WORKSHEET TO ANALYZE WHY SIX CONSUMER PRODUCTS FAILED

PRODUCT	TARGET MARKET	REASON(S) FOR FAILURE							POSSIBLE MARKETING RESEARCH
		1 Bad Pt. of Diff.	2 Bad Prod/ Mkt Def.	3 Too Small Mkt	4 Bad Mkt Mix Exec	5 Poor Prod Qual	6 Bad Time	7 Poor Access to Buyers	
A. Body Smarts	Nutrition-conscious adults	√				√			Consumer taste tests
B. Surge	18 – 34 year old males	√					√	√	Paired-comparison taste test with Mountain Dew
C. Wheaties Dunk-A-Balls	Kids	√	√		√				Ask moms about product concept
D. Garlic Cake	Adults	√	√	√	√				Consumer education & taste tests
E. Special K Plus	Health-conscious adults				√			√	Package tests on consumers and retailers
F. Dr. Care Tooth-paste	Families	√	√		√				Ask moms and dads about product concept

© McGraw-Hill Companies, Inc. 2003

CHAPTER 11: MANAGING PRODUCTS AND BRANDS

ICA11-1: IN-CLASS ACTIVITY

MANAGING THE PRODUCT LIFE CYCLE

Learning Objectives. To have students learn about the strategies firms use in managing and extending the product life cycle (PLC) of their products and brands by having them suggest specific actions for Golden Valley Microwave Foods (GVMF) to use with its ACT II® Microwave Butter Popcorn.

Definitions. The following marketing terms are referred to in this in-class activity (ICA):

- Market Modification: Strategy in which a company tries to find new customers, increase a product's use among existing customers, or create new use situations.

- Product Life Cycle: The stages a new product goes through in the marketplace: introduction, growth, maturity, and decline.

- Product Modification: Altering a product's characteristic, such as its quality, performance, or appearance, to try to increase and extend the product's sales.

- Product Repositioning: Changing the place a product occupies in a consumer's mind relative to competitive products.

Nature of the Activity. To have student teams start with a single product of GVMF ACT II Microwave Butter Popcorn as it existed several years ago and then address the challenging task of developing new PLC ideas for microwave popcorn only. [NOTE: Ideas outside the popcorn line are not within the scope of this ICA.]

Estimated Class Time. 30 minutes.

Materials Needed.

- The packages of ACT II Microwave Extreme Butter Popcorn and ACT II Microwave Kettle Corn Popcorn from the *Instructor's Survival Kit* box.

- A transparency of TM11-1 (or use Slide 4 from ICA11-1.ppt of the ISK PowerPoint CD): Ideas for Managing and Extending the Product Life Cycle (PLC) for ACT II Microwave Extreme Butter Popcorn.

- Copies of transparency TM11-1 for each student.

- The ISK PowerPoint CD from the *Instructor's Survival Kit* box. See the instructions for use of this CD on page 4 of this manual if you use this CD in class.

Preparation Before Class. Follow the steps below:

1. Read the section in Chapter 11 on "Managing the Product Life Cycle" (pages 302-304) and Video Case 22-1 on GVMF (pages 609-611) as well as the material below.

2. Make a transparency of TM11-1 (or use Slide 4 from ICA11-1.ppt of the ISK PowerPoint CD).

3. Make copies of TM11-1 to hand out to students.

Instructions. Follow the steps below to conduct this ICA:

1. Divide the class into 3-person teams to develop the ideas.

2. Give the following background mini-lecture:

    "When a firm has a strong brand or product, it is critical that the firm find ways to exploit it—often through managing and extending its product life cycle. This is exactly the situation for Golden Valley Microwave Foods and its microwave popcorn. Now, let's assume you're a consulting team contracted to help GVMF come up with ideas for generating additional revenue from its microwave popcorn. To simplify your task, let's also make these assumptions:

    a. The time is right after GVMF was founded and it has only one product—ACT II Microwave Extreme Butter Popcorn. (Show the package from the *Instructor's Survival Kit* and/or show Slide 3).

    b. Because an agreement with General Mills precluded it from marketing its microwave popcorn through supermarkets for 10 years, GVMF chose to rely initially on the non-grocery channels, such as vending machines, convenience stores, mass-merchandisers, memberships warehouse clubs, and drug stores.

    c. Consider only microwave popcorn and not other snack foods, such as chips.

    Now in your teams, take 10 minutes to come up with ideas for GVMF to generate more revenues from its ACT II Microwave Extreme Butter Popcorn using the strategies shown on this transparency."

3. Show the transparency made from TM11-1 (or show Slide 4).

4. Pass out copies of TM11-1 to the student teams to use as worksheets.

5. After 10 minutes, ask the student teams for their ideas and write them down.

6. After the student teams have shared their ideas, tell the class what some of the actions of GVMF have been, as summarized in the table below. Also note that there is some "overlap" among the strategies.

PLC STRATEGY	IDEA	GVMF USES?	
		YES	NO
Modify the Product • Add New Features • Change the Package	• Add new flavors: Kettle Corn (show Slides 5-6) and Buttery Kettle Corn (show Slide 7). • Increase individual package size from normal to "jumbo" to reach heavy users. • Add a single-serve and 6-pack to reach light and heavy users respectively. • Increase package size to reach institutions. Not practical: they generally use either the regular packages or ready-to-eat popcorn.	✔ ✔ ✔	 ✔
Modify the Market • Find New Users • Increase the Use • Create New Use Situations	• Appeal to corn-lovers segment with "Corn-on-the-Cob" flavor (show Slide 8). • Use co-operative advertising with video rental stores during winter months (show Slide 9). • Market as snack to college students through vending machines on campus.	✔ ✔ ✔	
Reposition the Product • React to Competitor's Position • Reach New Markets • Catch a Rising Trend • Change the Value Offered	• Enter supermarkets, video rental stores, etc. and offer retailers convenient point-of-purchase display (show Slide 10). • Enter global markets. • Position as a more sophisticated cocktail snack. Not practical today. • Appeal to corn-lovers segment with Corn-on-the-Cob popcorn (see above). • Increase popped popcorn with new strains or better packaging technology. • Put more popcorn in the package. Not practical because of serving size.	✔ ✔ ✔ ✔	 ✔ ✔

Marketing Lessons. It is critical for firms to use creative marketing strategies to manage and extend the product life cycle for their key brands and products. Also, it is usually far less expensive and risky to do that, rather than try to come up with successful new-to-the-company or new-to-the-world products.

Websites. Golden Valley Microwave Foods was recently purchased by ConAgra Foods, which is a marketer of a variety of consumer packaged goods and snacks, and whose website is www.conagra.com. The website for its ACT II popcorn product line is www.actii.com.

TM11-1

IDEAS FOR MANAGING AND EXTENDING THE PRODUCT LIFE CYCLE (PLC) FOR ACT II® MICROWAVE EXTREME BUTTER POPCORN

PLC STRATEGY	IDEA
Modify the Product • Add New Flavors • Change the Package	
Modify the Market • Find New Users • Increase the Use • Create New Use Situations	
Reposition the Product • React to Competitor's Position • Reach New Markets • Catch a Rising Trend • Change the Value Offered	

© McGraw-Hill Companies, Inc. 2003

CHAPTER 11: MANAGING PRODUCTS AND BRANDS

ICA11-2: IN-CLASS ACTIVITY

USING BRAINSTORMING AND N/3 TECHNIQUES FOR BREATHE RIGHT® NASAL STRIPS

Learning Objectives. To have students: (1) experience an actual brainstorming session with a fun and rather outrageous product; and (2) evaluate the emerging ideas using an N/3 ("N over 3") rating process to assess some of the strengths and weaknesses of both techniques.

Definition. The following marketing term is referred to in this in-class activity (ICA):

- Brainstorming: To generate ideas about products, services, processes, or ideas.

Nature of the Activity. To have students engage in brainstorming and N/3 activities based on specific guidelines to generate advertising featuring the Breathe Right nasal strip.

Estimated Class Time. 25 minutes.

Materials Needed.

- The sample of Breathe Right® nasal strips from the *Instructor's Survival Kit* box.

- [OPTIONAL: Purchase a package(s) of tan and/or clear adult (small/medium) Breathe Right nasal strips from the grocery or drug store (found in the cough/colds section). Retail price: $4.99 per box of 12 strips.]

- Transparencies of:

    a. TM11-2A (or use Slide 4 from ICA11-2.ppt of the ISK PowerPoint CD): Brainstorming Ground Rules.

    b. TM11-2B (or use Slide 5 from ICA11-2.ppt of the ISK PowerPoint CD): N/3 Ground Rules.

- The ISK PowerPoint CD from the *Instructor's Survival Kit* box. See the instructions for use of this CD on page 4 of this manual if you use this CD in class.

Preparation Before Class. Follow the steps below:

1. Read the material below to be able to give background mini-lecture on Breathe Right.

2. Go to the Breathe Right nasal strip website at www.breatheright.com to learn more about the product and its uses.

3. OPTIONAL: Go to the store and purchase a package of Breathe Right nasal strips.

4. Make transparencies of:

    a. TM11-2A (or use Slide 4 from ICA11-2.ppt of the ISK PowerPoint CD).

    b. TM11-2B (or use Slide 5 from ICA11-2.ppt of the ISK PowerPoint CD).

5. Practice placing a Breathe Right nasal strip on your nose to be able to demonstrate the procedure to students in class.

Instructions. Follow the steps below to conduct this ICA:

1. Give the following background mini-lecture (or show Slide 3):

"Breathe Right nasal strips became popular among both professional athletes and consumers to open their nasal passages and improve their breathing when San Francisco 49ers' Jerry Rice used one during an outstanding Super Bowl performance. CNS, the maker of Breathe Right nasal strips, has also used a number of well-known public domain personalities, like Mona Lisa and The Statue of Liberty (pass the ads around), to advertise its Breathe Right nasal strips (or show Slides 4-5).

In 1995, the U.S. Food and Drug Administration allowed CNS to claim that use of its Breathe Right nasal strips reduced nighttime snoring. Your goal is to <u>brainstorm and give ideas of characters or situations for use in advertisements for a Breathe Right nasal strip could be highlighted to target the "snorers" market segment.</u> (Write the underlined goal on the board.)

2. Have 2-3 student volunteers try on the Breathe Right nasal strip from either the sample in the *Instructor's Survival Kit* box or those purchased from the store.

3. Show the transparency made from TM11-2A: Brainstorming Ground Rules (or show Slide 6). Explain that brainstorming is often used to come up with new product ideas as well as advertising ideas. Answer any questions students may have concerning this technique and its ground rules before proceeding with this part of the ICA.

4. Ask students to take 7 minutes to generate as many advertising ideas (characters or use situations) as possible during the time allotted. Ideas will be evaluated later, so encourage students to be as creative as they want and strive for at least 30 or 40 ideas.

5. List the advertising ideas on either the board or transparency made from TM11-2A.

6. After the 7 minutes, stop the brainstorming session and show the transparency made from TM11-2B: N/3 Ground Rules (or show Slide 7). Answer any questions students may have concerning this technique and its ground rules before proceeding.

7. Ask students to take 7 minutes to evaluate which are the better advertising ideas. Have them identify the top ten advertising characters and use situations.

8. Show students examples of CNS' advertising characters and use situations (show Slides 8-13). Do any match the characters or use situations the students came up with? Have students comment on the effectiveness of both the print and TV ads in communicating both benefits and process of applying a Breathe Right nasal strip.

   - Slide 8: Tan & clear strips
   - Slide 9: Vicks for colds
   - Slide 10: NYC marathon
   - Slide 11: Improves breathing (TRT 0:30)
   - Slide 12: Reduces snoring (TRT: 1:00)
   - Slide 13: Vicks w/ strip (TRT: 0:30)

9. Summarize the advantages and disadvantages of the brainstorming technique:

   - <u>Advantages</u>: (1) helps focus a group of people on generating a list of alternative solutions to a defined problem; (2) enables "piggybacking," which often leads to more creative solutions among the group; and (3) gives a time deadline to generate the creative solutions rather than it out over a longer period.

   - <u>Disadvantages</u>: (1) limits the list of candidate solutions to those given by a specific group of people at one specific time; (2) possibly generates many trivial, impractical candidates; and (3) does not provide for systematic screening of the generated ideas (which is one of the benefits of the N/3 technique).

10. Summarize the advantages and disadvantages of the N/3 technique:

    - <u>Advantages</u>: (1) provides a ranking that utilizes judgments from a knowledgeable cross-section of people; and (2) allows, through the 3, 2, 1, 0 point system, peoples' judgments to be weighted to reflect their personal priorities.

    - <u>Disadvantages</u>: (1) may be biased by an individual's voting for his/her ideas submitted in the brainstorming session; (2) omits inclusion of other ideas not coming from the brainstorming session; and (3) utilizes initial impressions for the evaluation judgments rather than greater in-depth business analysis.

    NOTE: It will be interesting to see if the class develops ideas for male snorers only since about 40 percent of women are snorers. Moreover, women make approximately 65 to 70 percent of Breathe Right nasal strip purchases.

<u>Marketing Lessons.</u> Marketers use brainstorming and N/3 techniques to develop and evaluate new or refine existing products and services in terms of their features, as well as price, promotion (advertising), and distribution strategies and tactics.

<u>Websites.</u> Connect to either the CNS website, marketers of Breathe Right nasal strips (www.cns.com) or the Breathe Right website (www.breatheright.com) for more information about: (1) the target markets for Breathe Right nasal strips (i.e. congestion, allergies, athletic and exercise performance enhancement, etc.; (2) a demo of what they are and how they work; and (3) a detailed discussion of the causes of snoring.

TM11-2A

BRAINSTORMING GROUND RULES

1. Strive for quantity of ideas, without special concern about quality.

2. "Piggybacking" on another person's ideas is OK, and is even encouraged.

3. Stress creativity by looking at a problem from another point of view in order to develop new ideas.

4. No evaluation or criticism allowed in the brainstorming session.

© McGraw-Hill Companies, Inc. 2003

TM11-2B

N/3 GROUND RULES

1. Divide the total number of ideas generated (N) by 3 to get the "points" each student can allocate.

    Example: If 30 ideas are generated, then N/3 = 30/3 = 10 points.

2. Have each student allocate her/his 10 points to the 30 items, with 3, 2, 1, or 0 points to each item—the maximum being 3 points for a given item.

3. Read down the list and have students hold up 1, 2, or 3 fingers for each item.

© McGraw-Hill Companies, Inc. 2003

CHAPTER 11: MANAGING PRODUCTS AND BRANDS

ICA11-3: IN-CLASS ACTIVITY

CREATING CUSTOMER VALUE THROUGH PACKAGING AND LABELING

Learning Objectives. To have students assess the packaging and labeling of an exciting new consumer product from Frito-Lay™ in terms of (1) direct benefits to consumers and (2) global concerns.

Definitions. The following marketing terms are referred to in this in-class activity (ICA):

- Label: An integral part of the package that typically identifies the product or brand, who made it, where and when it was made, how it is to be used, and package contents and ingredients.

- Packaging: Any container in which a product is offered for sale and on which label information is communicated.

- Stock Keeping Unit (SKU): A unique identification number that defines an item for ordering or inventory purposes.

Nature of the Activity. To have students assess the effectiveness of Frito-Lay's new Go Snacks™ canister packaging and labeling from both a consumer and societal point of view.

Estimated Class Time. 20 minutes.

Materials Needed.

- The Cheetos® Asteroids™ Go Snacks canister from the *Instructor's Survival Kit* box.

- [OPTIONAL: Purchase additional canisters in several other flavors from grocery stores, mass merchandisers, convenience stores, and drug stores. Retail price: $1.29.]

- Transparencies of:

    a. TM11-3A (or use Slide 11 from ICA11-3.ppt of the ISK PowerPoint CD): Go Snacks Package and Label Analysis Worksheet.

    b. TM11-3B (or use Slide 12 from ICA11-3.ppt of the ISK PowerPoint CD): An Analysis of the Go Snacks Package and Label.

- Copies of transparency TM11-3A for each student.

- The ISK PowerPoint CD from the *Instructor's Survival Kit* box. See the instructions for use of this CD on page 4 of this manual if you use this CD in class.

Preparation Before Class. Follow the steps below:

1. Read the material below to give background mini-lecture on Frito-Lay's Go Snacks.

2. Go to the Go Snacks website at www.gosnacks.com to learn more about the product.

3. Make transparencies of:

   a. TM11-3A (or use Slide 11 from ICA11-3.ppt of the ISK PowerPoint CD).

   b. TM11-3B (or use Slide 12 from ICA11-3.ppt of the ISK PowerPoint CD).

4. Make copies of TM11-3A to hand out to students.

5. OPTIONAL: Go to the store and purchase additional Go Snacks canisters in several other flavors.

Instructions. Follow the steps below to conduct this ICA:

1. Give the following background mini-lecture:

"In January 2002, Frito-Lay launched Go Snacks, a fun and convenient canister that contains mini shapes of America's top-selling snack foods in 'first-of-its-kind' packaging to fit the fast-paced lifestyles of today's consumers (or show Slides 3-4).

- "Cheerleaders" TV ad (TRT: 0:30) • "Queen's Bedroom" TV ad (TRT: 0:30)

With a $20 million national TV, print, and outdoor (billboard) advertising campaign and other promotional sale support, Frito-Lay has introduced the following stock-keeping units (SKUs) or flavors during the first half of 2002—5 in January and 3 in April (or show Slides 5-9):

- Doritos Mini 3Ds Nacho Cheese
- Doritos Mini 3Ds Zesty Ranch
- Cheetos Asteroids Original
- Cheetos Asteroids Flamin' Hot
- Fritos Hoops Honey BBQ
- Lays Original Crisps
- Lays Sour Cream & Onion Crisps
- Funyuns Onion Rings

Go Snacks come in a compact, 8"-tall, hour-glass designed canister that 'makes carrying them a breeze.' The crush-proof plastic packaging is designed for easy portability and fits perfectly into a car's cup-holder. Its screw-on lid means you can close and reopen Go Snacks anytime, and the lid doubles as a bowl for 'mess-free snacking anywhere.' Go Snacks is sold in supermarkets, mass merchandisers, convenience stores, and drug stores at a suggested retail price of $1.29 per canister[1]

---

[1] Information obtained from Pepsico press release. See http://www.pepsico.com/press/20020118f.shtml.

2. Form students into four-person teams.

3. Pass out the handouts made from TM11-3A: Go Snacks Package and Label Analysis Worksheet.

4. Pass around the Go Snacks Cheetos Asteroids Original canister from the *Instructor's Survival Kit* (or other Go Snacks canisters in several other flavors that you purchased). Have a student open it, pour some snacks into the lid (cup), and let the class sample the snack (or show Slide 10).

5. Show the transparency made from TM11-3A: Go Snacks Package and Label Analysis Worksheet (or show Slide 11). Ask students to identify and assess features of the package and label that relate to: (1) direct consumer benefits and (2) global concerns.

6. Give the teams 7 minutes to complete the TM11-3A worksheet.

7. Ask each student team to identify and assess a feature and let other class members comment. Write down their assessments on either the board or transparency made from TM11-3A.

8. Show transparency TM11-3B and use it as a short, closing wrap-up lecture note to the class discussion (or show Slide 12).

Marketing Lesson. Creative, consumer-beneficial, environmentally-sensitive packaging and labeling can give consumer product marketers like Frito-Lay a competitive edge in today's marketplace among both its channels of distribution (supermarkets, mass merchandisers, convenience stores, and drug stores) and its targeted consumers.

Websites. Connect to either the Frito-Lay website, marketers of Go Snacks (www.fritolay.com) or the Go Snacks website (www.gosnacks.com) for more information about the product, new flavors, and the "eploids" auction program.

TM11-3A

GO SNACKS PACKAGE & LABEL ANALYSIS WORKSHEET

ASSESSMENT AREA	SPECIFIC ISSUE	FEATURE ASSESSMENT
DIRECT CONSUMER BENEFITS	Communication Benefits	
	Functional Benefits	
	Perceptual Benefits	
GLOBAL CONCERNS	Environmental Recycling	
	Health and Safety	

© McGraw-Hill Companies, Inc. 2003

TM11-3B

AN ANALYSIS OF THE GO SNACKS PACKAGE & LABEL

ASSESSMENT AREA	SPECIFIC ISSUE	FEATURE ASSESSMENT
DIRECT CONSUMER BENEFITS	Communication Benefits	• Label's appeal: Attention-getting, colorful cartoon character Chester Cheetah • Picture of product: Shows consumer what the snack is inside the package • Stand-up package: Gives clear shelf facing to prospective buyers
	Functional Benefits	• Rigid "crush-proof" package: Reduces breakage of the snack in transit, on retail shelf, in back pack, etc. • Reclosable package: Increases convenience; snack stays fresh if not fully consumed in one "snacking" period • "Cup" cap and canister: Can be used to hold snacks for convenient eating • Hour-glass canister design: Allows consumers to easily grip the package
	Perceptual Benefits	• Product image: Colorful, modern label suggests innovative, contemporary, high-quality product in consumer's mind
GLOBAL CONCERNS	Environmental Recycling	• Recycling: Plastic package can be recycled • Recycling: Label encourages recycling
	Health and Safety	• Sealed package: Reduces likelihood of tampering in store compared to traditional snack or potato chip packages • Reclosable package: Reduces likelihood of bugs or dirt spoiling the snack after it is opened

© McGraw-Hill Companies, Inc. 2003

CHAPTER 12: MANAGING SERVICES

ICA12-1: IN-CLASS ACTIVITY

AIRLINE CUSTOMER SERVICE AND SOUTHWEST AIRLINES

Learning Objectives. To have students (1) identify key measures of customer service that airlines might use, (2) understand the importance that Southwest Airlines places on customer service, and (3) discover how Southwest Airlines and other U.S. airlines compare on a U.S. Department of Transportation (DOT) measure of customer complaints.

Definitions. The following marketing terms are referred to in this in-class activity (ICA):

- Customer Service: The ability of logistics management to satisfy users in terms of time, dependability, communication, and convenience.

- Gap Analysis: An evaluation tool that compares expectations about a service offering to the actual experience a consumer has with a service.

Nature of the Activity. To have students (1) identify candidate measures of customer service for airlines based on their own airline travel experiences, (2) compare the relative performance of major U.S. airlines from information obtained from the DOT website about customer complaints, and (3) discuss the importance Southwest Airlines places on customer service—and making it memorable by showing its inflatable airplane in class.

Estimated Class Time. 20 minutes.

Materials Needed.

- The Southwest Airline inflatable airplane from the *Instructor's Survival Kit* box.

- A transparency of TM12-1 (or use Slide 3 from ICA12-1.ppt of the ISK PowerPoint CD): Customer Complaint Categories from the DOT's Air Travel Consumer Report.

- Copies of the following to hand out to students:

    a. TM12-1: Air Travel Consumer Report: Consumer Complaint Categories.

    b. The DOT's most recent Consumer Complaint Rankings from the Air Travel Consumer Report. [OPTIONAL: Classroom access to the DOT website to assess the current Air Travel Consumer Report online.]

- The ISK PowerPoint CD from the *Instructor's Survival Kit* box. See the instructions for use of this CD on page 4 of this manual if you use this CD in class.

Preparation Before Class. Follow the steps below:

1. Read the section in Chapter 12 on service quality (pp. 330-333, Marketing NewsNet).

2. Familiarize yourself with the DOT website at www.dot.gov/airconsumer/index1.htm to learn more about the measures and rankings of airline service quality. Click on the "Most Recent Report" link to view, download, and print the most recent "Consumer Complaint Rankings" table. To locate this table, check the Table of Contents. Under the section "Consumer Complaints," scroll down to the table called "Rankings" (month). [NOTE: Adobe Acrobat Reader or Microsoft Word are required to view and print this report. Go to www.adobe.com to download the latest reader, if necessary.]

3. While at the DOT website, go to www.dot.gov/airconsumer/categories.htm and see the "Complaint Categories" or service quality dimensions the DOT uses in its "gap analysis." These are the categories listed in TM12-1.

4. Make a transparency of TM12-1 (or use Slide 3 from ICA12-1.ppt of the ISK PowerPoint CD).

5. Make copies of the following to hand out to students:

    a. TM12-1: Air Travel Consumer Report: Consumer Complaint Categories.

    b. The DOT's most recent Consumer Complaint Rankings from the Air Travel Consumer Report.

6. Familiarize yourself with the Southwest Airlines website at www.southwest.com to learn about how the firm strives to deliver excellent service quality to its customers.

Instructions. Follow the steps below to conduct this ICA:

1. Give the following background mini-lecture on service quality:

    "This ICA is about assessing customer service for airline flights. The process used to evaluate customer service is called 'gap analysis,' which involves asking consumers to compare the actual service delivered with what was expected relative to several service quality dimensions, such as time, dependability, communications, and convenience.

    The Department of Transportation (DOT) produces the monthly Air Travel Consumer Report, which tracks the service quality for the airline industry. The report provides consumers with information on the quality of airline services delivered and helps airlines identify and remedy any 'gaps' with respect to the service quality dimensions that are measured. Many airlines, such as Southwest Airlines, have used the favorable rankings they received to promote the quality of their service."

2. During the next 5 minutes, ask students the following two questions, writing only answers to the first question on the board or a blank transparency.

- <u>Question 1</u>: What are some key customer service factors you think of when flying on an airline?

    <u>Answers</u>: Flight leaving or arriving on time, fare was not changed between time of reservation and flight, flight not over-booked, baggage not damaged or lost, food quality, leg room, competent and courteous ticket agents and flight attendants, etc.

- <u>Question 2</u>: Can you describe a recent experience with an airline that illustrates an especially good or bad example of customer service on that factor?

    <u>Answers</u>: Multiple responses possible.

3. Ask students what measures of "airline customer service" the DOT might use and what the best one might be. Class discussion will probably turn up measures like percentage of on-time departures, percentage of on-time arrivals, and percentage of flight cancellations. Perhaps the best, all-inclusive measure is "rate of complaints per 100,000 enplanements" (or passengers), which is the one the DOT uses.

4. Pass out the handouts made from TM12-1: Consumer Complaint Categories from the DOT's Air Travel Consumer Report.

5. Show the transparency made from TM12-1 (or show Slide 3) and compare the customer service factors students identified with the "Complaint Categories" from the DOT's Air Travel Consumer Report. Have students identify which of these categories are most important to them when engaging in air travel.

6. Hand out copies of the DOT's most recent Air Travel Consumer report table that ranks U.S. airlines in terms of the fewest consumer complaints per enplanement.

7. Briefly discus the table, noting the ranking of the airlines that students fly the most. Ask students to comment on the ranking of their preferred airline. Any "gaps" that need to be analyzed?

8. Display the Southwest Airlines inflatable airplane from the *Instructor's Survival Kit* box (or show Slide 4).

9. Give the following background mini-lecture on Southwest Airline's commitment to service quality:

"For March 2002 (the latest data available at the time this manual was prepared), the DOT's Air Travel Consumer Report stated that among U.S. airlines, Southwest Airlines ranked No. 1 in terms of the lowest number of complaints per 100,000 enplanements (0.42). This was less than half that of the next best airline!

For many Americans, the 'gold standard' for high-quality customer service among U.S. airlines is Southwest Airlines. Southwest not only stresses its low fares for airline service between restricted pairs of U.S. cities but also emphasizes its commitment to delivering the highest-quality customer service possible. In fact, Southwest's mission statement says,

'The mission of Southwest Airlines is dedication to the highest quality of Customer Service delivered with a sense of warmth, friendliness, individual pride, and Company Spirit."

Note that both "Customer Service" and "Company Spirit" are in capitals. And during the past decade, Southwest Airlines has consistently achieved superior rankings in terms of the fewest consumer complaints per enplanement according to the DOT.

10. Briefly discuss the marketing implications for Southwest and other service providers, such as banks and hotels, that stress the delivery of high-quality services to their customers. Students should respond by saying that while costly, delivering services that meet or exceed customer expectations, both in the short- and long-term, can lead to increased sales and profits due to enhanced customer value.

<u>Marketing Lesson.</u> Assessing the quality of customer service is becoming more important as airlines and other service providers face increasing competition. The DOT provides actual statistics regarding the key dimensions of customer service for airline passengers. Such reports can help airlines identify any service quality gaps, which then can be remedied to improve overall service and ultimately, enhance sales and profits.

<u>Websites.</u> Connect to both the U.S. Department of Transportation website, Air Travel Report (www.dot.gov/airconsumer/index1.htm) and the Southwest Airlines website (www.southwest.com) for more information about how the former measures and reports airline service quality delivered by Southwest and other airlines and how the latter is committed to providing the best service quality it can.

TM12-1

AIR TRAVEL CONSUMER REPORT: CONSUMER COMPLAINT CATEGORIES

- **Flight Problems**: Cancellations, delays, or any other deviations from schedule.

- **Oversales**: Passengers who hold confirmed reservations and are denied boarding ("bumped") from a flight because it is oversold.

- **Reservations, Ticketing, and Boarding**: Airline or travel agent mistakes in reservations and ticketing, problems in making reservations and obtaining tickets due to busy phone lines, waiting in line, or delays in mailing tickets. Problems boarding the aircraft.

- **Fares**: Incorrect or incomplete information about fares, discount fare conditions or availability, overcharges, fare increases and levels.

- **Refunds**: Problems in obtaining refunds for unused or lost tickets or fare adjustments.

- **Baggage**: Claims for lost, damaged or delayed baggage, charges for excess baggage, and carry-on problems.

- **Customer Service**: Rude or unhelpful employees, inadequate meals or cabin service, treatment of delayed passengers.

- **Disability**: Civil rights complaints by air travelers with disabilities.

- **Advertising**: Advertising that is unfair, misleading or offensive.

- **Discrimination**: Civil rights complaints by air travelers based on race, national origin, religion, etc.

- **Animals**: Loss, injury or death of an animal during air transport provided by an air carrier.

- **Other**: Frequent flyer, smoking, credit, problems with scheduled or charter tour packages, cargo problems, security, airport facilities, claims for bodily injury, etc. not classified above.

© McGraw-Hill Companies, Inc. 2003

CHAPTER 13: BUILDING THE PRICE FOUNDATION

ICA13-1: IN-CLASS ACTIVITY

PRICING A PANASONIC DVD PLAYER

Learning Objectives. To have students learn the concept of value as it pertains to setting prices for a DVD player.

Definitions. The following marketing terms are referred to in this in-class activity (ICA):

- Price: The money or other considerations (including other goods and services) exchanged for the ownership or use of a good or service.

- Value: The ratio of perceived benefits to price (Value = Perceived Benefits/Price).

Nature of the Activity. To have students discuss the pricing of a Panasonic DVD player.

Estimated Class Time. 15 minutes.

Materials Needed.

- A transparency of TM13-1 (or use Slide 4 from ICA13-1.ppt of the ISK PowerPoint CD): MSRPs for Panasonic DVD Players as Listed on Panasonic's Consumer Electronics Website.

- The ISK PowerPoint CD from the *Instructor's Survival Kit* box. See the instructions for use of this CD on page 4 of this manual if you use this CD in class.

Preparation Before Class. Follow the steps below:

1. Read the material below to give background mini-lecture on DVD players.

2. Make a transparency of TM13-1 (or use Slide 4 from ICA13-1.ppt of the ISK PowerPoint CD).

3. Visit the Panasonic website, which is at www.panasonic.com, locate the consumer electronics link, and then click on the "DVD" link to explore Panasonic's DVD product lines (DVD-Video, DVD-Audio, DVD-Recorder, etc.). Then, visit the Best Buy website, which is at www.bestbuy.com, to view its selection and prices of DVD players from a variety of manufacturers.

4. OPTIONAL: Bookmark the Panasonic and Best Buy websites on your classroom computer.

Instructions. Follow the steps below to conduct this ICA:

1. Show Slide 3: Panasonic DVD Video Recorder Player from ICA13-1.ppt of the ISK PowerPoint CD and ask students to identify the function of a generic DVD player.

2. Give the following background mini-lecture:

   "The DVD format has revolutionized the home entertainment industry by offering image and sound quality nearly twice that of standard of VHS videotape. DVD players come in several configurations: (Read list)."

   - DVD Video Home Players
   - Portable DVD Video Players
   - DVD/VCR Combo Video Players
   - TVDVD/VCR Combo Video Players
   - DVD Video Recorder Players

3. Ask students what they think the price of a DVD player is. Write some of their responses on the board to obtain a price range based in the features offered.

4. Ask students to estimate how little as well as how much DVD player could sell for to establish a perceived minimum and maximum price range.

5. Show the transparency made from TM13-1: MSRPs for Panasonic DVD Players as Listed on Panasonic's Consumer Electronics Website (or show Slide 4). [NOTE: prices at retailers, such as Best Buy, may be lower.]

6. Ask students to explain the wide range of prices for the Panasonic DVD Players shown. In particular, how could anyone justify paying over $$1.499.95 for a DVD Video Recorder Players if they could buy a "no name" brand for $59.92?

   [NOTE: In May 2002 when this manual was prepared, Best Buy had the Mintek DVD Player that plays DVD movies CDs, MP3-encoded CD-R/RWs and Kodak Picture CDs as its "This Week's Picks." Its MSRP was $69.99 but was on sale for $59.92; go to bestbuy.com. and click on the "Home and Audio" menu option on its home page. Then click on the "DVD players" link.]

7. Lead the discussion that might develop these points:

   a. Brand name, such as Panasonic.
   b. Features and functions of the DVD player.
   c. Reliability or durability.
   d. Compatibility of the DVD player with specific brands or models of TVs.
   e. Marketing expenses associated with promoting the product.
   f. Aesthetics of the DVD player.

  g. Brand loyalty and satisfaction with previous purchases of Panasonic products.

  h. Type of DVD player wanted: DVD only; Portable DVD; DVD/VCR Combo; TV/DVD/VCR Combo; and DVD Recorder.

  i. Fit: as an integrated part of a component home entertainment system.

  j. Price versus value.

8. Show transparency TM11-3B and use it as a short, closing wrap-up lecture note to the class discussion (or show Slide 12).

  <u>Marketing Lessons.</u> Price is not simply cost plus some margin or mark-up. Price is only as good as the value delivered to the customer *in the eyes of the customer*. Customers who are not interested in aesthetics or do not perceive any functional difference in DVD products probably will not be willing to pay much for a DVD player. On the other hand, certain customers and market segments are willing to pay much more for a DVD player. Smart marketers recognize these differences in market segments in order to target customers and to influence customer perceptions of value through the marketing mix.

  <u>Websites.</u> Connect to the Panasonic website at www.panasonic.com to obtain more information on updated models of its DVD players. Also, check out www.bestbuy.com to find out the latest pricing of Panasonic and other manufacturer's DVD players and prices.

TM13-1

MSRPS FOR PANASONIC DVD PLAYERS AS LISTED ON PANASONIC'S CONSUMER ELECTRONICS WEBSITE

DVD PLAYER	MSRP
❑ **DVD-Video Home Players**	
• DVD-RV32S (DVD-Video Player with CD-R/RW & MP3 Playback)	$199.95
• DVD-RP56 (DVD-Video Player with Home Theater Features)	$299.95
• DVD-RV45K (DVD-Video/CD Player with Karaoke Function)	$449.95
❑ **Portable DVD-Video Players**	
• DVD-PV40 (Portable DVD-Video/CD Player; No Monitor)	$449.95
• DVD-LA95 (Portable DVD-Video/CD Player with Built-in 7" Monitor)	$1,099.95
❑ **DVD/VCR Combo Players**	
• PV-D4742 (Basic DVD/VCR Combo Deck with 4-Head Hi-Fi VCR)	$279.95
• PV-D4761 (Enhanced DVD/VCR Combo Deck with 4-Head Hi-Fi VCR)	$479.95
❑ **TV/DVD/VCR Combo Players**	
• PV-DF2002 (20" diagonal TV with Built-in DVD/VCR Combo Deck)	$699.95
• PV-DF2700 (27" diagonal TV with Built-in DVD/VCR Combo Deck; 2 Tuner with Picture-in-Picture; FM Radio)	$1,299.95
❑ **DVD-Recorder Players**	
• DMR-E20B (DVD Video Recorder with 4.7 Gb DVD-RAM disc to digitally record and edit TV programs)	$1,499.95

© McGraw-Hill Companies, Inc. 2003

CHAPTER 14: ARRIVING AT THE FINAL PRICE

ICA14-1: IN-CLASS ACTIVITY

EXTRA VALUE MEAL BUNDLE PRICING AT MCDONALD'S

Learning Objectives. To have students (1) analyze the bundle pricing practice of a fast food restaurant and (2) realize that it is based on applying the 3 C's (customer, company, and competition) discussed in the text.

Definitions. The following marketing terms are referred to in this in-class activity (ICA):

- Bundle Pricing: The marketing of two or more products in a single "package" price.

- Value: The ratio of perceived benefits to price (Value = Perceived Benefits/Price).

Nature of the Activity. To have students discuss the reasons why McDonald's would adopt an "Extra Value Meals" (EVM) product bundle pricing strategy.

Estimated Class Time. 20 minutes.

Materials Needed.

- Transparencies of:

    a. TM14-1A (or use Slide 3 from ICA14-1.ppt of the ISK PowerPoint CD): "Extra Value Meal" Bundle Pricing at McDonald's."

    b. TM14-1B (or use Slide 4 from ICA14-1.ppt of the ISK PowerPoint CD): Why McDonald's Uses Bundle Pricing for "Extra Value Meals."

- The ISK PowerPoint CD from the *Instructor's Survival Kit* box. See the instructions for use of this CD on page 4 of this manual if you use this CD in class.

Preparation Before Class. Follow the steps below:

1. Try an "Extra Value Meal" at your local McDonald's restaurant to add a personal example to the class discussion. Write down the prices this restaurant charges for the Big Mac®, the Quarter Pounder with Cheese™, and the Chicken McGrill™ to compare them with those listed in TM14-1A.

2. Make transparencies of:

    a. TM14-1A (or use Slide 3 from ICA14-1.ppt of the ISK PowerPoint CD).

    b. TM14-1B (or use Slide 4 from ICA14-1.ppt of the ISK PowerPoint CD).

Instructions. Follow the steps below to conduct this ICA:

1. Ask students if they are familiar with McDonald's Extra Value Meals. Briefly explain that they include a sandwich (either a burger, chicken, or fish), a large fries, and a medium soft drink—all for a single price that is lower than if the three items were purchased separately.

2. Show transparency TM14-1A (or show Slide 3), which identifies the bundled EVM prices for a Big Mac, a Quarter Pounder with Cheese, and a Chicken McGrill as well as the unbundled prices if each item was purchased separately.

3. Give the following background mini-lecture:

"As TM14-1A shows, the prices McDonald's charges may vary by type of sandwich. Popular sandwiches, or ones with more costly ingredients, may be priced higher (e.g. the Big Mac EVM: $3.59; the Quarter Pounder w/ Cheese EVM: $3.69; and Chicken McGrill EVM: $4.39). Prices may also be higher at a McDonald's restaurant located in airports, highway rest stops, or prime downtown locations in major cities. Furthermore, prices may vary according to whether the restaurant is owed by McDonald's or a franchisee. Finally, each restaurant may charge its own price based on competitive or promotional considerations (e.g. a Big Mac EVM is $3.59 at location 'A' vs. $3.39 at location 'B', which is two miles from 'A')."

4. Ask students why McDonald's would use a bundle pricing strategy. Why not just sell the items separately and charge the higher prices?

5. Show transparency TM14-1B (or show Slide 4).

6. Have students individually or in teams suggest reasons why McDonald's would use bundle pricing based on the three factors that influence price: customer, company, and competition. Write the reasons down on TM14-1B or the board. Typical student answers include:

- Customer Factors:

    a. **To get customers to buy more**. This is done in two ways: (a) buys additional items, such as fries, even if they weren't intending to because the item is only a few cents more with the EVM or (b) buys the larger item, such as fries, because a customer who would normally buy a small fries finds it more profitable to buy an Extra Value Meal, thereby purchasing the large fries for slightly more on a per item cost basis, but receiving the entire meal at an aggregate cost savings. This is a form of "trade-up bundling" according to Eppen, et. al.[1]

---

[1] Gary D. Eppen, Ward A. Hanson and R. Kipp Martin, "Bundling – New Products, New Markets, Low Risk," Sloan Management Review, (Summer, 1991), pp. 7 - 14.

A recent strategy by McDonald's (and other fast food restaurants) is to "Super Size" the Extra Value Meal to increase the value to customers even further by upgrading the large fries to a super size fries and a medium soft drink to a large one for a modest price increase of $0.49.

b. **To give customers a unique value from the product bundle**. This is to expedite the ordering process due to the myriad number of menu offerings at restaurants like McDonald's. For example, McDonald's segregates its EVMs on its menu boards both inside and at the drive-thru from the itemized listing of sandwiches, fries, and soft drinks. Moreover, it gives each EVM a number (e.g. the Big Mac EVM is a #1, the Quarter Pounder w/ Cheese EVM is a #3, and the Chicken McGrill EVM is a #10) to expedite customer orders, thereby increasing the time value of the purchase experience.

With a sense of humor, this can also be related to the idea of "joint performance bundling,"[2] since with the salty food and fries, the meal is definitely enhanced with some form of beverage, making the bundle superior to a meal without a drink.

Ask students the following pricing-related question:

- Question: Why not just give customers lower prices on individual items if saving consumers money is the goal?

  Answer: The lower price of an Extra Value Meal gets people to try items they might not have normally tried and then they will value them in the future.

c. **To reach the meal segment**. The bundle is actually the product aimed at a specific "meal" market segment, and the individual items are aimed at the "niche" customer segments (a form of "aggregation bundling").[3] Also, EVM's are designed to target particular sandwich preferences (beef, chicken, or fish) and time of day (breakfast and lunch/dinner).

- Company Factors:

  a. **To get customers to buy higher margin items.** The highest-margin items at fast food restaurants are soft drinks. For a $0.99 soft drink, the cost to a restaurant is less than 10 cents, with the cup costing the most. Fries are also one of the highest-margin food items. This is a form of "margin spread bundling."[4]

  b. **To reduce the time for transactions and order processing**. This has two benefits. First, it reduces the length of the queue, thereby reducing the time spent in the cashiers' line by customers, which generates more orders during peak traffic times. Second, it reduces the labor costs associated with processing orders, which a form of "production efficiency bundling."[5]

---

[2] Ibid.
[3] Ibid.
[4] Ibid.
[5] Ibid.

c. **To obtain additional cost efficiencies**. There are additional production efficiencies in being better able to plan orders and buying items that will see increased volume because they are included in Extra Value Meals. This is another aspect of "production efficiency bundling."[6]

- Competition Factor: **To compete better with other fast food restaurants**.

    Value meals were first introduced in the late 1980's when Taco Bell introduced its new "value pricing" strategy to the fast food industry. Taco Bell's strategy was to price all of its items under $1.00, with items such as tacos priced as low as $0.59. This shocked the fast food industry. McDonald's initial response to Taco Bell's strategy was to cut the price of its basic hamburger to $0.59.

    Ask students the following question:

    - Question: Which costs more to make: a taco or a burger?

        Answer: Some students will say that a taco is much less expensive to make than a burger (or chicken or fish) because it is made up of much less expensive ingredients. If so, McDonald's is at a competitive disadvantage on an item-for-item basis with Taco Bell. Yet, if McDonald's can compete on a meal-for-meal basis, it can lessen its relative competitive disadvantage.

        For example, to feel satisfied when eating a lunch or dinner meal, it may take 5 tacos from Taco Bell to feel satisfied compared to an EVM (a burger, large fries, and a medium soft drink) from McDonald's. Some students will say it is to match the competition, which is what happened with McDonald's and its competitors since the late 1980s.

Marketing Lesson. McDonald's Extra Value Meal bundle pricing strategy has been one of the most successful pricing strategies ever devised. The underlying logic for product bundle pricing is the same as for other marketing decisions—the 3 C's: customer, company, and competition.

Website. McDonald's website is www.mcdonalds.com. To obtain a reprint of the Eppen, et. al. article on product bundle pricing, visit the *Sloan Management Review* website at www.mit-smr.com.

---

[6] Ibid.

TM14-1A

"EXTRA VALUE MEALS" BUNDLE PRICING AT MCDONALD'S

■ **THE BIG MAC EXTRA VALUE MEAL (#1):**

ITEM	UNBUNDLED PRICE (ITEMS BOUGHT SEPARATELY)	BUNDLED PRICE (EXTRA VALUE MEAL)
• Big Mac	$2.19	✓
• Large Fries	$1.29	✓
• Medium Soft Drink	$1.09	✓
TOTAL	**$4.57**	**$3.59**

- **So the bundle price saves $0.98**

■ **THE QUARTER POUNDER W/ CHEESE EXTRA VALUE MEAL (#3):**

ITEM	UNBUNDLED PRICE (ITEMS BOUGHT SEPARATELY)	BUNDLED PRICE (EXTRA VALUE MEAL)
• Quarter Pounder w/ Cheese	$2.19	✓
• Large Fries	$1.29	✓
• Medium Soft Drink	$1.09	✓
TOTAL	**$4.57**	**$3.69**

- **So the bundle price saves $0.88**

■ **THE CHICKEN MCGRILL EXTRA VALUE MEAL (#10):**

ITEM	UNBUNDLED PRICE (ITEMS BOUGHT SEPARATELY)	BUNDLED PRICE (EXTRA VALUE MEAL)
• Chicken McGrill	$2.99	✓
• Large Fries	$1.29	✓
• Medium Soft Drink	$1.09	✓
TOTAL	**$5.37**	**$4.39**

- **So the bundle price saves $0.98**

© McGraw-Hill Companies, Inc. 2003

TM14-1B

WHY MCDONALD'S USES BUNDLE PRICING FOR "EXTRA VALUE MEALS"

FACTOR	REASONS FOR BUNDLE PRICING
• Customer	
• Company	
• Competition	

CHAPTER 15: MANAGING MARKETING CHANNELS AND WHOLESALING

ICA15-1: IN-CLASS ACTIVITY

MARKETING CHANNELS FOR APPLE COMPUTER

Learning Objectives. To have students learn about the marketing channels currently used by Apple Computer to sell its computers, digital devices, and software products to consumers.

Definitions. The following marketing terms are referred to in this in-class activity (ICA):

- Direct Channel: A marketing channel where a producer and ultimate consumer deal directly with each other.

- Dual Distribution: An arrangement by which a firm reaches buyers by employing two or more different types of channels for the same basic product.

- Indirect Channel: A marketing channel where intermediaries are situated between the producer and consumers and perform numerous channel functions.

- Marketing Channel: Individuals and firms involved in the process of making a product or service available for use or consumption by consumers or industrial users.

- Strategic Channel Alliance: A practice whereby one firm's marketing channel is used to sell another firm's products.

Nature of the Activity. To have students identify the channel members that sell Apple products and classify the channel strategies used by Apple, and in one case, Microsoft.

Estimated Class Time. 20 minutes.

Materials Needed.

- The ISK PowerPoint CD from the *Instructor's Survival Kit* box. See the instructions for use of this CD on page 4 of this manual if you use this CD in class.

Preparation Before Class. Read the material in Chapter 15 on channel structure and organization (pp. 402-406).

Instructions. Follow the steps below to conduct this ICA:

1. Show Slide 3: Apple Computer Products Distributed Through Marketing Channels from ICA15-1.ppt of the ISK PowerPoint CD.

2. Ask students if any have recently purchased a product (computer, digital device, software, etc.) manufactured or sold by Apple Computer and where they purchased it to determine how familiar students are with Apple's channel structure.

3. After 2 minutes of discussion, inform students that they will now analyze Apple Computer's channel structure. [NOTE: The structure presented here is not exhaustive; only representative examples are depicted and analyzed.]

4. Ask students the following questions:

- Question 1: Since the late 1990s, Apple has allowed consumers to purchase its products online via its Apple Store. If you were to purchase an Apple product from the **Apple Store**, (a) identify the channels members as either producer, wholesaler, or retailer and (b) classify the channel strategy used by Apple and its channel members as either direct, indirect, dual distribution, or strategic channel alliance.

    Answer (a): Channel members are "Producer (Apple) → Consumer."

    Answer (b): Channel strategy is "Direct Channel."

    Rationale: Show Slide 4: Apple Online Store. Apple and consumers interact directly with each other through its Internet website. There is no intermediary and therefore Apple must perform all channel functions.

- Question 2: By mid-2002, Apple had opened about 30 retail stores with plans to open others in the near future. If you were to purchase an Apple product from an **Apple Retail Store**, (a) identify the channels members as either producer, wholesaler, or retailer and (b) classify the channel strategy used by Apple and its channel members as either direct, indirect, dual distribution, or strategic channel alliance.

    Answer (a): Channel members are "Producer (Apple) → Consumer."

    Answer (b): Channel strategy is "Direct Channel."

    Rationale: Show Slide 5: Apple Retail Store. Again, Apple and consumers interact directly with each other through its retail stores so there is no intermediary. Therefore, Apple must perform all channel functions.

- Question 3: Under its Authorized Apple Reseller program, Apple has established relationships with many firms to sell Apple products. One such reseller is CompUSA, the nation's largest computer superstore reseller of personal computer-related products and services, with approximately 220 Superstores in 85 major metropolitan markets. However, under a unique arrangement with Apple, CompUSA has established a "store-with-a-store" that is staffed by employees trained and paid solely by Apple. Presumably, CompUSA receives a sales commission or other compensation for allowing Apple to use some of its store space.

If you were to purchase an Apple product from **CompUSA**, (a) identify the channels members as either producer, wholesaler, or retailer and (b) classify the channel strategy used by Apple and its channel members as either direct, indirect, dual distribution, or strategic channel alliance.

Answer (a): Channel members are "Producer (Apple) → Consumer."

Answer (b): Channel strategies are "Direct Channel," "Strategic Channel Alliance," and "Dual Distribution."

Rationale: Show Slide 6: CompUSA. Apple and consumers interact directly with each other ("direct channel"), even though sales occur within an "Apple store," which is located within a specific area within a CompUSA retail store. Apple and CompUSA have entered into a "strategic channel alliance" whereby Apple performs some channel functions (provides inventory management, sales employees, financing, etc.) in exchange for space in additional retail outlets while CompUSA performs other channel functions (provides retail floor space, transactional services, etc.) in exchange for sales commissions and other considerations. Some students may also say that Apple uses a "dual distribution" channel strategy since CompUSA is the second kind of channel member now affiliated with Apple (the first being Apple itself).

- Question 4: Under its Authorized Apple Reseller program, Apple has also established a relationship with Micro Center, which has about 20 stores across the U.S. In the early 1980s, Micro Center created the first computer superstore and originated the "store-within-a-store" departmental approach. Each store's layout is organized into the following departments: Macintosh, Brand Names, Book, Communications, Digital Imaging, Furniture, Books, Portable Devices, Office Supplies, and Computer Supplies. The Macintosh department contains Apple computers and software products and is staffed by experienced Micro Center employees. Each Micro Center location carries more than 700 product categories and nearly 36,000 products.

    Assume that Micro Center obtains its entire inventory from **Ingram Micro**, the nation's largest distributor of technology products, carrying over 280,000 products from over 1,700 manufacturers, including Apple.

    If you were to purchase an Apple product from **Micro Center**, (a) identify the channels members as either producer, wholesaler, or retailer and (b) classify the channel strategy used by Apple and its channel members as either direct, indirect, dual distribution, or strategic channel alliance.

    Answer (a): Channel members are "Producer (Apple) → Wholesaler (Ingram Micro) → Retailer (Micro Center) → Consumer."

    Answer (b): Channel strategies are "Indirect Channel" and "Dual Distribution."

Rationale: Show Slide 7: Micro Center. Intermediaries exist between Apple and consumers. Specifically, Ingram Micro (wholesaler) takes delivery of computers, digital devices, and software from Apple in bulk (logistical function), and then breaks it down in smaller units for retailers, such as Micro Center. Micro Center, in turn, performs other facilitating channel functions, such as sales, transactional, technical support, financing, etc. Some students may also say that Apple uses a "dual distribution" strategy since Micro Center is a distinct channel member through which Apple also uses to sell its products.

- Question 5: Under its Authorized Apple Reseller program, Apple has also established a relationship with MacMall, which sells Apple products online and by telephone through its catalog.

    If you were to purchase an Apple product from **MacMall**, (a) identify the channels members as either producer, wholesaler, or retailer and (b) classify the channel strategy used by Apple and its channel members as either direct, indirect, dual distribution, or strategic channel alliance.

    Answer (a): Channel members are "Producer (Apple) → Retailer (MacMall) → Consumer."

    Answer (b): Channel strategies are "Indirect Channel" and "Dual Distribution."

    Rationale: Show Slide 8: MacMall. An intermediary exists between Apple and consumers. Specifically, MacMall (retailer) takes delivery of computers, digital devices, and software from Apple (logistical function) and performs other facilitating channel functions, such as sales, transactional, technical support, financing, etc. Some students may also say that Apple uses a "dual distribution" strategy since MacMall is a distinct channel member through which Apple also uses to sell its products.

- Question 6: Finally, Microsoft sells its Office v. X software for Apple Macintosh computers through both the Apple Store (online) and the Apple Retail Store.

    If you were to purchase Microsoft's Office v. X software from either the **Apple Store (online) and the Apple Retail Store**, (a) identify the channels members as either producer, wholesaler, or retailer and (b) classify the channel strategy used by **Microsoft** and its channel members as either direct, indirect, dual distribution, or strategic channel alliance.

    Answer (a): Channel members are "Producer (Microsoft) → Retailer (Apple) → Consumer."

    Answer (b): Channel strategies are "Indirect Channel," "Strategic Alliance," and "Dual Distribution."

Rationale: Show Slide 9: Microsoft. An intermediary exists between Microsoft and consumers. Specifically, Apple (both a "producer" and "retailer" depending on the situation) takes delivery of software from Microsoft (logistical function) and performs other facilitating channel functions, such as sales, transactional, technical support, financing, etc. Moreover, since Microsoft uses Apple's online and retail channels to sell its products, it uses a "strategic channel alliance" strategy. Some students may also say that Microsoft uses a "dual distribution" strategy since Apple is one of many channel members through which Microsoft uses to sell its products.

Marketing Lesson. Producers, such as Apple Computer and Microsoft, use multiple channel members and channel strategies to sell their products and services to ultimate consumers. In some cases, such as with Apple, a firm can be both a producer and retailer channel member as well as simultaneously engaging in multiple channel strategies.

Websites. Go to the following websites to learn more about the companies mentioned in this ICA: Apple's website is www.apple.com; CompUSA's website is www.compusa.com; Micro Center's website is www.microcenter.com; Ingram Micro's website is www.ingrammicro.com; MacMall's website is www.macmall.com; and Microsoft's Office v. X website is www.microsoft.com/mac.

CHAPTER 16: INTEGRATING SUPPLY CHAIN AND LOGISTICS MANAGEMENT

ICA16-1: IN-CLASS ACTIVITY

THE "FOAM FACTORY" PROCESS IMPROVEMENT EXERCISE[1]

Learning Objectives. To have students discover the difference between "process improvement," which can lead to a 10 to 20 percent improvement in performing an activity, and "reengineering," a process that can lead to improvements of several hundred percent. Logistics management and order fulfillment are marketing activities that have been primary targets for process improvement and reengineering efforts.

Definition. The following marketing term is referred to in this in-class activity (ICA):

- Logistics Management: The practice of organizing the cost-effective flow of raw materials, in-process inventory, finished goods, and related information from point of origin to point of consumption to satisfy customer requirements.

Nature of the Activity. To have the instructor play the role of a production-line manager who leads a student "team" through an exercise that (1) shows how hard it is to change and improve old processes (the process improvement activity) and (2) demonstrates how giving workers real information from the environment can force a shift in thinking that can lead to breakthrough improvements of hundreds of percent (the reengineering process). In this experiment the "information from the environment" is the speed with which competitive groups have been able to accomplish the task.

Estimated Class Time. 20 minutes.

Materials Needed.

- A transparency of TM16-1 (or use Slide 3 from ICA16-1.ppt of the ISK PowerPoint CD): The Foam Factory: A Group Exercise.

- 12 1" x 1" foam cubes (made by cutting up 1-inch insulation foam) plus a small box to hold them. (Alternatively, use 12 small beanbags 12 toy building blocks.)

- A small table in the classroom around which seven students can stand.

- The ISK PowerPoint CD from the *Instructor's Survival Kit* box. See the instructions for use of this CD on page 4 of this manual if you use this CD in class.

---

[1] Adapted from "The Beanbag Exercise" in Christopher Meyer, Fast Cycle Time (New York: The Free Press, 1993), pp. 54 - 57.

Preparation Before Class. Follow the steps below:

1. Read material below to be able to conduct the exercise in class. Make sure you understand the movement of the cubes (or beanbags).

2. Make a transparency of TM16-1 (or use Slide 3 from ICA16-1.ppt of the ISK PowerPoint CD).

Instructions. Follow the steps below to conduct this ICA:

1. Select seven "volunteers" from the class and a "timekeeper" who has a watch with a second hand.

2. Arrange the seven class members around a table (no chairs) as shown in TM16-1.

3. Show the transparency made from TM16-1 (or show Slide 3).

4. Read the instructions to the team (and class) shown within the quotations.

    a. Production Run #1: The Old Process. "You are members of a production line team. You have 5 minutes to read the rules on the transparency and practice passing a foam block (bean bag) or two through the process so you understand it."

    Timekeeper: Time the team as they move the 12 blocks from a loose pile at the start until they are all packed in the box. Typical times to complete the "old process" will be 25 to 35 seconds.

    b. Production Run #2: An Improved Process. "Team, you have two minutes to figure out how to improve the process, and to try it again. Try to improve how you did the old process in Production Run #1."

    Timekeeper: Time the team again. Typical times to complete the "improved process" will be 20 to 30 seconds.

    c. Production Run #3: A Reengineered Process. "Team, you have just learned that the competition can do this process in 10 seconds. If the company is to remain in business, you must match or beat this time. Please reconsider the rules, and get creative in your redesign. Something has to change! You have five minutes to make your breakthrough."

    Timekeeper: Time the team one last time. Typical times to complete the "reengineered process" will be 7 to 10 seconds.

5. The reengineering breakthrough the team should uncover is to: (1) put all twelve cubes in the center of the table; (2) have six team members place and remove their hands on top of the cubes, thereby having touched or "handled" all of them; and (3) have the seventh team member put all the cubes into the box at once.

__Marketing Lessons.__ Point out how your instructions as their manager influenced the team's behavior and results, and how real data from the environment can have a dramatic impact when shared with the workers. Draw a parallel to actual marketing activities, such as warehousing, order filling, and other supply chain and logistics processes, which are a primary target for process improvement and reengineering efforts. Explain that additional information, such as knowing competitors can perform the activity in 10 seconds, can cause the team to recast the problem and solve it in creative new ways. The team may wish to debate whether its reengineered process meets the meaning of "handle cubes" used in the transparency.

TM16-1

THE FOAM FACTORY: A GROUP EXERCISE

Rules:

1. All cubes go from start pile into the box at the end.

2. All people must handle all cubes.

3. All people must handle cubes in the sequence shown below.

4. Cubes must enter the box one at a time.

Sequence:

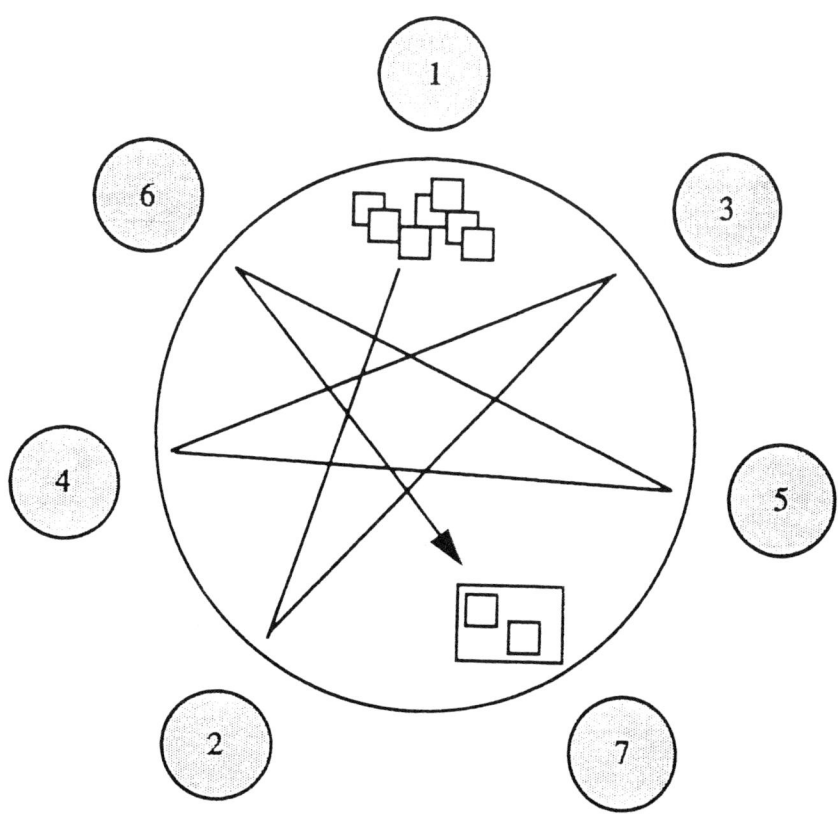

© McGraw-Hill Companies, Inc. 2003

CHAPTER 17: RETAILING

ICA17-1: IN-CLASS ACTIVITY

RETAIL SHOPPING ONLINE: COMPARING PRICES FOR A DIGITAL CAMERA

Learning Objectives. To have students shop for a digital camera online from a manufacturer, selected retailers, and "bots" to compare their respective prices.

Definitions. The following marketing terms are referred to in this in-class activity (ICA):

- Bots: Electronic shopping agents or robots that comb websites to compare prices and product or service features.

- Shopping Goods: Items for which the consumer compares several alternatives on criteria such as price, quality, or style.

Nature of the Activity. To have students access the websites of Kodak, manufacturer of the EasyShare DX 4900 digital camera, retailers that may carry this particular brand and model from Kodak, and shopping agents (or "bots") to experience online retail comparative shopping for this particular product.

Estimated Class Time. 20 minutes, which consists of:

- 5 minutes to explain the nature of this ICA and distribute the Online Retail Shopping Handout to student teams.

- 15 minutes to present summaries by student teams during the next class period.

- [NOTE: Students will spend 45 minutes outside class to complete their assignment.]

Materials Needed.

- Copies of the Online Retail Shopping Handout for each student.

- Student access to the Internet.

- The ISK PowerPoint CD from the *Instructor's Survival Kit* box. See the instructions for use of this CD on page 4 of this manual if you use this CD in class.

Preparation Before Class. Read the material in Chapter 15 on channel structure and organization (pp. 402-406).

1. Read the material in Chapter 17 on online retailing (pp. 455-456) and in Chapter 21 on why consumers shop and buy online (pp. 569-572).

2. Familiarize yourself with websites referred to in this ICA.

3. Make copies of the Online Retail Shopping Handout for each student.

4. Develop in-class discussion questions, if desired.

<u>Instructions.</u> Follow the steps below to conduct this ICA:

1. Give copies of the Online Retail Shopping Handout to each student.

2. Form students into four-person teams during one class period.

3. Take 5 minutes to explain the nature of this ICA by giving the following background mini-lecture (or show Slide 3: Kodak's EasyShare DX4900 Digital Camera from ICA17-1.ppt of the ISK PowerPoint CD).

   "Between now and the next class period, each team will go to pre-selected websites listed in the Online Retail Shopping Handout to shop for a Kodak EasyShare DX4900 digital camera that has 4.0 mega pixel resolution and Compact Flash memory card.

   [NOTE: Do not have students shop for the accompanying attachments, such as the EasyShare docking station, which allows users to transfer images captured by the camera into a PC and costs an additional $80 or the Compact Flash memory card.]

   For each website listed, locate the Kodak EasyShare DX4900 digital camera by using the 'Search' engine to expedite the shopping process, clicking on a 'digital camera' link that may be present on the home page, etc. When you have located the camera, write down its price on the space provided in the handout. Ignore the costs of accessories, including the EasyShare docking station, which costs about $80. Also, ignore any sales taxes or delivery charges.

   For the shopping "bots" listed, write down the identities and prices of the retailers with the lowest and highest prices.

   [NOTE: If a website does not carry the product, have students leave the price blank.]

   Finally, call or visit 3 local digital camera retailers that sell the Kodak EasyShare DX4900 digital camera to obtain a price."

4. Have the students write a 2-page brief that responds to the following questions:

   a. Comment on <u>each</u> shopping website with respect to its ease of navigation, visual layout, time to find the product, variety of product categories offered, and the price offered for the product. Also, were the shopping "bots" helpful? (1 page).

   b. If you were in the market, would you actually purchase this Kodak EasyShare DX4900 digital camera from one of these online websites? If "Yes," which ones and why? If "No," why not? (1 page).

5. The MSRP for the Kodak EasyShare DX4900 Digital Camera is $499.99. The retailers and prices obtained by students should be similar to those shown below:

Kodak EasyShare DX4900 Digital Camera Websites	Retailer Name	Prices Found at the Time This Manual Was Published
• **Kodak**: www.kodak.com	Shop@Kodak	Not Sold Online

[NOTE: At the time of this manual's publication, Kodak did not sell this camera on its Shop@Kodak online store, perhaps since the camera was recently introduced; other DX models were available.]

- **America Online**: (bot): www.aol.com. Scroll down to Shop@AOL and click on the 'Digital Camera' link or type in 'Kodak' in the search engine. Find these three retailers:

  - Amazon.com (retailer): www.amazon.com ... N/A $379.95
  - Rita Camera (retailer): www.ritz.com .... N/A $399.99
  - Wolf Camera (retailer): www.wolf.com .... N/A $399.99

- **Buy.com**: www.buy.com
  Click on the 'Electronics' link to find 'digital cameras' $399.00

- **mySimon**: (bot): www.mysimon.com
  - Lowest price retailer: .... Beach Camera $353.00
  - Highest price retailer: .... computers4sure.com $399.99

- **Yahoo!**: (bot): www. shopping.yahoo.com
  - Lowest price retailer: .... Shop Digital $339.00
  - Highest price retailer: .... i4Digital $499.00

- **Local retailer1**: (Best Buy) .... bestbuy.com $399.99
- **Local retailer2**: (Sears) .... sears.com $499.99
- **Local retailer3**: (Student's Choice) .... ?

6. At the beginning of the next class period, select 3 or 4 student teams to give a brief report on its experience with online comparative shopping.

<u>Marketing Lessons.</u> Manufacturers, traditional retailers, and online retailers all offer online shopping. In addition, shopping agents or "bots" can assist consumers in locating retailers that carry a desired product item for the lowest price. Consumers can compare prices obtained online with those from traditional "brick & mortar" retailers to get the best possible price, which realistically would include delivery and sales tax charges.

<u>Websites.</u> See above. Check www.kodak.com to see if the Kodak EasyShare DX4900 digital camera is offered for sale at Kodak's online store, Shop@Kodak.

ONLINE RETAIL SHOPPING HANDOUT

1. For each website, shopping "bot," and local retailer, write down both the name of the retailer (if different from the website) and the price of a Kodak EasyShare DX4900 digital camera on this Handout. Only write down the price of the digital camera itself, excluding delivery and sales tax charges. [NOTE: If a website does not carry the Kodak EasyShare DX4900 digital camera, leave the price blank.]

Website	Retailer(s) Where Item Can Be Bought	Price of the Kodak EasyShare DX4900 Digital Camera
Kodak (www.kodak.com)		_____

America Online (bot): www.aol.com
Shop@AOL: click to the following:

- Amazon.com (retailer): www.amazon.com _____
- Rita Camera (retailer): www.ritz.com _____
- Wolf Camera (retailer): www.wolf.com _____

Buy.com (online retailer): www.buy.com _____

mySimon (bot): www.mysimon.com

- Lowest price retailer: _____ _____
- Highest price retailer: _____ _____

Yahoo! (bot): www.shopping.yahoo.com

- Lowest price retailer: _____ _____
- Highest price retailer: _____ _____

2. Write a 2-page brief that responds to the following questions:

   a. Comment on <u>each</u> shopping website with respect to its ease of navigation, visual layout, time to find the product, variety of product categories offered, and the price offered for the product. Also, were the shopping "bots" helpful? (1 page).

   b. If you were in the market, would you actually purchase this Kodak EasyShare DX4900 digital camera from one of these online websites? If "Yes," which ones and why? If "No," why not? (1 page).

3. Hand in your briefs and be prepared to discuss them during the next class period.

CHAPTER 18: INTEGRATED MARKETING COMMUNICATIONS AND DIRECT MARKETING

ICA18-1: IN-CLASS ACTIVITY

AN IMC FOR THE TORO® iMOW™ ROBOTIC MOWER

Learning Objectives. To have students (1) suggest elements of an integrated marketing communications (IMC) program and (2) describe how these elements can generate revenues for an innovative new consumer product—Toro's iMow Robotic Mower.

Definitions. The following marketing terms are referred to in this in-class activity (ICA):

- Advertising: Any paid form of nonpersonal communication about an organization, good, service, or idea by an identified sponsor.

- Direct Marketing: A promotional element that uses direct communication with consumers to generate a response in the form of an order, a request for further information, or a visit to a retail outlet.

- Integrated Marketing Communications (IMC): The concept of designing marketing communications programs that coordinates all promotional activities—advertising, personal selling, sales promotion, public relations, and direct marketing—to provide a consistent message across all audiences.

- Personal Selling: The two-way flow of communication between a buyer and seller, often in a face-to-face encounter, designed to influence a person's or group's purchase decision.

- Public Relations A form of communication management that seeks to influence the feelings, opinions, or beliefs held by customers, prospective customers, stockholders, suppliers, employees, and other publics about a company and its products or services.

- Sales Promotion: A short-term inducement of value offered to arouse interest in buying a good or service.

Nature of the Activity. To have students work in teams to identify integrated marketing communications (IMC) actions that Toro might take to reach innovative and early adopters that may be willing to buy a revolutionary new product such as Toro's iMow Robotic mower, one "that can mow a lawn without human direction."

Estimated Class Time. 25 minutes.

Materials Needed.

- The Toro iMow Robotic Mower brochure from the *Instructor's Survival Kit* box.
- Transparencies of:

    a. TM18-1A (or use Slide 11 from ICA18-1.ppt of the ISK PowerPoint CD): Summary of Features for the Toro iMow Robotic Mower.

    b. TM18-1B (or use Slide 12 from ICA18-1.ppt of the ISK PowerPoint CD): An IMC for the Toro iMow Robotic Mower.

    c. TM18-1C: An IMC for the Toro iMow Robotic Mower.

- Copies of TM18-1B: An IMC for the Toro iMow Robotic Mower.
- Copies of TM18-1C: An IMC for the Toro iMow Robotic Mower.
- The ISK PowerPoint CD from the *Instructor's Survival Kit* box. See the instructions for use of this CD on page 4 of this manual if you use this CD in class.

Preparation Before Class. Follow the steps below:

1. Read pages 294-296 about the introduction stage of the product life cycle and pages 300-302 about the diffusion of innovation, particularly the characteristics of consumers who are either "innovators" or "early adopters" of new products.

2. Make transparencies of TM18-1A (or use Slide 11), TM18-1B (or use Slide 12), and TM18-1C.

3. Make copies of TM18-1B and TM18-1C for each student.

4. Review possible answers contained in TM18-1C.

Instructions. Follow the steps below to conduct this ICA:

1. Show Slide 3 from ICA18-1.ppt of the ISK PowerPoint CD: "History's Greatest Innovations," which is a promotional video about the Toro iMow Robotic Mower (TRT: 2:51).

2. Pass the Toro iMow Robotic Mower brochure around the class (or show Slides 4-8).

3. Divide the class into four-person teams.

4. Give the following background mini-lecture:

"Gaining awareness and actually making sales of an innovative new product—like the Toro 'Hands-Free' iMow Robotic Mower—is a very difficult task. This is one reason why marketers find it necessary to identify and reach the 'innovators' and 'early adopters' among product adopters during the introduction stage of the product life cycle. These are the 'opinion leaders' that other consumers will later follow. This is probably one reason why Toro developed the 'History's Greatest Innovation' promotional video as part of its IMC for the iMow Robotic Mower to reach these important consumers.

As we have seen, the Toro iMow Robotic Mower clearly qualifies as a genuine new product innovation. This lawn mower is far different than those that generations of Americans are familiar with. Therefore, the communications task is far more difficult in selling this machine that retails for $499 than selling a new food product that retails for $2.99.

A truly complete IMC will include communications that are targeted at both wholesalers and retailers in the channel of distribution as well as those targeted at ultimate consumers. In fact, Toro has developed a major IMC effort directed at its channel members to encourage and support them in their decision to stock and sell the Toro iMow Robotic Mower (or show Slides 9-10)."

Show transparency TM18-1A (or show Slide 11). "To better understand the capabilities of the new Toro iMow Robotic Mower, here is a summary of its features. As you can see, the iMow isn't for every yard and Toro's advertising points out the mower's key limitations, product features, and pricing.

So, let's now develop an IMC program for the Toro iMow Robotic Mower."

5. Show transparency TM18-1B (or show Slide 12). Explain that the top of TM18-1B identifies the:

   a. Target audience or market—American homeowners with lawns that meet the criteria and who are "innovators" or "early adopters" and are willing to buy a revolutionary lawn mower.

   b. Promotional objectives: (1) generate awareness and (2) achieve sales of the Toro iMow Robotic Mower.

6. Inform students of the difficulty and importance of developing an effective IMC. In this case, the IMC is assumed to have promotional objectives of both (1) generating awareness and (2) obtaining actual sales of the Toro iMow Robotic Mower among target consumers.

7. Hand out copies of TM18-2B and have the teams take 10 minutes to complete it.

8. Ask the teams to share their ideas regarding an IMC for the Toro iMow Robotic Mower from transparency TM18-2B.

9. Use transparency TM18-3C to provide you with some initial ideas for the Toro iMow Robotic Mower IMC. After the discussion of ideas, hand out copies to students.

10. Show Slides 13-14 that depict examples of the IMC Toro developed to reach consumers for the iMow.

Marketing Lesson. Developing an effective IMC program requires creativity and attention to detail. This becomes especially true when a relatively expensive new consumer product like the Toro iMow Robotic Mower is involved.

Website. To view the new the Toro iMow Robotic Mower, go to www.toro.com.

TM18-1A

SUMMARY OF FEATURES FOR THE TORO® iMOW™ ROBOTIC MOWER

KEY LIMITATIONS	
Yard Size	No more than 5,000 square feet of lawn to mow
Yard Slope	The yard must be relatively flat; no slopes > 15°
Obstacles (Trees, etc.)	The yard must be free of excessive obstacles
Safety	Users must follow all safety instructions
Product Specifications	
Width of Cut	21"
Mulching	Standard
Run Time	2 hours
Battery Charge Time	24 hours
Weight	70 lbs.
Warranty	3 year mower; 1 year battery; 60-day satisfaction guarantee
Prices	
iMow	$499
Battery (additional)	$129.95
Battery Charger	$79.95
Perimeter Switch (additional)	$74.95
Perimeter Wire/Pegs (additional)	$19.95 (per 100 ft.)/ $12.95 (50 per bag)
Replacement Blades	$54.95 (3 per pack)

© McGraw-Hill Companies, Inc. 2003

TM18-1B

AN IMC FOR THE TORO® iMOW™ ROBOTIC MOWER

- Target audience or market—American homeowners with lawns who are "innovators" or "early adopters" and potentially willing to buy a revolutionary lawn mower.
- Promotional objectives—(1) create awareness and (2) achieve sales of the iMow.

ELEMENT OF THE IMC	IMC ACTION	HOW THE ACTION PRODUCES REVENUES
Advertising		
Personal Selling		
Public Relations		
Sales Promotions		
Direct Marketing		

© McGraw-Hill Companies, Inc. 2003

TM18-1C

AN IMC FOR THE TORO® iMOW™ ROBOTIC MOWER

- Target audience or market—American homeowners with lawns who are "innovators" or "early adopters" and potentially willing to buy a revolutionary lawn mower.
- Promotional objectives—(1) create awareness and (2) achieve sales of the iMow.

ELEMENT OF THE IMC	IMC ACTION	HOW THE ACTION PRODUCES REVENUES
Advertising	• Advertise innovative iMow on national and cable (HGTV) TV • Develop co-operative advertising program with Home Depot (a major Toro retailer), local hardware or lawn & garden stores to run ads on local radio, in newspapers, etc.	• Generates consumer awareness about the iMow and possibly visits to retail outlets or Toro's website • Long-term: generate actual sales at retail outlets identified in the co-operative ads
Personal Selling	• Conduct training seminars for retail salespeople • Have sales brochures and training videotapes available for salespeople	• Provides retail salespeople with detailed information to answer consumer questions about the iMow and actually complete a sale
Public Relations	• Issues press releases and product announcements to gain feature magazines, newspapers and TV news coverage.	• Generates awareness through reading feature newspapers or magazine articles or TV news coverage. Example: "Toro! Toro! Toro" _Fortune_ article July 9, 2001
Sales Promotions	• Have attention-getting point-of-purchase displays in Home Depot stores and other Toro dealers	• Generates consumer awareness for the iMOW in retail outlets where attentive salespeople might actually make a sale
Direct Marketing	• Put excitement into description of iMow's capabilities on Toro's website with "iMow virtual tour." • Let consumers be able to order an iMow on Toro's website • Send customers of other Toro products (sprinkler/irrigation) a direct mail piece with coupon	• Gains awareness and interest among consumers with the iMow virtual tour • Make actual iMOW sales on the website via Amazon.com • Generates sales from already loyal Toro customers

© McGraw-Hill Companies, Inc. 2003

CHAPTER 18: INTEGRATED MARKETING COMMUNICATIONS AND DIRECT MARKETING

ICA18-2: IN-CLASS ACTIVITY

AN IMC FOR THE HERMITAGE MUSEUM

Learning Objectives. To have students (1) suggest elements of an integrated marketing communications (IMC) program and (2) describe how these elements can generate revenues for a specialized service—Russia's Hermitage Museum, a world-class art museum.

Definitions. The following marketing terms are referred to in this in-class activity (ICA):

- Advertising: Any paid form of nonpersonal communication about an organization, good, service, or idea by an identified sponsor.

- Direct Marketing: A promotional element that uses direct communication with consumers to generate a response in the form of an order, a request for further information, or a visit to a retail outlet.

- Integrated Marketing Communications (IMC): The concept of designing marketing communications programs that coordinates all promotional activities—advertising, personal selling, sales promotion, public relations, and direct marketing—to provide a consistent message across all audiences.

- Personal Selling: The two-way flow of communication between a buyer and seller, often in a face-to-face encounter, designed to influence a person's or group's purchase decision.

- Public Relations A form of communication management that seeks to influence the feelings, opinions, or beliefs held by customers, prospective customers, stockholders, suppliers, employees, and other publics about a company and its products or services.

- Sales Promotion: A short-term inducement of value offered to arouse interest in buying a good or service.

Nature of the Activity. To have students work in teams to identify integrated marketing communications (IMC) actions the Hermitage Museum might take to reach an American target audience (i.e. market). This ICA shows the wide applicability of marketing concepts because it involves marketing a non-profit service across international boundaries.

Estimated Class Time. 25 minutes.

Materials Needed.

- Copies of the Web Link box handout on p. 24 of *Marketing*, 7th edition: Marketing the Hermitage, a World-Class Art Museum – with a Virtual Tour.

- A transparency of TM18-2A (or use Slide 7 from ICA18-2.ppt of the ISK PowerPoint CD): An IMC Analysis for the Hermitage Museum.

- Copies of TM18-2B: An IMC Analysis for the Hermitage Museum.

- The ISK PowerPoint CD from the *Instructor's Survival Kit* box. See the instructions for use of this CD on page 4 of this manual if you use this CD in class.

Preparation Before Class. Follow the steps below:

1. Read the Hermitage Museum Web Link box on p. 24 of *Marketing*, 7th edition and the accompanying text.

2. Make a transparency of TM18-2A (or use Slide 7 from ICA18-2.ppt of the ISK PowerPoint CD).

3. For each student, make copies of:

    a. the Hermitage Museum Web Link box on handout p. 24 of *Marketing*, 7th edition.

    b. transparency TM18-2A: An IMC Analysis r the Hermitage Museum.

    c. transparency TM18-2B: An IMC Analysis for the Hermitage Museum.

4. Visit the Hermitage Museum website, which is www.hermitagemuseum.org, and explore the "Virtual Visit" or the "Virtual Viewings" areas.

5. Bookmark the Hermitage Museum website on your classroom computer and check to see if the computer has the recommended site technology installed.

6. Review possible answers contained in TM18-2B: An IMC Analysis for the Hermitage Museum.

Instructions. Follow the steps below to conduct this ICA:

1. Pass out copies of the Hermitage Museum Web Link box handout and have students read the material.

2. Take students on a brief "Virtual Tour" of the Hermitage Museum by going to the Hermitage website, which is www.hermitagemuseum.org (or show Slides 3 – 6).

3. Divide the class into four person teams.

4. Show transparency TM18-2A (or show Slide 7). Explain that the top of TM18-2A identifies the:

   a. Target audience or market—Americans with interests in art who may be tourists in Russia or those who never leave the U.S.

   b. Long-term promotional objective—generate revenues for the Hermitage Museum located in St. Petersburg, Russia.

5. Inform students of the difficulty and importance of developing an effective IMC. Point out that some IMC elements don't conveniently fall into a single category. This is the reason for the bottom row on "Partnerships with U.S. Art Museums," which is filled out on TM18-2A to help students in their IMC plan.

6. Hand out copies of TM18-2A and have the teams take 10 minutes to complete it.

7. Ask the teams to share their ideas regarding an IMC analysis of the Hermitage Museum targeted at American consumers from transparency TM18-2A.

8. Use transparency TM18-2B to provide you with some initial ideas for the Hermitage IMC. After the discussion of ideas, hand out copies to students.

9. Use transparency TM18-2B to provide you with some initial ideas for the Hermitage IMC.

10. Hand out copies of transparency TM18-2B to students after concluding the discussion of students' ideas.

Marketing Lesson. Developing an effective IMC program requires creativity and attention to detail. This becomes especially true when services offered by institutions like the Hermitage Museum are marketed internationally.

Website. To view the Hermitage Museum website, go to www.hermitagemuseum.org.

TM18-2A

AN IMC ANALYSIS FOR THE HERMITAGE MUSEUM

- Target audience or market—Americans with interests in art who may be tourists in Russia or those who never leave the U.S.
- Long-term promotional objective—generate revenues for the Hermitage Museum located in St. Petersburg, Russia.

ELEMENT OF THE IMC	IMC ACTION	HOW THE ACTION PRODUCES REVENUES
Advertising		
Personal Selling		
Public Relations		
Sales Promotions		
Direct Marketing		
Partnerships with U.S. Art Museums	• Partner with the Guggenheim Museum of NYC to open a "Jewel Box" museum in Las Vegas	• Short-term: Sales of tickets to U.S.-partnered shows, posters, etc. • Long-term: Encourage Americans to visit the Hermitage in St. Petersburg

© McGraw-Hill Companies, Inc. 2003

TM18-2B

AN IMC ANALYSIS FOR THE HERMITAGE MUSEUM

- Target audience or market—Americans with interests in art who may be tourists in Russia or those who never leave the U.S.
- Long-term promotional objective—generate revenues for the Hermitage Museum located in St. Petersburg, Russia.

ELEMENT OF THE IMC	IMC ACTION	HOW THE ACTION PRODUCES REVENUES
Advertising	• Advertise in U.S and St. Petersburg Museums	• Generates ticket sales in the U.S. and among American tourists in St. Petersburg
Personal Selling	• Have St. Petersburg art experts give guest lectures around the U.S.	• Generates short-term awareness that may lead to longer-term sales
Public Relations	• Place feature articles in U.S. newspapers • Arrange for TV interviews with Hermitage art experts	• Generates short-term awareness that may lead to longer-term sales for the museum
Sales Promotions	• Use coupons or price discounts as part of St. Petersburg tour activities	• Generates visits of Americans on a package tour to visit the Hermitage Museum
Direct Marketing	• Develop online "virtual tour" of the Hermitage Museum	• Short-term: Could result in sales of posters and art books • Long-term: Encourage visits by Americans to the Hermitage in St. Petersburg
Partnerships with U.S. Art Museums	• Partner with the Guggenheim Museum of NYC to open a "Jewel Box" museum in Las Vegas	• Short-term: Sales of tickets to U.S.-partnered shows, posters, etc. • Long-term: Encourage Americans to visit the Hermitage in St. Petersburg

© McGraw-Hill Companies, Inc. 2003

CHAPTER 19: ADVERTISING, SALES PROMOTION, AND PUBLIC RELATIONS

ICA19-1: IN-CLASS ACTIVITY

RECOGNIZING ADVERTISING SLOGANS

Learning Objectives. To have students realize the difficulty advertisers face when trying to help consumers remember their company or brands.

Definition. The following marketing term is referred to in this in-class activity (ICA):

- Slogan: The verbal or written portion of an advertising message that summarizes the main idea in a few memorable words." From the Dictionary of Marketing Terms, 2nd edition, Peter Bennett, Ed. (Lincolnwood: NTC Publishing Group, 1995), p. 264.

Nature of the Activity. To have students identify the company or product associated with an advertising slogan.

Estimated Class Time. 10 minutes.

Materials Needed. A transparency of TM19-1: Match Each Slogan to the Company or Product and copies of it to hand out to students.

Preparation Before Class. Make a transparency of TM19-1 and copies of it to hand out to students.

Instructions. Follow the steps below to conduct this ICA:

1. Ask students to identify the company or product for each slogan. The answers are:

Company/Product:	Advertising Slogan:	Answer
1. Tylenol	"Take Comfort in Our Strength"	I
2. Chevy Trucks	"Like a Rock"	T
3. IBM	"People who get it. People who get it done."	L
4. Volkswagen	"Drivers Wanted"	F
5. New York Times	"All the News That Fit to Print"	N
6. Sears	"Where else?"	Q
7. GE	"We Bring Good Things to Life"	A
8. American Express	"Make Life Rewarding"	W
9. PowerBar	"Be Great"	O
10. Apple Computer	"Think Different"	K
11. VISA	"It's Everywhere You Want to Be"	S

Company/Product:	Advertising Slogan:	Answer:
12. Xerox	"The Document Company"	B
13. DuPont	"The Miracles of Science"	C
14. Allstate Insurance	"You're in Good Hands"	Z
15. Nissan	"Driven"	D
16. Verizon Wireless	"Make Progress Every Day"	H
17. Accenture	"Innovation delivered"	G
18. Energizer Batteries	"The Power to Keep You Going, and Going…"	J
19. Ford Motor Co.	"No Boundaries"	M
20. L.L.Bean	"Start here. Go anywhere."	Y
21. Wendy's	"Taste The Difference Fresh Makes"	R
22. Lexus	"The Passionate Pursuit of Perfection"	E
23. Toyota	"Get the Feeling"	X
24. Outward Bound	"Same world. Different place."	P
25. Wal Mart	"Always Low Prices. Always."	U
26. BMW	"The Ultimate Driving Machine"	V

2. Share the following "classic" slogans for students to identify the company or product:

Advertising Slogan:	Company/Product:
A. "The Quicker, Picker Upper"	Bounty
B. "It's the Real Thing"	Coca Cola
C. "Please Don't Squeeze the…"	Charmin Toilet Tissue
D. "Does She or Doesn't She"	Clairol Hair Coloring
E. "Finger-Lickin' Good"	KFC
F. "Good to the Last Drop"	Maxwell House Coffee
G. "Takes a Lickin' and Keeps on Tickin'"	Timex Watches
H. "Just Do It"	Nike
I. "Nobody Doesn't Like…"	Sara Lee
J. "Fly the Friendly Skies"	United Airlines
K. "Breakfast of Champions"	Wheaties
L. "Let Your Fingers Do the Walking"	Yellow Pages
M. "Melts in Your Mouth, Not in Your Hand"	M&M's
N. "M'm M'm Good"	Campbell's Soup
O. "Where's the Beef?"	Wendy's
P. "A Mind is a Terrible Thing to Waste"	United Negro College Fund
Q. "Betcha Can't Eat Just One"	Lay's Potato Chips
R. "A Little Dab'll Do Ya"	Brylcreem
S. "Be All That You Can Be"	U. S. Army

Marketing Lesson. One of the challenges of a successful advertising campaign is to break through the clutter with a slogan or ad that is remembered favorably by consumers.

Website. See *Advertising Age's* top 10 slogans at www.adage.com/century/slogans.html.

TM19-1

MATCH EACH SLOGAN TO THE COMPANY OR PRODUCT

SLOGAN		COMPANY/PRODUCT
1. "Take Comfort in Our Strength"	____	A. GE
2. "Like a Rock"	____	B. Xerox
3. "People who get it. People who get it done."	____	C. DuPont
4. "Drivers Wanted"	____	D. Nissan
5. "All the News That Fit to Print"	____	E. Lexus
6. "Where else?"	____	F. Volkswagen
7. "We Bring Good Things to Life"	____	G. Accenture
8. "Make Life Rewarding"	____	H. Verizon Wireless
9. "Be Great"	____	I. Tylenol
10. "Think Different"	____	J. Energizer Batteries
11. "It's Everywhere You Want to Be"	____	K. Apple Computer
12. "The Document Company"	____	L. IBM
13. "The Miracles of Science"	____	M. Ford Motor Company
14. "You're in Good Hands"	____	N. New York Times
15. "Driven"	____	O. PowerBar
16. "Make Progress Every Day"	____	P. Outward Bound
17. "Innovation delivered"	____	Q. Sears
18. "The Power to Keep You Going, and Going…"	____	R. Wendy's
19. "No Boundaries"	____	S. VISA
20. "Start here. Go anywhere."	____	T. Chevy Trucks
21. "Taste the Difference Fresh Makes"	____	U. Wal Mart
22. "The Passionate Pursuit of Perfection"	____	V. BMW
23. "Get the Feeling"	____	W. American Express
24. "Same world. Different place."	____	X. Toyota
25. "Always Low Prices. Always."	____	Y. L.L. Bean
26. The Ultimate Driving Machine"	____	Z. Allstate Insurance

© McGraw-Hill Companies, Inc. 2003

CHAPTER 19: ADVERTISING, SALES PROMOTION, AND PUBLIC RELATIONS

ICA19-2: IN-CLASS ACTIVITY

WHAT MAKES A MEMORABLE TV COMMERCIAL?

Learning Objectives. To have students identify the factors that makes a memorable television commercial.

Definitions. The following marketing terms are referred to in this in-class activity (ICA):

- Advertising: Any paid form of non-personal communication about an organization, good, service, or idea by an identified sponsor.

- Commercial: An advertisement broadcast on radio or television.

Nature of the Activity. To have students (1) observe three TV ads in class, (2) classify each TV ad seen as either a product or institutional ad, (3) identify the appeal used, and (4) discuss why the ad was memorable.

Estimated Class Time. 20 minutes.

Materials Needed. The ISK PowerPoint CD from the *Instructor's Survival Kit* box. See the instructions for use of this CD on page 4 of this manual if you use this CD in class.

Preparation Before Class. Read the material in Chapter 19 on the types of advertising (pp. 498-500) and message content (502-503).

Instructions. Follow the steps below to conduct this ICA:

1. Give students this background mini-lecture:

"The Clio Awards hosts the world's largest and most famous advertising awards competition in the international advertising. At its 43rd annual Clio Festival in 2002, Fallon Worldwide won two Grand Clio Awards, the highest award given, for its BMW "*The Hire*" campaign. Fallon has won several other prestigious advertising awards since it was founded in 1981. Examples of its award-winning ads include Rolling Stone's "Perception/Reality" campaign, MTV's "Jukka Brothers," and the EDS "Cat Herders" TV spot. One of its early TV spots that won acclaim was its "Gold'n Plump Chicken" ad that aired in the early-1980s." [NOTE: Fallon's BMW "*The Hire*" campaign is comprised of five "movie ads" that can be seen at bmwfilms.com. A brief snippet of *The Follow* is part of ICA 21-1.]

2. Show Slide 3 from the ICA19-2.ppt of the ISK PowerPoint CD: "Gold'n Plump Chicken" TV ad and have students respond to the following questions:

- <u>Question 1</u>: Is the "Gold'n Plump Chicken" TV spot a product or institutional ad?

    <u>Answer</u>: This ad is a product ad since its focus is on the Gold'n Plump brand of chicken.

- <u>Question 2</u>: Is the "Gold'n Plump Chicken" TV commercial a pioneering (or informational), competitive (or comparative), reminder (or reinforcement), or an advocacy ad?

    <u>Answers</u>: This ad is a competitive ad since it promotes this brand as better than those from "the south."

- <u>Question 3</u>: What kind of appeal does this ad use?

    <u>Answer</u>: This ad uses a humorous appeal to convey its message to the target audience.

- <u>Question 4</u>: Why do you think this ad was memorable and worthy of an award?

    <u>Answer</u>: This ad creatively uses humor to motivate target consumers to purchase the brand, which it successfully did.

3. Give students this background mini-lecture:

    "Pepsi Cola has produced several award winning TV ads over the years in its battle with Coca-Cola (as has Coca-Cola) for the hearts and minds of soft drink consumers worldwide. A few of these TV spots are either in the Clio Hall of Fame or cited as one of the best ads ever. In 1999, *TV Guide* polled advertising agencies to rank the "Fifty Greatest TV Commercials of All Time." The following ad not only is in the Clio Hall of fame but was ranked #41 by those polled by *TV Guide*:"

4. Show Slide 4 from the ICA19-2.ppt of the ISK PowerPoint CD: Diet Pepsi's 1987 "Apartment 10G" TV ad and have students respond to the following questions:

- <u>Question 1</u>: Is Diet Pepsi's "Apartment 10G" TV spot a product or institutional ad?

    <u>Answer</u>: This ad is a product ad since its focus is on selling Diet Pepsi.

- <u>Question 2</u>: Is the Diet Pepsi TV commercial a pioneering (or informational), competitive (or comparative), reminder (or reinforcement), or an advocacy ad?

    <u>Answers</u>: This ad is a reinforcement ad because it informs its target market about its a good-taste and sugar free (notice the NutraSweet logo).

- <u>Question 3</u>: What kind of appeal does this ad use?

Answer: This ad uses a humorous appeal (Michael J. Fox will do anything for Gail O'Grady) to convey its message to the target audience that Diet Pepsi is worth the extra effort to obtain.

- Question 4: Why do you think this ad was memorable and worthy of an award?

Answer: This ad uses humor with information to motivate target consumers to purchase the brand, which it successfully did. Also, according to those polled by *TV Guide*, the ad "epitomized Diet Pepsi as '80s cool."[1]

5. Give students this background mini-lecture:

"Pepsi's" Security Camera" TV spot was ranked #21 by those polled by *TV Guide* in its "Fifty Greatest TV Commercials of All Time" and has won other awards as well."

6. Show Slide 5 from the ICA19-2.ppt of the ISK PowerPoint CD: "Security Camera" TV ad and have students respond to the following questions:

- Question 1: Is the Pepsi "Security Camera" TV spot a product or institutional ad?

Answer: This ad is a product ad since its focus is on selling Pepsi.

- Question 2: Is the Pepsi TV commercial a pioneering (or informational), competitive (or comparative), reminder (or reinforcement), or an advocacy ad?

Answers: This ad is a competitive (comparative) ad because it creatively demonstrates the Coke delivery guy's preference of Pepsi over Coke—his employer!

- Question 3: What kind of appeal does this ad use?

Answer: This ad uses a humorous appeal (to the tune of "Your Cheatin' Heart") to convey its message to the target audience that Pepsi is better than Coke and that Coke drinkers may feel guilty in trying or switching to Pepsi.

- Question 4: Why do you think this ad was memorable and worthy of an award?

Answer: This ad creatively uses humor and music without any dialog (except the lyrics of the song) to encourage Coke drinkers to boldly, not timidly switch to Pepsi.

7. Give students this background mini-lecture:

"The last TV spot we're going to view has been voted the best TV commercial ever created by advertising agencies, advertisers, and of course *TV Guide*. It also is a prestigious member in the Clio Hall of Fame because this TV ad changed how advertisers think about the ways ads are created. It set a new standard for cinematic style. In fact, a famous Hollywood movie director directed the ad. This TV spot cost over $400,000 to make (a huge amount back then) and cost an additional $500,000 to

---

[1] Dottie Enrico, "The Fifty Greatest TV Commercials of All Time," *TV Guide* (July 3, 1999: Vol. 47; No. 27), pp. 2-34.

air. The ad aired only once—during Super Bowl XVIII in 1984. However, because of its success, it started the Super Bowl ad extravaganza we see today, when a 60-second TV spot can cost over $3 million! Finally, the ad was not only a creative success, but also a commercial one as well. After the ad ran, it generated sales of over 500,000 units during the next year. Here now is the best TV commercial ever made:"

8. Show Slide 6 from the ICA19-2.ppt of the ISK PowerPoint CD: Apple Computer's "1984" TV ad and have students respond to the following questions:

- Question 1: Is Apple's "1984" TV commercial a product or institutional ad?

  Answer: The ad is mainly an institutional ad since its Orwellian imagery and story, which was directed by Ridley Scott (Alien, etc.) advocates PC users to rebel against the tyranny and status quo of 'Big Brother' (a creative link to IBM's nickname, which was 'Big Blue'). Only at the end of the commercial do we know that it is for the Apple's Macintosh, giving it a little product advertisement flavor.

- Question 2: Is the Apple "1984" commercial a pioneering (or informational), competitive (or comparative), reminder (or reinforcement), or an advocacy ad?

  Answers: This ad is a competitive ad because it creatively distinguishes between IBM PC users and the new Macintosh users. In addition, this ad is a pioneering ad since it introduces the Macintosh PC.

- Question 3: What kind of appeal does this ad use?

  Answer: This ad uses a fear appeal. The woman, who is the only character in color, is running away from the police and throws a sledgehammer against the view screen to convey the message to the target audience that she can avoid the negative experience of an IBM PC.

- Question 4: Why do you think this ad was memorable and worthy of an award?

  Answer: This ad was hugely successful on a number of levels because it: (1) sold a huge number of Macintosh PCs; (2) established the Super Bowl advertising craze we see today; (3) brought Hollywood production and cinematic flair to a 60-second TV spot; and (4) created brand name recognition for small PC manufacturer at the time.

Marketing Lessons. Over 20,000 TV commercials are created and aired in the U.S. each year. Marketers and advertisers struggle with the problem of creating memorable messages that (1) promotes the idea, product, or service being featured without getting in the way of the message, (2) satisfies the objectives developed for the ad campaign, and (3) falls within a budget that the sponsor can afford.

Websites. To view a list of Advertising Age's top 100 campaigns, go to www.adage.com/century/campaigns.html. Unfortunately, the link to *TV Guide's* list of the "Fifty Greatest TV Commercials of All Time" does not now exist. To view current and past Clio award winners and a list of ads that are in its Hall of Fame, go to www.clioawards.com.

CHAPTER 19: ADVERTISING, SALES PROMOTION, AND PUBLIC RELATIONS

ICA19-3: IN-CLASS ACTIVITY

PRODUCT SAMPLING PROMOTION

Learning Objectives. To have students (1) learn about the practice of product sampling, an important and growing segment of marketing and (2) apply the concepts learned using an actual example of a product sampling promotion developed by a leading firm in the field.

Definitions. The following marketing terms are referred to in this in-class activity (ICA):

- Consumer-Oriented Sales Promotion: Sales tools used to support a company's advertising and personal selling efforts directed to ultimate consumers, such as coupons, sweepstakes, and samples.

- Free Standing Insert (FSI): A full-color booklet featuring advertisements with coupons and other promotional offers, inserted in the Sunday newspaper.

- Product Sampling: Offering a free (or at a reduced price) trial of a product to consumers in an effort to create awareness, stimulate trial, and induce repeat purchases.

- Sales Promotion: A short-term inducement of value offered to arouse interest in buying a good or service.

Nature of the Activity. To have students (1) learn about the product sampling industry and (2) propose product sampling strategies for the Caress® Product Sample Promotion managed by Valassis Communications.

Estimated Class Time. 20 minutes.

Materials Needed.

- The Caress product sample from the *Instructor's Survival Kit* box.

- A transparency of TM19-3A (or use Slide 11 from ICA19-3.ppt of the ISK PowerPoint CD): Caress Product Sample Promotion.

- A transparency of TM19-3B (or use Slide 12 from ICA19-3.ppt of the ISK PowerPoint CD): Other Product Sampling Strategies for Caress.

- Copies of TM19-3A and TM19-3B for each student.

- The ISK PowerPoint CD from the *Instructor's Survival Kit* box. See the instructions for use of this CD on page 4 of this manual if you use this CD in class.

Preparation Before Class. Follow the steps below:

1. Read the section in Chapter 19 on product sampling (pp. 515-521).

2. Read the material below.

3. Make transparencies of:

   a. TM19-3A (or use Slide 11 from ICA19-3.ppt of the ISK PowerPoint CD): Caress Product Sample Promotion.

   b. TM19-3B (or use Slide 12 from ICA19-3.ppt of the ISK PowerPoint CD): Other Product Sampling Strategies for Caress.

4. Make copies of TM19-3A and TM19-3B for each student.

Instructions. Follow the steps below to conduct this ICA:

1. Give students this background mini-lecture on the sales promotion industry:

   "According to *Promo Magazine's* Industry Report 2002, organizations spent an estimated $98.7 billion on consumer-oriented sales promotion in 2001, down almost 4 percent from 2000. This was due to the economic slowdown that had begun earlier in the year and was exacerbated by the September 11, 2001 tragedy. However, product sampling, which accounts for only 1.2 percent of total consumer-oriented sales promotion spending, increased almost 3 percent to $1.2 billion in 2001.

   For 2002 and the near term, marketers may increasingly target their product sampling efforts. Instead of taking 'one million samples and just throw them out there,' marketers may rely more on branding sampling, in which 500,000 samples are given to 'the right people at the right time.' This targeted approach is designed to strengthen existing customer relationships rather than attract new ones."[1]

2. Give students this background mini-lecture on Valassis Communications:

   "Valassis Communications, Inc., based in Livonia, MI, is one of the largest full-service sales promotion firms in the U. S., with 2001 sales of $850 million. Many of you are familiar with the sales promotion and product sampling techniques developed by Valassis on behalf of its clients. This firm pioneered the coupon booklets that we receive in our local Sunday newspaper, which are called free-standing inserts or FSI's. The FSI represents 84 percent of all coupons distributed! Valassis itself distributes over 102 billion coupons each year (or show Slide 3).

   [NOTE: For more info on the sales promotion industry, see the Valassis "Educating the Brand Marketers of Tomorrow" PowerPoint that is included in the ISK CD.]

---

[1] "Sampling: A Softer Sell," *Promo Magazine's* Industry Report 2002, (April 1, 2002). See www.promomagazine.com.

Valassis has also created these other product sampling vehicles:

- Newspouch®: A newspaper is placed in a plastic bag that contains a product sample in a pouch attached to the side or end of the bag (or show Slide 4).
- Brand Bag+™: Similar to the Newspouch, the Brand Bag+ is a full-color polybag "billboard" for a high visibility advertising message. It also has a perforated space at the end of the bag to contain a product sample.
- Newspac®: A full-color, 4-page brochure with an attached sample packet that is placed into the newspaper's promotion section. This promotional vehicle is the focus of our discussion today."

3. Give students this background mini-lecture on Caress (or show Slides 5-6):

"Caress is the #1 leader in the experiential skin care segment. Its product portfolio includes bar soap, bath and shower gel, body wash, body lotion, and body spray. Caress is one brand within the brand portfolio of the skin care division of Unilever Home & Personal Care products. Caress products are sold in supermarkets (Safeway or Kroger), drug stores (Walgreen's or CVS/Pharmacy), mass merchandisers (Wal-Mart or Target) and club stores (Costco or BJ's). Caress Body Washes come in 12- and 18-oz. sizes while Caress Body Lotions come in 3-, 9- and 16-oz. sizes."

4. Give students this background mini-lecture on the Caress Product Sample Promotion (or show Slides 7-10):

In the 4th quarter of 2000, Valassis created the Caress Product Sample Promotion. The promotional strategy consisted of the following:

- The Newspac sampling vehicle was used to deliver Caress Silkening Body Lotion and Body Wash variants to over 2 million targeted households in the U. S.
- The target audience was women, who are 18-34 years old, experiential shampoos or lotions users, and have household incomes of $40,000 or more.
- The objectives of the promotion were to (a) generate awareness and trial for Caress' new Waterfresh Breeze Silkening Body Lotions and these Body Wash fragrances: Waterfresh Breeze, Botanical Bliss and Luscious Nectar and (b) build awareness, interest, and trial of the full range of Caress product forms (bar soap, bath and shower gel, body wash, body lotion, and body spray) and fragrances (Nature's Silk, Spring Blush, Luscious Nectar, Waterfresh Breeze, Wild Blossom, and Botanical Bliss) to promote a 'fragrance layering across all skin care needs.'
- The Newspac brochure had 4 product samples attached to it: a 0.34-oz. sample of Caress Waterfresh Breeze Body Wash, a 0.17 oz. sample of Caress Waterfresh Breeze Silkening Body Lotion, a 0.34 oz. sample of Caress Botanical Bliss Body Wash, and a 0.34 oz. sample of Caress Luscious Nectar Body Wash."

5. Show transparency TM 19-3A (or show Slide 11). Ask students to list the advantages and disadvantages of the promotion strategy developed for the Caress Product Sample Promotion. Write down their responses on either the blackboard or the transparency made from TM19-3A. Compare their responses to those identified by both Valassis and Caress for the Caress Product Sample Promotion:

Caress Product Sample Promotion	
Advantages	**Disadvantages**
<ul><li>Full-color.</li><li>Separate brochure; not part of a larger coupon booklet.</li><li>Uses category (CDI) and brand development (BDI) indices on purchase behavior to select target audience.[2]</li><li>Newspac can be effective in generating awareness and trial if tracking data are conclusive.</li><li>Cover of Newspac identifies the target market: women, ages 18-34 years old.</li><li>Newspac has four separate samples to choose from.</li><li>Brochure effectively conveys product benefits.</li><li>Each sample is affixed securely to the brochure so they won't become loose.</li><li>Each sample is contained in a strong plastic envelope that resists tearing.</li></ul> [2] NOTE: CDI=((category volume in market/market pop.)/ (category volume US/US pop.)) [2] NOTE: BDI=((brand volume in market/market pop.)/ (brand volume US/US pop.))	<ul><li>Cost/benefit to marketer: how many trials and adoptions after the sample id deliverd? Is further sampling needed to maintain sales?</li><li>How does Valassis measure the effect on purchase behavior of competitors' products?</li><li>Target audience may be loyal to current brands.</li><li>No coupon offered to stimulate trial.</li><li>Bad weather could spoil newspaper and the brochure.</li><li>Target audience might not see the brochure and therefore not try the sample.</li><li>Men (not the target audience) might throw the brochure away.</li><li>Target audience may not subscribe to or read Sunday newspaper.</li><li>Target audience didn't opt into sampling program and therefore trial and repeat purchase behavior may be low.</li></ul>

6. Ask students to propose five other product sampling strategies for Caress. Write down and discuss the advantages and disadvantages of each strategy proposed on either the blackboard or a transparency made from TM19-3B (or show Slide 12).

<u>Marketing Lesson.</u> Marketers use product sampling to increase awareness, trial, and adoption of new products, build brand loyalty for existing products, among others.

<u>Websites.</u> To more obtain information about Valassis, go to www.valassis.com. To obtain more information about the sales promotion industry, go to www.promomagazine.com.

TM19-3A

CARESS® PRODUCT SAMPLE PROMOTION

ADVANTAGES	DISADVANTAGES
•	•
•	•
•	•
•	•
•	•

TM19-3B

OTHER PRODUCT SAMPLING STRATEGIES FOR CARESS®

STRATEGY	ADVANTAGES	DISADVANTAGES
• #1:	• • •	• • •
• #2:	• • •	• • •
• #3:	• • •	• • •
• #4:	• • •	• • •
• #5:	• • •	• • •

© McGraw-Hill Companies, Inc. 2003

CHAPTER 19: ADVERTISING, SALES PROMOTION, AND PUBLIC RELATIONS

ICA19-4: IN-CLASS ACTIVITY

PRODUCT PLACEMENT IN MOVIES AND TV

Learning Objective. To have students learn about growing popularity of product placement in movies, television programs, and other media as a promotional tool for marketers.

Definition. The following marketing term is referred to in this in-class activity (ICA):

- Product Placement: Using a brand-name product in a movie, television show, video, or commercial for another product.

Nature of the Activity. To have students match a list of movies with a list of products that were used or displayed in these movies.

Estimated Class Time. 10 minutes.

Materials Needed.

- A transparency of TM19-4:
- Copies of TM19-4 for each student.
- The ISK PowerPoint CD from the *Instructor's Survival Kit* box. See the instructions for use of this CD on page 4 of this manual if you use this CD in class.

Preparation Before Class. Follow the steps below:

1. Read the section in Chapter 19 on product placement (p. 520).

2. Read the material below.

3. Make a transparency of TM19-4A.

4. Make copies of TM19-4 for each student.

Instructions. Follow the steps below to conduct this ICA:

1. Show Slide 3 from the ICA19-4.ppt of the ISK PowerPoint CD: A List Entertainment Product Placement Video.

2. Ask students why marketers would place their products in a movie or television show. Responses should include the following:

   a. Increases sales—sales of Reese's Pieces, featured in ET: The Extra-Terrestrial, exploded by 60 percent while sales of Ray Ban sunglasses increased as a result of being placed in *Top Gun* and *Men in Black*. With respect to TV, Pepsi, GM, and others have repeatedly placed their products in *Survivor* due to increased sales.

   b. Gives movies and TV shows a sense of realism since people in real life eat, drink, and wear brand-named products.

   c. Reinforces a character's personality, such as James Bond driving a sports car.

   d. Creates an implied endorsement by the characters and the high-profile celebrities who play them.

   e. Gains significant exposure of the brand in both domestic and foreign markets.

   f. Is a lower cost alternative in terms of the cost per thousand (CPM) since some products are placed for free and others for a nominal fee (product placements usually cost between $10,000 and $1 million, and average about $50,000).

   g. Reduces the advertising "clutter" present in other media.

   h. Provides a captive audience—most people don't leave when the product is "advertised" during the movie or TV show. And with the advent of TiVo and other devices that can skip over TV commercials, TV viewers won't want to skip over a character consuming a product as part of the story.

5. Show the transparency made from TM19-4. Ask students to match the movies and TV shows with the list of products shown. The answers are:

Movies & TV Shows:	Product(s) Placed:	Answer:
1. You've Got Mail	America Online; Starbucks*	N, F
2. ET: The Extra-Terrestrial	Reese's Pieces	H
3. Mission Impossible	Apple Computer	O
4. Jurassic Park	Ford Explorer	U
5. Golden Eye	BMW Z3 Roadster	Q
6. Top Gun	Ray Ban Sunglasses	A
7. The Matrix	Duracell Batteries	S
8. Forrest Gump	Dr. Pepper	W
9. Good Will Hunting	Dunkin' Donuts	R
10. Men In Black	Ray Ban Sunglasses	A
11. Jerry Maguire	Reebok**	E
12. Life or Something Like It	Oreos	G
13. Batman & Robin	Frito Lay	I
14. Charlie's Angels	Nokia Mobile Phone	B

Movies & TV Shows:	Product(s) Placed:	Answer:
15. Austin Powers III	MINI Cooper S	J
16. Bridget Jones Diary	Microsoft Hotmail	C
17. Seinfeld	Junior Mints	K
18. Friends	7-Up	L
19. Survivor	Mountain Dew, Reebok, Frito Lay	M, E, I
20. Will & Grace	Polo Shirts	V
21. Who Wants to be a Millionaire?	AT&T	D
22. 7th Heaven	Miracle Whip	P
23. ER	Best Buy	T

* Most of the movies listed had more than one product placement. For example, *The Lost World* had Burger King, General Mills, JVC, Kodak, Mercedes-Benz, Timberland, and Tropicana.

** In the movie *Jerry Maguire*, Reebok had wanted to air full-length commercial in the movie. However, not only was it left on the cutting room floor, but also one of the characters actually "insulted" the company in the movie! Reebok demanded that TriStar Pictures "Show us the money!" and settled a breach of contract suit for $10 million!

Marketing Lessons. The popularity of product placements has grown in recent years because marketers believe that using brands in movies and TV shows is a subtle way of gaining exposure, particularly with younger audiences. Several marketers place their products in multiple movies and TV shows to increase their exposure to target audiences. Movie and television producers like the practice because it makes their movies and TV shows more realistic while providing additional revenues. Other potential venues for product placements include: video games, sporting events (where a product or ad is digitally inserted on the field of play, scoreboard, etc.), and even novels!

Website. To more obtain information about product placements, go to A List Entertainment's website, which is www.alistentertainment.com.

TM19-4

CAN YOU MATCH THESE PRODUCTS TO THESE MOVIES AND TV SHOWS?

MOVIES & TV SHOWS	**PRODUCT PLACEMENTS**
1. You've Got Mail _____	A. Ray Ban Sunglasses
2. ET: The Extra-Terrestrial _____	B. Nokia Mobile Phone
3. Mission: Impossible _____	C. Microsoft Hotmail
4. Jurassic Park _____	D. AT&T
5. Golden Eye _____	E. Reebok
6. Top Gun _____	F. Starbucks
7. The Matrix _____	G. Oreos
8. Forrest Gump _____	H. Reese's Pieces
9. Good Will Hunting _____	I. Frito Lay
10. Men In Black _____	J. MINI Cooper S
11. Jerry Maguire _____	K. Junior Mints
12. Life or Something Like It _____	L. 7-Up
13. Batman & Robin _____	M. Mountain Dew
14. Charlie's Angels _____	N. AOL
15. Austin Powers III _____	O. Apple Computer
16. Bridget Jone's Diary _____	P. Miracle Whip
17. Seinfeld _____	Q. BMW Z3 Roadster
18. Friends _____	R. Dunkin' Donuts
19. Survivor _____	S. Duracell Batteries
20. Will & Grace _____	T. Best Buy
21. Who Wants to be a Millionaire? _____	U. Ford Explorer
22. Friends _____	V. Polo Shirts
23. ER _____	W. Dr. Pepper

© McGraw-Hill Companies, Inc. 2003

CHAPTER 19: ADVERTISING, SALES PROMOTION, AND PUBLIC RELATIONS

ICA19-5: IN-CLASS ACTIVITY

DESIGNING A PUBLICITY CAMPAIGN FOR THE SEGWAY™ HT

Learning Objectives. To have students (1) understand the elements of the public relations process, (2) learn the importance of publicity in the launch of a new product, and (3) develop a simple publicity campaign for a new product.

Definitions. The following marketing terms are referred to in this in-class activity (ICA):

- Public Relations: A form of communication management that seeks to influence the feelings, opinions, or beliefs held by customers, prospective customers, stockholders, suppliers, employees, and other publics about a company and its products or services.

- Publicity: A nonpersonal, indirectly paid presentation of an organization, good, or service.

- Publicity Tools: Methods of obtaining nonpersonal presentation of an organization, good, or service without direct cost. Examples include news releases, news conferences, special events, and public service announcements.

Nature of the Activity. To have students work in teams to develop a simple publicity campaign for the new Segway™ Human Transporter (HT).

Estimated Class Time. 30 minutes.

Materials Needed.

- Copies of TM19-5: Publicity Tools Handout.

- A transparency of TM19-5 (or use Slide 7 from ICA19-5.ppt of the ISK PowerPoint CD): Publicity Tools Handout.

- The ISK PowerPoint CD from the *Instructor's Survival Kit* box. See the instructions for use of this CD on page 4 of this manual if you use this CD in class.

Preparation Before Class. Follow the steps below:

1. Make a transparency of TM19-5: Publicity Tools Handout (or use Slide 4).

2. Make copies of TM19-5: Publicity Tools Handout.

Instructions. Follow the steps below to conduct this ICA:

1. Pass out copies of TM19-5: Publicity Tools Handout.

2. Give students this background mini-lecture (or show Slide 3; TRT: 3:11):

   "On December 3, 2001, renowned inventor and entrepreneur Dean Kamen unveiled The Segway™ Human Transporter (HT). The 85-pound Segway HT commercial model is a two-wheeled personal transportation device that is self-balancing, travels up to 12.5 miles and hour, and has a range of 17 miles on a single battery charge. Users control the speed and direction of the Segway HT by shifting their weight and manually turning a handle on the user interface."

3. Divide the class into four person teams to begin the ICA.

4. Give students this background mini-lecture on public relations and publicity:

   "Public relations (PR) is a form of communications management that seeks to favorably influence the image of an organization and its products. Typically, four steps are involved in the PR process: (1) identifying the issues and audience(s) that require a PR campaign, such as launching a new product among target consumers, minimizing the impact of a problem or crisis among employees or the general public, etc.;
   (2) determining the objectives of the PR campaign, such as generating awareness and/or stimulating sales of a product, enhancing credibility, reducing the impact of a negative situation, etc.; (3) executing the PR campaign using tools, such as publicity; and (4) evaluating the results of the PR campaign. Public relations is becoming an increasingly important part of an organization's integrated marketing communication (IMC) program. The principal reasons are that (1) PR in general and publicity in particular generates immediate impact, and (2) the cost is lower than engaging in an advertising and/or sales promotion campaign and the results generated are regarded as 'earned' rather than 'paid' media.

   One of the more frequently used strategies in a PR campaign is publicity. Typical publicity tools include the news release, a news conference, a media or press kit, a special event, etc. When used for a new product, publicity provides information about its uses and benefits to the following publics: (1) target consumers that may purchase the product; (2) media representatives who will report on and analyze the product; (3) governmental agencies that may regulate the product; and (4) employees and shareholders who have a stake in the successful launch of the product."

5. Give students this background mini-lecture on Burson-Marsteller:

   "Burson-Marsteller, headquartered in New York City and with 34 offices worldwide, developed the PR campaign for the product launch of the new Segway™ HT. Burson-Marsteller is a leading global public relations and communications counseling firm. It provides its clients with strategic thinking and program execution across a full range of public relations, public affairs, advertising, and other communications services.

The firm worked with Segway LLC, the developer of the Segway HT, to provide it with strategic brand development and public relations services. Later on, we will show you what Burson-Marsteller did to promote the new the Segway HT. But for now, you will act as the public relations firm for Segway LLC and develop a simple publicity campaign to inform various publics about this new, innovative product."

6. Show transparency TM19-5 (or show Slide 4). Have students take 20 minutes to write down their answers to the following questions on their Publicity Tools Handout.

    - Question 1: What are the elements that should be included in a news release for the launch of a new product, such as the Segway HT? Write them down on the Publicity Tools Handout. [5 minutes.]

    Answers: Standard news releases should contain the following elements (or show Slides 5-7):

    a. Contact information, which includes the name, telephone number, and e-mail address of the primary person responsible for answering any media or customer inquiries about the product.

    b. An attention-getting headline that informs the reader as to what the news release is all about.

    c. The dateline of the news release, along with the city, state, and country (if necessary) of origin.

    d. A brief but complete description of the new product, such as its features, benefits, and intended applications and/or targeted customers.

    e. A brief description of the company that is marketing the product.

    - Question 2: What items should be included in a kit for the media and/or potential customers? Write them down on the Publicity Tools Handout. [5 minutes.]

    Answers: A media kit include the following:

    a. News releases of the launch of the product (see Slides 5-7).

    b. Company background sheet (see Slide 8).

    c. Key personnel background sheet (see Slide 9).

    d. Product description sheet (see Slide 10).

    e. Product specifications sheet (see Slide 11).

    f. Product photos in a CD (see Slide 12).

- Question 3: What special publicity event would your team develop to launch the new Segway HT? Write it down on the Publicity Tools Handout. [10 minutes.]

    Answers: Burson-Marsteller developed the following publicity special events and activities to launch the new Segway HT:

    a. Secured an exclusive arrangement with ABC News' "*Good Morning America*" national morning TV program, which earned the show the highest ratings for 2001. The firm created an environment at New York City's Bryant Park with the show's producers to showcase the Segway HT to the public for the first time. [OPTIONAL: To view the exclusive coverage of the launch of the Segway HT, go to the ABC News *Good Morning America* website, which is http://abcnews.go.sections/GMA/GoodMorningAmerica/GMA011203What_IT_is.html]

    b. Placed a six-page story in *Time* magazine and a front-page, business section story in the *New York Times* newspaper.

    c. Created an event/demonstration site at Studio 450 in New York City where representatives of the media could see and photograph the new Segway HT in action. Over 50 national and international media outlets attended the event.

    d. Hosted more than 25 one-on-one media briefings and demonstrations during a two-day period. Also, remotes from CNN, the BBC, Nippon TV and others were conducted.

    e. Created a dedicated media hotline and e-mail address to respond to media inquiries.

    f. Developed an electronic press kit with dedicated website so that media and interested publics could download the media kit, engage in an interactive Flash video demonstration of the product, and find out more about Segway LLC. [OPTIONAL: To view these resources, go to the Segway HT online newsroom, which is www.segway.com/news.]

Marketing Lessons. Developing an effective PR campaign and publicity program requires creativity and attention to detail. Organizations like Segway LLC hire public relations and marketing consulting firms like Burson-Marsteller to help develop PR strategies and execute PR campaigns that will accomplish the organization's objectives in a more cost-efficient manner than advertising or sales promotion. Increasingly, PR is becoming an integral part of a firm's IMC.

Websites. To view the Segway HT website, go to www.segway.com. To find out more about Burson-Marsteller, go to www.bm.com.

TM19-5

PUBLICITY TOOLS HANDOUT

PUBLICITY TOOL	ITEMS TO INCLUDE OR ACTIONS TO TAKE
News Release	
Media Kit	
Special Event	

CHAPTER 20: PERSONAL SELLING AND SALES MANAGEMENT

ICA20-1: IN-CLASS ACTIVITY

STUDENT PERCEPTIONS OF SELLING

Learning Objectives. To have students investigate the stereotypes of sales and selling.

Definition. The following marketing term is referred to in this in-class activity (ICA):

- Personal Selling: The two-way flow of communication between a buyer and seller, often in a face-to-face encounter, designed to influence a person's or group's purchase decision.

Nature of the Activity. To have students take a quick quiz on sales and selling and then compare their attitudes and ideas to actual practice.

Estimated Class Time. 10 minutes.

Materials Needed.

- A transparency of TM20-1 (or use Slide 3) from ICA20-1.ppt of the ISK PowerPoint CD): Sales and Selling Quiz.

- The ISK PowerPoint CD from the *Instructor's Survival Kit* box. See the instructions for use of this CD on page 4 of this manual if you use this CD in class.

Preparation Before Class. Read through the instructions below.

Instructions. Follow the steps below to conduct this ICA:

1. Explain that the media have reinforced negative stereotypes of personal selling held by society. Not surprisingly, many students hold these same negative opinions. However, many of today's college graduates will begin their marketing career as a sales representative or in a customer service job.

2. Ask students to describe what salespeople do as part of their selling jobs.

3. Ask students if any of them plan on a sales career. For those who say, "Yes," ask them why they want to go into sales. Write down these responses on the board. If no one indicates any interest, ask none would consider a sales career.

4. Show transparency TM20-1 (or show Slide 3). Cover the responses and reveal them after each question is answered. Ask the class to respond to the questions asked and give their reasons. The responses should all be fallacious.

5. Respond to the students' comments with the "key observations" from the Sales and Selling Quiz: Some Key Observations activity below:

1. **Sales people push products on people.**

   Observations. The most successful companies and sales forces increasingly are taking a marketing orientation. Consider the following:

   - "We have a simple premise or philosophy, 'Know your customer and his needs.'"—Martin L. Andreas, Senior Vice President, Archer-Daniels-Midland.

   - "We're telling our sales reps, you need to think more broadly than just selling. You need to put on your business hat. I think that works to the advantage of everybody, especially to our customers' advantage. Now sales reps are in partnership with customers, helping them to run their business."—Michael Morley, Vice President and General Manager for US Marketing and Sales, Consumer Imaging Division, Kodak.

   - Bethlehem Steel Corporation's sales philosophy is, "To have a well trained, highly motivated sales force dedicated to developing and satisfying customer needs."

2. **Anybody can get a job in sales. You don't need a degree to work in sales.**

   Observations. Consider the following: "Our salespeople go to colleges and recruit."—David M. Beinner, General Manager of Sales, Bethlehem Steel Corporation. About half its sales force has a technical background.

3. **Sales people are born, not trained.**

   Observations. Knowledge is key for a successful sales person. This means more than valuable sales skills such as listening and probing to understand needs. It means product, industry, and customer knowledge. Consider the following:

   - "Our sales people have to know the big picture. Sometimes that means legislative issues, politics, trade. We want them to be the best source of information in the industry."—Martin L. Andreas, Senior Vice President, Archer-Daniels-Midland.

   - Kodak sales recruits take 90 days of intensive training before being sent into the field.

   Marketing Lessons. Sales and selling will continue to change. After all, if you were a buyer, would you want to waste your time talking to the stereotypical pushy, obnoxious sales person? Selling will continue to emphasize "finding solutions to customers problems."[1]

---

[1] Sources: Allison Lucas "Portrait of a Salesperson," Sales and Marketing Management (June, 1995), p. 13 and Thomas R. Wotruba, "The Evolution of Personal Selling and Sales Management," Journal of Personal Selling and Sales Management (Summer, 1995), pp. 1-12.

TM20-1

SALES AND SELLING QUIZ:

Are the following statements "Fact" or "Fallacy"?

1. Sales people push products on people.

2. Anybody can get a job in sales. You don't need a degree to work in sales.

3. Sales people are born, not trained.

CHAPTER 20: PERSONAL SELLING AND SALES MANAGEMENT

ICA20-2: IN-CLASS ACTIVITY

EXPENSE ACCOUNT ROLE-PLAY

Learning Objectives. To have students (1) understand the ethical dimensions involved being a sales person within an organization and (2) distinguish between the two different models of ethical behavior in Chapter 4 of the textbook as it applies to salespeople: moral idealism and utilitarianism.

Definitions. The following marketing terms are referred to in this in-class activity (ICA):

- Code of Ethics: A formal statement of ethical principles and rules of conduct.

- Ethics: The moral principles and values that govern the actions and decisions of an individual or group.

- Moral Idealism: A personal moral philosophy that considers certain individual rights or duties as universal, regardless of the outcome.

- Utilitarianism: A personal moral philosophy that focuses on the "greatest good for the greatest number" by assessing the costs and benefits of the consequences of ethical behavior.

Nature of the Activity. To have a few students conduct a role-play by assuming different characters to demonstrate an ethical issue related to salespeople within an organization.

Estimated Class Time. 20 minutes.

Materials Needed.

- 3 copies of the script that appears at the end of this ICA.

- 3 name cards, one for each of the student participants in the role-play.

Preparation Before Class. Follow the steps below:

1. Read the material in Chapter 4, pp. 105-108 that discusses (1) corporate culture and codes of ethics and (2) personal moral philosophy and ethical behavior.

2. Read the material below for background.

3. Prepare name cards for each of the characters.

4. Make 3 copies of the role-play, one for each of the participants.

5. Highlight the particular parts for each character's script.

6. Set up a table and chairs in front of the classroom for the "meeting."

<u>Instructions.</u> Follow the steps below to conduct this ICA:

1. Recruit three students (2 males & 1 female) to play the characters in the role-play. Seat the characters at a table in front of the class and give each the corresponding "script" for his or her character.

2. While the role-playing students are reviewing the scripts, the instructor should give the following background and then introduce the characters:

"What you are about to see is a reenactment of a real situation. Julia has been with Emco for 6 months and is back at headquarters for her first sales department quarterly review. On the last day of the meeting, Julia finds herself at lunch, seated between two veteran sales representatives, Dan and Mike in the company cafeteria. Listen closely and take note of the dilemma portrayed in this situation. Here are the three characters in our drama:

<u>Character</u>

- Julia: New Emco sales representative
- Dan: Veteran Emco sales representative
- Mike: Veteran Emco sales representative

3. Introduce the cast and his/her job title.

4. Have the students read the expense account role-play script in front of the class.

5. When finished with the role-play, say: "So, we now leave Emco's company cafeteria. Let's discuss what we've observed by answering some questions."

6. Ask students the questions below to facilitate the buying center discussion:

- <u>Question 1</u>: What are the relevant facts in the case?

    <u>Answers</u>:

    a. Julia is meeting sales goals with her current expenses.

    b. Dan and Mike perceive Julia's sales and entertainment expenses to be significantly lower than those for the rest of the sales force.

- Question 2: What are some of the ethical issues or questions presented?

    Answers:

    a. Are expenses appropriate to sales objectives/goals?

    b. Should Julia conform to sales force expense norms?

    c. What is the company's code of ethics with regarding this practice?

    d. To what extent does Julia have a responsibility to keep her expenses at a minimum while meeting her objectives?

    e. How did Mike and Dan find out about Julia's sales expenses in the first place?

    f. Do customers expect to be entertained? Is there a culture of "quid pro quo?"

- Question 3: Who are people that are affected by this situation?

    Answers: Julia, Emco's stakeholders (shareholders, other employees, etc.), Emco sales force (including Dan and Mike), the Emco sales manager, and Emco customers.

- Question 4: What are the alternatives in this situation?

    Answers:

    a. Increase the amount of expenses claimed.

    b. Begin entertaining customers more frequently and more lavishly.

    c. Discuss the situation with the sales manager.

    d. Discuss the situation with the sales manager.

    e. Quit.

- Question 5: What evaluation criteria (from the two ethical perspectives) should be applied to the alternatives? The analysis of the alternatives will depend on the particular perspective taken.

    Moral Idealism Perspective:

    a. What does each stakeholder have the right to expect?

    b. Which alternative(s) would you not want imposed on you if you were Julia? Dan and Mike? The sales manager? Customers?

    c. Which stakeholder carries the greatest burden if Julia decides to do nothing?

    d. What is the upper limit on expense budget?

    e. Will exceeding the as yet unknown "average" sales expense may invite scrutiny of past and current sales expenses?

Utilitarian Perspective:

a. Which alternative would provide the greatest benefit to the greatest number?

b. How would costs be measured? How much value should be placed on the:

1. Good will of Dan and Mike, the rest of the sales department?
2. Benefits of the expenditures to the customer, to the firm, and to Julia's sales performance?
3. Costs of bringing this up to the sales manager?

c. Which stakeholder carries the greatest burden if Julia decides to do nothing?

d. What is the practical upper limit on the expense budget?

e. Will exceeding the as yet unknown "average" sales expense may invite scrutiny of past and current sales expenses?

- Question 6: What action should Julia take?

a. What alternative would you chose in her situation? Why?

b. Which ethical theories make the most sense in this particular situation?

1. Could argue for doing nothing. The sales manager has not indicated any problems with Julia's performance or expenses. However, if Julia really should be doing more entertaining and this is an important part of building relationships and selling, she may be negatively affecting a number of stakeholders because she is not operating at her potential.

2. Discussing the situation with the sales manager has some merit, but this has the potential for drawing attention to other sales people who are spending more. This gets sales people like Mike and Don "in trouble" or unnecessarily draws attention to Julia's activities. Still, this seems to be the most sensible way to address the situation. Julia could approach the sales manager for feedback on her own performance and not referencing others' expenses.

3. Increasing the amount of entertaining expenses without increasing the amount of sales without any real justification would be unethical. This has a negative impact on a number of stakeholders under both models.

Marketing Lesson. A number of stakeholders are affected by the ethical decisions of a company's salespeople. Marketers need to consider the impact of these decisions on organizational and societal stakeholders.

SCRIPT: EXPENSE ACCOUNT ROLE-PLAY

Mike: "Julia, the accounting guys are giving us grief about our expenses. You're making us look bad. I've heard that you have the lowest sales expenses of anyone in the whole company."

Dan: "You shouldn't be cutting corners on entertainment with your customers, Julia. And you owe it to yourself when you're on the road to stay in nice hotels and eat well. Pass the pepper, Mike."

Mike: "Yeah. Remember, your expense account is one of the benefits of this job. Say, did you see the game last night? The Chicago Cubs were incredible."

As Mike and Dan continue their conversation (softly ad lib), Julia stands, faces the audience and wonders out loud:

Julia: "Have my sales expenses been too low?"

"Sales for my territory have been steadily growing since I took over the area 6 months ago. I'm meeting my sales goals. I wonder if I should be entertaining my customers more often. Maybe I'd generate more sales if I wined and dined my customers like Mike and Dan. I'm not altogether comfortable asking customers to dinner, although I do frequently take them to lunch.

"I stay in modest hotels while I'm on the road. I usually order room service and work on my call reports in the evenings. Still, I don't feel that I have been miserly with my own personal expenses.

"I wonder if I should discuss the situation with my boss, the sales secretary, or someone in accounting. Or maybe I should find a copy of Emco's Code of Ethics. On the other hand, perhaps that would only draw more attention to the situation and make matters worse. After all, the sales manager has said nothing about my expenses."

[End of the Role-Play]

CHAPTER 20: DEVELOPING NEW PRODUCTS AND SERVICES

ICA20-3: IN-CLASS ACTIVITY

PERSONAL SELLING PROCESS

Learning Objectives. To have students utilize the personal selling process to try to sell a Sunday insert coupon to a consumer-packaged goods firm to illustrate the kind of sales job many marketing graduates will have right out of college.

Definitions. The following marketing terms are referred to in this in-class activity (ICA):

- Partnership Selling: The practice whereby buyers and sellers combine their expertise to create customized solutions; commit to joint planning; and share customer, competitive, and company information for mutual benefit, and ultimately the customer. Sometimes called enterprise selling.

- Personal Selling: The two-way flow of communication between a buyer and seller, often in face-to-face encounter, designed to influence a person's or group's purchase decision

- Personal Selling Process: Sales activities occurring before and after the sale itself, consisting of six stages:

    a. Prospecting Stage: The search for and qualification of potential customers.

    b. Preapproach Stage: Involves obtaining further information about the prospect and deciding on the best method of approach.

    c. Approach Stage: The initial meeting between the salesperson and prospect, where the objectives are to gain the prospect's attention, stimulate interest, and build the foundation for the sales presentation itself and the basis for a working relationship.

    d. Presentation Stage: Its objective is to convert the prospect into a customer by creating a desire for the product or service.

    e. Closing Stage: Involves obtaining a purchase commitment from a prospect.

    f. Follow-up Stage: Making sure the customer's purchase has been properly delivered and installed and difficulties experienced with using the product are addressed.

- Relationship Selling: The practice of building ties to customers based on a salesperson's attention and commitment to customer needs over time.

Nature of the Activity. To have students participate in the personal selling process for News America Marketing's SmartSource Magazine, the most widely circulated publication in the U.S. Each Sunday, it offers over a dozen coupons from well-known consumer product firms.

Estimated Class Time. 25 minutes.

Materials Needed.

- The News America Marketing SmartSource Magazine (booklet of coupons) from the *Instructor's Survival Kit* box.

- Transparencies of:

    a. Selected pages of the News America Marketing SmartSource Magazine coupon booklet (or use Slides 3-11).

    b. TM20-3 (or use Slide 12 from ICA20-3.ppt of the ISK PowerPoint CD): Personal Selling Process Worksheet for News America Marketing.

- Copies of:

    a. Selected pages of the News America Marketing SmartSource Magazine coupon booklet (or use Slides 3-11).

    b. TM20-3 (or use Slide 12 from ICA20-3.ppt of the ISK PowerPoint CD): Personal Selling Process Worksheet for News America Marketing.

- The ISK PowerPoint CD from the *Instructor's Survival Kit* box. See the instructions for use of this CD on page 4 of this manual if you use this CD in class.

Preparation Before Class. Follow the steps below:

1. Read the material in Chapter 20 on the on the personal selling process (pp. 535-541) in Chapter 19 on coupons (pp. 516-517).

2. Read the material below.

3. Make a transparency of TM20-3 (or use Slide 12): Personal Selling Process Worksheet for News America Marketing.

4. OPTIONAL: Make copies of selected pages of the News America Marketing SmartSource Magazine coupon booklet (or use Slides 3-11) to hand out to students.

Instructions. Follow the steps below to conduct this ICA:

1. Give the following background mini-lecture:

"According to *Promo Magazine's* Industry Report 2002, coupons represented 6.6 percent of total promotion spending or $98.7 billion in 2001. However, due to the slowdown in the U.S. economy and the September 11, 2001 tragedy, marketers reduced their spending and use of coupons as a promotional tool in 2001. Specifically, coupon spending declined 6.1 percent to $6.5 billion in 2001 while coupon distribution dropped 3.5 percent to 239 billion, the largest percentage drop in 5 years. Moreover, the face value of a coupon (50¢ or $1.00 off) offered by marketers declined for the first time ever from 79¢ to 75¢. Finally, 25 percent of coupons offered by marketers required the purchase of 2 or more products.

Coupons redeemed by consumers also fell in 2001. This is surprising given that consumers normally **increase** their redemption behavior during recessions to save money. Specifically, unit coupon redemption fell a staggering 11 percent in 2001 to 4 billion while dollar redemption plummeted 17 percent to $3 billion. The consumer redemption rate also dipped slightly, from 1.8 percent to 1.7 percent, in 2001.[1]

The News America Marketing SmartSource magazine is the nation's most widely circulated publication. The magazine consists of coupons from over a dozen premier consumer product firms in the U.S. Each week, the SmartSource Magazine reaches an audience of 63 million households or 102 million people in over 700 Sunday newspapers 46 times per year. News America Marketing also offers special issues of its SmartSource Magazine, which are usually in conjunction with the Super Bowl, Major League Baseball's All-Star Game, and the Easter Seal Society Telethon."[2]

According to News America Marketing, coupons:

- Generate awareness and stimulate trial of a product.
- Motivate switching from competitors' brands to the firm's own brand.
- Generate repeat purchase to drive sales volume and build brand equity.

However, coupons:

- Reduce gross revenues by lowering the average price paid by loyal customers.
- Cost up to 3 times more than its face value due to advertising, handling, and other costs associated with their promotion and redemption.
- Are increasingly subject to fraud due to misredemption by consumers.

---

[1] "Sampling: A Softer Sell," *Promo Magazine's* Industry Report 2002, (April 1, 2002). See www.promomagazine.com.

[2] News America Marketing website. See www.newsamerica.com.

News America Marketing prides itself on its practice of relationship selling. Each salesperson is committed to building a long-term relationship with its customers in the consumer-packaged goods industry. In certain instances, News America Marketing goes one step further: it engages in partnership selling practices, in which it combines its expertise with selected customers to create customized solutions in their couponing programs.

With News America Marketing, like most firms with products and services to sell to its customers, engages in the personal selling process. This process consists of six stages: (1) prospecting; (2) preapproach; (3) approach; (4) presentation; (5) close; and (6) follow-up. As a salesperson for News America Marketing's SmartSource Magazine, you will now develop suggestions for one aspect of the personal selling process targeted to a specific prospective consumer-packaged good customer.

2. Divide the class into the following 9 separate and distinct teams, each representing a particular marketer that has purchased space in News America Marketing's SmartSource Magazine to offer consumers a coupon(s) on one of its products.

    - Team 1: Aqua Fresh (show Slide 3)
    - Team 2: Green Giant (show Slide 4)
    - Team 3: Hefty (show Slide 5)
    - Team 4: Huggies (show Slide 6)
    - Team 5: Oxi Clean (show Slide 7)
    - Team 6: Progresso (show Slide 8)
    - Team 7: Tums (show Slide 9)
    - Team 8: Tyson (show Slide 10)
    - Team 9: Vicks (show Slide 11)

3. Hand out copies of the Personal Selling Process Worksheet for News America Marketing (or show Slide 12).

4. Assign each student team one of the stages of the personal selling process according to the following order. Then, ask each team to spend 7 minutes developing ideas on how to accomplish its assigned personal selling process objective.

- Prospecting: Teams 1 (Aqua Fresh) and Team 9 (Vicks).

    Possible Ideas: Prospects identified through advertising, referrals, cold canvassing, trade associations, etc.

- Preapproach: Teams 2 (Hefty) and Team 8 (Tums).

    Possible Ideas: Information sources include, personal observation, other customers, own salespeople, previous sales attempts, etc.

- Approach: Teams 3 (Green Giant) and Team 7 (Tyson).

    Possible Ideas: Need to make a great first impression, cultivate a warm, business-like relationship, reference common acquaintances and interests, conduct a product demonstration, leave a brochure or other sales materials, etc.

- Presentation: Teams 4 (Huggies) and Team 6 (Progresso).

    Possible Ideas: Use suggestive selling, focus on benefits, cost-benefit analysis, probe by asking questions then listen and act on the responses, offer solution to client problems, if client has objections, handle them professionally using one of the techniques described in Chapter 20, etc.

- Close and Follow-up: Teams 4 (Oxi Clean)

    Possible Ideas: Close: Focus on body language and/or language used to indicate a ready-to-buy decision is forthcoming, ask the client to make a decision on some aspect or term of the sale, ask the client to make decisions on some attribute under the assumption the sales ahs been finalized, offer a time deadline (the offer is good until…), ask specifically for the order, etc.; and Follow-up: Make sure the product or service has been delivered, ask if you can do anything else to ensure their satisfaction with you and the firm, etc..

Marketing Lessons. Marketers use the personal selling process to develop satisfied, long-term customer relationships. When executed properly, it leads to satisfied customers who may generate additional sales through increased sales and referrals, which leads to the first stage of the process.

Website. To learn more about the marketing services of News America Marketing, go to www.newsamerica.com

TM20-3

PERSONAL SELLING PROCESS WORKSHEET FOR NEWS AMERICA MARKETING

STAGE	OBJECTIVE	IDEAS TO MEET OBJECTIVE IN THE PERSONAL SELLING PROCESS
Prospecting	Search for and qualify prospects	<ul><li></li><li></li><li></li></ul>
Preapproach	Gather information and decide how to approach the prospect	<ul><li></li><li></li><li></li></ul>
Approach	Gain prospect's attention, stimulate interest, and make the transition to the presentation	<ul><li></li><li></li><li></li></ul>
Presentation	Begin converting a prospect into a customer by creating a desire for the product or service	<ul><li></li><li></li><li></li></ul>
Close	Obtain a purchase commitment from the prospect and create a customer	<ul><li></li><li></li><li></li></ul>
Follow-up	Ensure that the customer is satisfied with the product or service	<ul><li></li><li></li><li></li></ul>

© McGraw-Hill Companies, Inc. 2003

CHAPTER 21: IMPLEMENTING INTERACTIVE AND MULTICHANNEL MARKETING

ICA21-1: IN-CLASS ACTIVITY

BUYING A BMW Z3 ROADSTER: "MARKETPLACE" VS. "MARKETSPACE" (PART 1)

Learning Objectives. To have students (1) understand the nature of interactive marketing and electronic commerce, (2) compare the traditional "marketplace" channel with the new "marketspace" channel (Part 1), and (3) experience an interactive marketing website that encourages prospective customers to "build-to-order" a product with the specific features, options, and price they want (Part 2).

Definitions. The following marketing terms are referred to in this in-class activity (ICA):

- Electronic Commerce: Any activity that uses some form of electronic communication in the inventory, exchange, advertisement, distribution, and payment of goods and services.

- Interactive Marketing: Two-way buyer-seller electronic communications in a computer-mediated environment in which the buyer controls the kind and amount of information received from the seller.

- Internet Marketing Channels: Channels that employ the Internet to make goods and services available for consumption or use by consumers or industrial buyers.

- Marketspace: An Internet/Web-enabled digital environment characterized by "face-to-screen" exchange relationships and electronic images and offerings.

Nature of the Activity. To have students compare the traditional "marketplace" channel for buying a BMW Z3 Roadster 3.0i from a BMW dealership with the new "marketspace" channel for buying a Z3 Roadster 3.0i at BMW's "Build Your Z" website. The entire activity consists of Part 1 (this ICA) and Part 2 (ICA21-2).

Estimated Class Time. 40 minutes, which consists of:

- 20 minutes for this ICA.

- 20 minutes for ICA21-2 during the subsequent class period.

- [NOTE: Some students will spend 45 minutes outside class to complete their assignment.]

Materials Needed.

- The 2002 BMW Z3 Roadster brochure from the *Instructor's Survival Kit* box (or use Slide 3 from ICA21-1.ppt of the ISK PowerPoint CD).

- A transparency of TM21-1 (or use Slide 8 from ICA21-1.ppt of the ISK PowerPoint CD): Using the Six "C" Framework to Suggest Reasons for Buying a BMW Z3 Roadster 3.0i.

- Copies of the BMW 2002 Pricing Sheet (or use Slide 9 from ICA21-1.ppt of the ISK PowerPoint CD).

- The ISK PowerPoint CD from the *Instructor's Survival Kit* box. See the instructions for use of this CD on page 4 of this manual if you use this CD in class.

Preparation Before Class. Follow the steps below:

1. Read Chapter 21 as well as the material below to give a background lecture.

2. Make a transparency of TM21-1 (or use Slide 8 from ICA21-1.ppt of the ISK PowerPoint CD).

3. Make copies the BMW 2002 Pricing Sheet (or use Slide 9 from ICA21-1.ppt of the ISK PowerPoint CD).

4. Visit the BMW website to explore the "Build Your BMW" build-to-order option.

Instructions. Follow the steps below to conduct this ICA:

1. Pass around the BMW Z3 brochure (or show Slide 3).

2. Give students this background mini-lecture on the "marketplace" channel:

"BMW, like other firms, pursues a multichannel marketing strategy when selling its products, such as the Z3 Roadster 3.0i, to target customers.

The first is the traditional "marketplace" channel for selling cars that we all are familiar with. For example, we see TV, radio, magazine, or other advertising and promotional campaigns (or show Slides 4-5) that attract our attention or we see one of our colleagues or classmates driving a Z3 Roadster 3.0i that stimulates a want. To satisfy this want, we go to the local BMW dealer and check out the Z3 Roadsters in the showroom or on the lot (or show Slides 6-7).

We are met by a salesperson who gives us a brochure of the Z3 Roadster line (which you now are looking at) and asks us about the model we want (Z3 Roadster 3.0i) and the specific features and options we desire (manual transmission, hardtop, etc.).

Then, the salesperson gives us an initial price on that car (or show Slide 8) and asks us to take a test drive. After taking the exhilarating test drive, the salesperson asks us how we want to finance the car (amount of down payment, the type of financing, either loan or lease, and the terms of the financing) and what kind of car we have to trade-in. She or he then informs us of any rebates to reduce the price of the car. Finally, if we're <u>truly</u> interested, we begin to negotiate over the final price and terms of the purchase with the salesperson."

3. Give students this background mini-lecture on the "marketspace" channel:

"BMW also uses an Internet marketing channel to sell its cars. This channel involves the use of both interactive marketing, in which information about the Z3 Roadster product line has been placed on the website, and electronic commerce, in which we are given the opportunity to "build-to-order" the Z3 Roadster 3.0i based on the features and options we select. For BMW's "Build Your BMW" Internet website, like those of other firms, consumers can request additional information, have a salesperson from a local dealership contact them to answer any questions or arrange for a test drive, and finance the purchase of their car through BMW Financial Services."

4. Conclude this background mini-lecture:

"Consumers choose to use interactive marketing websites to purchase products because of the convenience, cost, choice, customization, communication, and control they receive. These reasons apply to both the traditional "marketplace" channel and the new "marketspace" channel."

5. Hand out copies of transparency TM21-1 (or show Slide 9).

6. Using the six "C" framework, ask students to suggest specific reasons why consumers would choose the traditional "marketplace" method for purchasing a Z3 Roadster 3.0i and write them on the blackboard or on the transparency made from TM21-1. Then ask students why they would choose the new "marketspace" method for purchasing a Z3 Roadster 3.0i and write them on the blackboard or on the transparency made from TM21-1. Some of the reasons students may suggest are listed on the next page.

<u>Marketing Lesson.</u> Both the "marketplace" and "marketspace" channels for buying products are now common, with the latter growing in importance. Students should understand the reasons some consumers may prefer one channel to the other.

<u>Website.</u> The BMW website is www.bmwusa.com.

USING THE SIX "C" FRAMEWORK TO SUGGEST REASONS FOR BUYING A BMW Z3 ROADSTER 3.0i

Traditional "Marketplace" Channel	New "Marketspace" Channel
Convenience: • Local dealer may be available • Relationship with dealer important for after-sale service; expedite repairs • Visually inspect the car before buying	**Convenience:** • Shop anytime and from anywhere; not dependent upon local dealer availability or hours of operation to compare features & prices
Cost: • May be able to negotiate lower price • May get more value for trade-in • May get better financing terms with one's own local bank	**Cost:** • Usually the same or lower than dealer • Lower due to lower inventory, order processing, communications, and commissions costs • Easier to adjust prices due to market conditions • Search costs lower (save time = money)
Choice: • May have good selection of BMW Z3 Roadster 3.0i's on dealer lot • May have more than one dealer in larger metropolitan markets to choose from	**Choice:** • Option of comparing BMW dealer with BMW "build-to-order" • Search other websites, such as Carpoint, to compare prices or purchase from other BMW dealers nationwide • Search websites for reviews on BMW Z3 Roadster 3.0i
Customization: • Dealers can create direct marketing programs for their local market; know profiles of customers better and therefore target programs more efficiently	**Customization:** • Create the product with only the features and options desired via the "Build Your Z" • Suggest specific features & options to different segments if customer profiles are captured
Communication: • IMC approach to generate awareness, trial, and purchase • Knowledgeable salespeople can be invaluable	**Communication:** • Can request e-mail or telephone response for additional information from an online salesperson • Can receive e-mail notices of product news, special offers, etc. automatically
Control: • Aggressive customers like to dictate the terms of the negotiation process (price, trade-in value, features & options, financing, etc.) • Concern over privacy and security of personal and financial information	**Control:** • Consumers can better dictate the amount of information they receive, the alternatives they wish to evaluate, and the terms of the purchase

TM21-1

USING THE SIX "C" FRAMEWORK TO SUGGEST REASONS FOR BUYING A BMW Z3 ROADSTER 3.0i

Traditional "Marketplace" Channel	New "Marketspace" Channel
• Convenience	• Convenience
• Cost	• Cost
• Choice	• Choice
• Customization	• Customization
• Communication	• Communication
• Control	• Control

© McGraw-Hill Companies, Inc. 2003

CHAPTER 21: IMPLEMENTING INTERACTIVE AND MULTICHANNEL MARKETING

ICA21-2: IN-CLASS ACTIVITY

BUYING A BMW Z3 ROADSTER: "BUILD YOUR BMW" (PART 2)

Learning Objectives. To have students (1) understand the nature of interactive marketing and electronic commerce, (2) compare the traditional "marketplace" channel with the new "marketspace" channel (Part 1), and (3) experience an interactive marketing website that encourages prospective customers to "build-to-order" a product with the specific features, options, and price they want (Part 2).

Definitions. The following marketing terms are referred to in this in-class activity (ICA):

- Electronic Commerce: Any activity that uses some form of electronic communication in the inventory, exchange, advertisement, distribution, and payment of goods and services.

- Interactive Marketing: Two-way buyer-seller electronic communications in a computer-mediated environment in which the buyer controls the kind and amount of information received from the seller.

- Internet Marketing Channels: Channels that employ the Internet to make goods and services available for consumption or use by consumers or industrial buyers.

- Marketspace: An Internet/Web-enabled digital environment characterized by "face-to-screen" exchange relationships and electronic images and offerings.

Nature of the Activity. To have students compare the traditional "marketplace" channel for buying a BMW Z3 Roadster 3.0i from a BMW dealership with the new "marketspace" channel for buying a Z3 Roadster 3.0i at BMW's "Build Your Z" website. The entire activity consists of Part 1 (ICA21-1) and Part 2 (this ICA).

Estimated Class Time. 40 minutes, which consists of:

- 20 minutes for ICA21-1 from the previous class period.

- 20 minutes for this ICA.

- [NOTE: Some students will spend 45 minutes outside class to complete their assignment.]

Materials Needed.

- The 2002 BMW Z3 Roadster brochure from the *Instructor's Survival Kit* box (or use Slide 3 from ICA21-1.ppt of the ISK PowerPoint CD).

- Copies of the BMW Z3 Roadster 3.0i Pricing Sheet.
- The ISK PowerPoint CD from the *Instructor's Survival Kit* box. See the instructions for use of this CD on page 4 of this manual if you use this CD in class.

Preparation Before Class. Follow the steps below:

1. Read Chapter 21 as well as the material below to give a background lecture.

2. Make a transparency of the BMW Z3 Roadster 3.0i Pricing Sheet.

3. Make copies of the BMW Z3 Roadster 3.0i Pricing Sheet.

4. Visit the BMW website and explore the "Build Your BMW" build-to-order option by going through this ICA.

5. Bookmark the BMW website on your classroom computer and check to see if the computer has the recommended site technology installed.

Instructions. Follow the steps below to conduct this ICA:

1. Pass around the BMW Z3 brochure (or show Slides 3–8 from ICA21-1.ppt).

2. Give students this background mini-lecture for review:

    "BMW, like other firms, pursues a multichannel marketing strategy when selling its products, such as the Z3 Roadster 3.0i, to target customers.

    BMW sells its cars both through its traditional dealership network and more recently its Internet website. Previously, we identified the reasons consumers might purchase this vehicle at a local dealer or from its marketing website using the six "C" framework. Consumers choose to use an organization's website to purchase products because of the convenience, cost, choice, customization, communication, and control they receive."

3. Show the blank transparency of TM21-1 that listed the students' responses from ICA21-1 for review.

4. Form teams of 4 to 5 students. Each team will share its collective decisions on the specific features and options it selects for the BMW Z3 Roadster 3.0i.

5. Hand out copies of the BMW Z3 Roadster 3.0i Pricing Sheet.

6. Step 1: Connect to the BMW website at www.bmwusa.com. Locate the "Choose a Model" on the screen and click on the "Z3" link. At the top of the webpage, click on the "3.0i" link to obtain an overview of the BMW Z3 Roadster 3.0i.

7. Step 2: To begin the "marketspace" experience, click on the "Build Your Z3 Roadster 3.0i" link, which goes to the "Exterior/Interior" webpage.

8. Step 3: Have each team select and write down the "Exterior" and "Interior" color options they want on the BMW Z3 Roadster 3.0i Pricing Sheet based on a consensus of the group. Scroll the cursor over the options to obtain a description. Note that some "Interior" color options are not available for a particular "Exterior" color.

9. Step 4: Have Team 1 identify its "Exterior" and "Interior" color selections. Note how the screen changes based on the selections made. Also, note that the MSRP (Manufacturer's Suggested Retail Price) changes in the upper right hand corner of the webpage as features and options are selected. When finished with the selections, click on the "Continue" button, which goes to the "Packages/Options" webpage.

10. Step 5: Have each team select and write down the "Package" and "Options" they want on the BMW Z3 Roadster 3.0i Pricing Sheet based on a consensus of the group.

11. Step 6: Have Team 2 identify its "Package" and "Options" selections. Again, notice how the screen and MSRP change. When finished with the selections, click the "Continue" button, which goes to the "Explore Financing" webpage.

12. Step 7: Have each team select and write down the financing options they want on the BMW Z3 Roadster 3.0i Pricing Sheet based on a consensus of the group. To do this, select the state where you are located. Then, select the financing method ("Lease," "OwnersChoice," "Traditional Finance," or "Performance Loan"). Next, select the term and annual mileage option. Finally, input the "Down Payment" and "Estimated Trade-in Value." When finished with the selections, click the "Continue" button, which goes to the "Summary" webpage.

    [NOTE: To obtain an estimate of the trade-in value of a car, go to the Kelley Blue Book website, which is www.kbb.com and follow the directions.]

13. Step 8: Have Team 3 identify its "Explore Financing" selections. When finished with the selections, click the "Continue" button, which goes to the "Summary" webpage.

14. Step 9: Scroll down the "Summary" webpage. Review the features, options, and financing arrangements that Teams 1 - 3 selected. If you want to change any, go back by clicking on the tab at the bottom of the webpage. When the class is satisfied with its selections, click on the "Save" tab. BMW will prompt you to register. If you only want to print the results, scroll down to the bottom of the webpage and click the "Printable Format" button. You are now finished with the "marketspace" portion of ICA21-2.

15. For the out-of-class assignment, have Team 4 (or another that volunteers) go to a local BMW dealer (or telephone one near by; to locate one, click on the "Locate a BMW Center" tab at the very bottom of each webpage). Kindly ask for a salesperson and explain that you want to obtain prices for the Z3 Roadster 3.0i configuration that is written on the BMW Z3 Roadster 3.0i Pricing Sheet. Tell them that you are doing this for a class project. Have the team write down their findings on the sheet and report them during the start of the next class period.

16. Have the following teams obtain prices for the BMW Z3 Roadster 3.0i from one of the following websites:

    - Team 5: Autobytel, which is www.autobytel.com.
    - Team 6: MSN Carpoint, which is www.carpoint.com.
    - Team 7: Edmunds, www.edmunds.com.

    [NOTE: Some of these car-buying websites require that the prospective buyer be a serious purchaser. Try the sites anyway and provide the required information. You may get an e-mail quote or a telephone call from a salesperson at the nearest BMW dealer.]

Marketing Lesson. The 21st century will see an expansion of purchases through marketing websites on the Internet. Even complex purchases, like automobiles, lends can be accomplished through this channel. Thus, as demonstrated in this ICA and ICA21-1, the new "marketspace" channel for shopping is a viable alternative to the more traditional "marketplace" channel for many of today's consumers.

Websites. The BMW website is www.bmwusa.com. The others are identified above.

BMW Z3 ROADSTER 3.0i PRICING SHEET

Item	Build Your "Z3 Roadster 3.0i" Price Quote	Item	BMW Dealer Price Quote	Item	Autobytel, Carpoint, or Edmunds Price Quote
Base Price:	_____	Base Price:	_____	Base Price:	_____
Dest. Charge:	_____	Dest. Charge:	_____	Dest. Charge:	_____
Exterior Color:	_____	Exterior Color:	_____	Exterior Color:	_____
Interior Color:	_____	Interior Color:	_____	Interior Color:	_____
Premium Package:	_____	Premium Package:	_____	Premium Package:	_____
Option #1:	_____	Option #1:	_____	Option #1:	_____
Option #2:	_____	Option #2:	_____	Option #2:	_____
Option #3:	_____	Option #3:	_____	Option #3:	_____
Option #4:	_____	Option #4:	_____	Option #4:	_____
Option #5:	_____	Option #5:	_____	Option #5:	_____
Option #6:	_____	Option #6:	_____	Option #6:	_____
Other Options:	_____	Other Options:	_____	Other Options:	_____
TOTAL MSRP:	_____	**TOTAL MSRP:**	_____	**TOTAL MSRP:**	_____
Trade-in Value:	_____	Trade-in Value:	_____	Trade-in Value:	_____
Down Payment:	_____	Down Payment:	_____	Down Payment:	_____
Months Financed:	_____	Months Financed:	_____	Months Financed:	_____
APR:	_____	APR:	_____	APR:	_____
Monthly Payment:	_____	Monthly Payment:	_____	Monthly Payment:	_____

CHAPTER 22: PUTTING IT ALL TOGETHER:
THE STRATEGIC MARKETING PROCESS

ICA22-1: IN-CLASS ACTIVITY

MARKETING PLANNING WORKSHEET

Learning Objective. To have students do a marketing plan that lets them apply the strategic marketing process to highlight the key issues in assessing a marketing opportunity.

Definitions. The following marketing terms are referred to in this in-class activity (ICA):

- Marketing Plan: A roadmap for the marketing activities of an organization for a specified future period of time, such as one or five years.

- Strategic Marketing Process: The approach whereby an organization allocates its marketing mix resources to reach its target markets.

Nature of the Activity. To have students complete the marketing planning worksheet for a simple marketing situation that might be either:

1. The one described below.

2. One the instructor selects.

3. The product or service the student or team will use for a marketing plan class project.

    If Choices #1 or #2 are used, this ICA will be used as a means of summarizing the course in conjunction with Chapter 22 of the textbook. Alternatively, the ICA may be used early in the course to help students undertake a preliminary structuring of the product or service used for their marketing plans (Choice #3 above).

Estimated Class Time. 20 minutes.

Materials Needed.

- A scenario, like the one below or Choices #2 or #3 described above.

- A transparency of TM22-1: Marketing Planning Worksheet for Team Development Sessions.

- Copies of the Marketing Planning Worksheet to hand out to each student.

Preparation Before Class. Follow the steps below:

1. Read the material below to use either the scenario below as a basis for the student activity or prepare one of your own.

2. Make a transparency of TM22-1: Marketing Planning Worksheet for Team Development Sessions.

3. Make copies of the Marketing Planning Worksheet to hand out to each student.

Instructions. Follow the steps below to conduct this ICA:

1. Give students this background mini-lecture:

   "A subsidiary of a community health center, specializing in private psychiatric care, has recently expanded into human resource development programs for business and industry. As the first in a series of offerings, the subsidiary is marketing an outdoor, adventure-based team development session for employee groups who work together to accomplish tasks. The center's subsidiary activities are intended to generate sufficient revenues to help fund new health programs."

2. Pass out copies of the Marketing Planning Worksheet.

3. Give students 15 minutes to complete the worksheet.

4. Inform students that the Marketing Planning Worksheet provides examples of possible responses to each of the planning factors.

5. Discuss the students' ideas and their marketing implications for the choice that was selected from above.

Marketing Lessons. Marketing managers are often faced with a number of alternative opportunities. The Marketing Planning Worksheet enables a marketer to quickly assess the key environmental and marketing factors. While this quick assessment cannot replace an in-depth analysis, it can often screen out impractical ideas.

MARKETING PLAN WORKSHEET FOR: _____

FACTOR	ISSUE	MARKETING PLAN
Consumer Analysis/Target Market Analysis	• Who Benefits?	
	• How Do They Benefit?	
	• Who Decides to Buy or Use?	
	• Point of Difference?	
Environmental (Uncontrollable) Factors	• Consumer/Social Factors	
	• Economic Factors	
	• Technological Factors	
	• Competitive Factors	
	• Legal/Regulatory Factors	
Developing the Marketing Plan	• Objective	
	• Research (Collect Info)	
	• Product/Service Offered	
	• Price	
	• Promotion – Advertising	
	– Sales Promotion	
	– Public Relations	
	– Personal Selling	
	• Place/Distribution	
Executing the Marketing Plan	• Budget	
	• Who is Responsible?	
	• Milestone Dates	
Evaluating the Marketing Plan	• Did it Work?	

© McGraw-Hill Companies, Inc. 2003

TM22-1

MARKETING PLAN WORKSHEET FOR TEAM DEVELOPMENT SESSIONS

FACTOR	ISSUE	MARKETING PLAN
Consumer Analysis/Target Market Analysis	• Who Benefits?	Employees, work groups, employers
	• How Do They Benefit?	Skill building: problem solving, creative thinking, communication
	• Who Decides to Buy/Use?	Owner, CEO, Director of Human Resources
	• Point of Difference?	Alternative, more experiential approach
Environmental (Uncontrollable) Factors	• Consumer/Social Factors	Perception of need, values to human resource-development
	• Economic Factors	Perceived as too expensive by many small-medium companies
	• Technological Factors	Only 8 - 10 people at one time—requires high technical and safety emphasis
	• Competitive Factors	One competitor—program not as inclusive or safe but it costs half the amount
	• Legal/Regulatory Factors	None
Developing the Marketing Plan	• Objective	Provide team building workshops to area companies leading to other businesses
	• Research (Collect Info)	Which companies now purchase such programs? What are their characteristics? What companies are considering more progressive management practices?
	• Product/Service Offered	2 hours of orientation and planning, 9-hour course w/ 2 meals, 2 hour debrief session
	• Price	$150
	• Promotion – Advertising	Professional/business journals
	– Sales Promotion	None
	– Public Relations	Professional meeting, free course exhibits, newspaper, TV, radio, fairs
	– Personal Selling	By facilitators and Marketing Director
	• Place/Distribution	4 hours in their office and 9 hours on course
Executing the Marketing Plan	• Budget	$100,000
	• Who is Responsible?	Marketing Director
	• Milestone Dates	Complete model by Aug. 1-2; free days by Oct. 1; Exec. Comm. & Bd. by Sep. 1
Evaluating the Marketing Plan	• Did it Work?	Meeting revenue targets

© McGraw-Hill Companies, Inc. 2003

CHAPTER 22: PUTTING IT ALL TOGETHER: THE STRATEGIC MARKETING PROCESS

ICA22-2: IN-CLASS ACTIVITY

BRAND EXTENSIONS: HOW FAR CAN GENERAL MILLS GO?

Learning Objectives. To have students (1) suggest some brand extensions for two General Mills brands, and (2) develop some generalizations about when a brand extension is or is not likely to work.

Definitions. The following marketing terms are referred to in this in-class activity (ICA):

- Brand Extension: The practice of using a current brand name to enter a completely different product class.

- Brand Name: Any word or device (design, shape, sound, or color) that is used to distinguish one company's products from a competitor's.

Nature of the Activity. To have students (1) suggest new products to extend (or "flank") the Wheaties® and Cheerios® brands, (2) assess which brand extension ideas make sense and which don't, and (3) suggest some guidelines for developing brand extensions. [NOTE: In contrast to ICA11-2 where students identified opportunities within the microwave popcorn product category, here students are encouraged to provide ideas outside the product category.]

Estimated Class Time. 20 minutes.

Materials Needed.

- The Wheaties and Wheaties Energy Crunch cereal boxes from the *Instructor's Survival Kit* box.

- A transparency of TM22-2 (or use Slide 7 from ICA22-2.ppt of the ISK PowerPoint

- The ISK PowerPoint CD from the *Instructor's Survival Kit* box. See the instructions for use of this CD on page 4 of this manual if you use this CD in class.

Preparation Before Class. Follow the steps below:

1. Read the material below to give a background lecture.

2. Make transparency of TM22-2 (or use Slide 7 from ICA22-2.ppt of the ISK PowerPoint CD).

Instructions. Follow the steps below to conduct this ICA:

1. Give students this background mini-lecture:

   "In 2001, the U. S. ready-to-eat (RTE) cereal market was $7.45 billion and General Mills had a 32% share of this market. For the past several years, the growth in the RTE cereal market has remained flat, as consumer demographics and tastes have changed. Some of these changes include the following:

   - Fewer people eat breakfast, and those that do want more convenience. As a result, General Mills recently introduced its Big G Milk 'n Cereal Bar product line, which combines cereal, such as Honey Nut Cheerios, with a milk-based layer (see ICA 9-1).

   - More consumers are concerned about eating healthier foods. As a result, General Mills recently introduced:

     a. Harmony, a "nutraceutical" cereal that is fortified with higher amounts of folic acid and calcium and is specifically targeted at women.

     b. Sunrise, an organic cereal targeted at those who want all-natural ingredients.

     c. Wheaties Energy Crunch, "The Breakfast of Everyday Champions," which combines added protein, carbohydrates, and B vitamins for people who engage in active lifestyles and want "all-day energy" (or show Slides 3-5).

2. Divide the class roughly in half and assign students to one of two "teams" that represent General Mills' two most popular cereal brands: Wheaties and Cheerios.

3. Pass around the boxes of Wheaties and Wheaties Energy Crunch from the *Instructor's Survival Kit* (or show Slide 6).

4. Show transparency TM22-2 (or show Slide 7).

5. Give students 5 minutes to come up with ideas for products that could extend their respective brand. [NOTE: As mentioned below, students who have read the textbook or shop in grocery stores can easily identify existing products or flavors <u>inside</u> the product line. Moving <u>outside</u> the product line is far more difficult.]

6. Ask both the "Wheaties Team" and the "Cheerios Team" for their respective brand extension ideas and write them on either the board or the transparency made from transparency TM22-2.

7. Ask for a quick show of hands from the students' on their reaction to the question "Does the extension work?" Check either the "Yes" or "No" column on the right side of TM22-2 that corresponds to the <u>majority</u> of student votes.

8. Here are some possible ideas, with an asterisk (*) showing those General Mills brand extensions that are currently on retailers' shelves today as well as the year of introduction in parentheses. [NOTES: (1) Wheaties Dunk-A-Balls is discussed in ICA 10-4; (2) Ideas with a '?' are currently being done by General Mills even though they are technically "outside the line."]

Basic Brand	Kind of Brand Extension	
	Inside the Line	Outside the Line
Wheaties	<ul><li>Wheaties* (1924)</li><li>Fruit & Bran Wheaties (1984)</li><li>Wheaties Honey Gold (1991)</li><li>Wheaties Dunk-A-Balls (1994)</li><li>Wheaties Quarterback Crunch (1994)</li><li>Frosted Wheaties* (1996)</li><li>Wheaties Raisin Bran* (1996)</li><li>Wheaties Energy Crunch* (2001)</li></ul>	<ul><li>Snack Pouch</li><li>Cereal/Granola Bars</li><li>Hot Cereal</li><li>Frozen Muffins</li></ul>
Cheerios	<ul><li>Cheerios* (1941)</li><li>Honey Nut Cheerios* (1979)</li><li>Apple Cinnamon Cheerios* (1987)</li><li>Multi-Grain Cheerios* (1991)</li><li>Frosted Cheerios* (1995)</li><li>Team Cheerios* (1997)</li><li>Big G Milk 'n Cereal Bar: Honey Nut Cheerios</li><li>Big G Snack 'n Dash: Honey Nut Cheerios</li></ul>	<ul><li>Cereal/Granola Bars (?)</li><li>Cocktail Snacks</li><li>Instant Breakfast</li><li>Hot Cereal</li><li>Snack Pouch (?)</li><li>Chocolate or Banana</li><li>Licensing: Toddler Clothes, Cereal Containers, etc.</li><li>NASCAR Race Car Sponsorship (?)</li></ul>

9. Looking at the list above, it is relatively easy to come up with ideas in the middle column, but not all ideas work. Wheaties Honey Gold didn't sell and was quickly withdrawn from the market. And 1994 was not a very good year: General Mills introduced two Wheaties brand extensions that were quickly pulled off the market.

10. Ask the students for their conclusions or guidelines for what might "work" and "not work" in developing brand extensions. Some guidelines to discuss are:

    - Guidelines for brand extensions that <u>do work</u>:

        a. Consumer credibility with the new brand/product under the old brand name umbrella.

        b. Potential for significant new incremental sales and profits.

        c. Sales don't steal or "cannibalize" those from the original brand.

        d. Little risk to original brand.

        e. A perception of high quality for the new brand/product that retains the high consumer regard for the original brand.

    - Guidelines for brand extensions that <u>don't work</u> are really the reverse of those just listed. Introducing Frosted Cheerios had to overcome the concern about guideline "c" above, as was the case in introducing Diet Coke by the Coca-Cola Company.

<u>Marketing Lessons.</u> Introducing brand extensions may look easy but it is a very complex, demanding, and costly process. Hopefully for General Mills, Wheaties Energy Crunch will be a successful brand extension.

<u>Websites.</u> To view General Mill's current cereal product lines, go to www.generalmills.com. Wheaties (www.wheaties.com), Wheaties Energy Crunch (www.wheatiesenergycrunch), and Cheerios (www.cheerios.com) all have their own websites.

TM22-2

FINDING BRAND EXTENSIONS FOR TWO GENERAL MILLS BRANDS

BASIC BRAND	EXTENSION INSIDE OR OUTSIDE PRODUCT LINE?	IDEA FOR EXTENSION OF BASIC BRAND	DOES EXTENSION WORK?	
			YES	NO
Wheaties	Inside	• • • • •		
	Outside	• • • • •		
Cheerios	Inside	• • • • •		
	Outside	• • • • •		

© McGraw-Hill Companies, Inc. 2003

CHAPTER 22: PULLING IT ALL TOGETHER: THE STRATEGIC MARKETING PROCESS

ICA22-3: IN-CLASS ACTIVITY

STRATEGIC MARKETING TRENDS

Learning Objectives. To enable students learn about the latest issues and trends in corporate and marketing strategy planning, implementation, and control.

Definition. The following marketing term is referred to in this in-class activity (ICA):

- Strategic Marketing Process: The approach whereby an organization allocates its marketing mix resources to reach its target markets.

Nature of the Activity. To have student teams access both current and back issues of The McKinsey Quarterly, a publication from the well-known management consulting firm to learn about its perspective on the latest issues and trends in corporate and marketing strategy planning, implementation, and control.

Estimated Class Time. 30 minutes, which consists of:

- 10 minutes to explain the nature of this ICA and distribute the McKinsey Quarterly Handout to student teams.
- 20 minutes to present summaries by student teams during the subsequent class period.
- [NOTE: Students will spend 45 minutes outside class to complete their assignment.]

Materials Needed.

- Copies of the McKinsey Quarterly Handout for each student.
- Student access to the Internet. [NOTE: Adobe Acrobat may be required to view and print some articles. If necessary, download the latest version at www.adobe.com.]

Preparation Before Class. Follow the steps below:

1. Read the material in Chapter 2 on linking corporate and marketing strategy and Chapter 22 on the strategic marketing process and strategy planning, implementation, and control.
2. Familiarize yourself with the McKinsey Quarterly website.
3. Make copies of the McKinsey Quarterly Handout for each student.
4. Develop in-class discussion questions, if desired.

Instructions. Follow the steps below to conduct this ICA:

1. Form students into four-person teams.

2. Pass out copies of the McKinsey Quarterly Handout to each student.

3. Have the student teams go to the McKinsey Quarterly website, which is www.mckinseyquarterly.com. Assign students the following tasks:

   a. Under the "Functions" menu at the left of the homepage, click on the "Marketing" link. Next, click on the "Featured Article" link at the top of the webpage. **[NOTE: Free registration is required to read the full text of the "Featured Article." Have one student team member complete the registration process to proceed with the ICA assignments below.]**

   ASSIGNMENT: Have student teams write a 1/2-page brief that summarizes the featured article.

   b. Still in the "Function: Marketing" area, scroll to the top of the webpage. Click on one of the menu options ('Editor's Choice,' 'Branding,' 'Channel Management,' …'Strategy'). Then, have teams click on an article of their choice.

   ASSIGNMENT: Have student teams write a 1/2-page brief that summarizes the article selected.

   c. Under the "Functions" menu at the left of the homepage, click on the "Strategy" link. Next, click on the "Featured Article" link at the top of the webpage or scroll down the webpage to have teams select an article of their choice.

   ASSIGNMENT: Have student teams write a 1/2-page brief that summarizes the article selected.

   d. Under the "Industries" menu at the left of the homepage, click on one of the industry sector links ('Automotive,' 'Electronic Commerce,' …'Transportation'). Next, click on the "Featured Article" link at the top of the webpage or scroll down the webpage to have teams select an article of their choice.

   ASSIGNMENT: Have student teams write a 1/2-page brief that summarizes the article selected.

   e. Have student teams hand in their summaries.

3. At the beginning of the next class period, select one student from 4 to 5 student teams to give 1 to 2 minute reports on the marketing and strategy articles they summarized.

Marketing Lesson. Because the global marketplace continues to undergo a sweeping transformation, many large and medium-size organizations use consulting firms to help them with their corporate and marketing strategy planning, implementation, and control. Students should develop a habit of monitoring the developments in corporate and marketing strategy to proactively respond to these changes in the global marketplace.

Website. The McKinsey Quarterly website is www.mckinseyquarterly.com.

ICA 22-3: STRATEGIC MARKETING TRENDS

MCKINSEY QUARTERLY HANDOUT

❏ Go to the McKinsey Quarterly website (www.mckinseyquarterly.com) and perform the following tasks…

1. Under the "Functions" menu at the left of the homepage, click on the "Marketing" link. Next, click on the "Featured Article" link at the top of the webpage.

   [NOTE: Free registration is required to read the full text of the "Featured Article." Have one student team member complete the registration process to proceed with the ICA assignments below.]

   ASSIGNMENT: Write a 1/2-page brief that summarizes the featured article.

2. Still in the "Function: Marketing" area, scroll to the top of the webpage. Click on one of the "Function: Marketing" menu options ('Editor's Choice,' 'Branding,' 'Channel Management,' …'Strategy'). Then, click on an article of your choice.

   ASSIGNMENT: Write a 1/2-page brief that summarizes the article selected.

3. Under the "Functions" menu at the left of the homepage, click on the "Strategy" link. Next, click on the "Featured Article" link at the top of the webpage or scroll down the webpage to select an article of your choice.

   ASSIGNMENT: Write a 1/2-page brief that summarizes the article selected.

4. Under the "Industries" menu at the left of the homepage, click on one of the industry sector links ('Automotive,' 'Electronic Commerce,' …'Transportation'). Next, click on the "Featured Article" link at the top of the webpage or scroll down the webpage to select an article of your choice.

   ASSIGNMENT: Write a 1/2-page brief that summarizes the article selected.

❏ At the beginning of the next class period, hand in your 2-page briefs. Be prepared to give a 1 to 2 minute report on the marketing and strategy articles you summarized.